D0998468

NC STATE BASKETBALL
100 YEARS
OF INNOVATION

TIM PEELER &
ROGER WINSTEAD

FOREWORD BY **SIDNEY LOWE**

NC State Basketball:
One Hundred Years of Innovation
© 2010 by NC State University Athletics Department

Distributed by:
The University of North Carolina Press
116 South Boundary St.
Chapel Hill, North Carolina 27514

Published by:
NC State University Athletics Department

Copy and Research by:
Tim Peeler

Design, Photo Editing and Typesetting by:
Roger Winstead

Additional copies of this publication may be
ordered from the UNC Press web site
(www.uncpress.unc.edu) or by calling
Longleaf Services at 800-848-6224.

ISBN 978-0-8078-3447-3

First Edition October 2010

PRINTED IN CANADA

CONTENTS

FOREWORD

by

Sidney **Lowe**

When I became NC State's basketball coach on May 6, 2006, no one had to explain to me the importance of my position.

During my four years as a player, under Norm Sloan and Jim Valvano, I learned all about the tradition of Everett Case and about the legendary players who came before me, from Dick Dickey to Ronnie Shavlik to David Thompson. Those are just a few of the names who made NC State basketball special during its first 100 years.

Coach Case, of course, is the "Father of Atlantic Coast Conference Basketball," someone every NC State fan should know and revere. If he had not come here in 1946, basketball might never have become a big-time college sport in the South. I'm sure glad that it did.

He started the pipeline from Indiana high schools to NC State, one that continues today. He made sure Reynolds Coliseum, the best college basketball venue in the nation, was completed. He set the standard for every other school in the Southern Conference and the ACC by winning nine tournaments in 10 years. Just think how amazing that is.

Coach Case brought so many things to the game of college basketball. We all know he brought the tradition of cutting down the nets after big basketball games, something I was honored to do on four occasions during my senior year of 1983. But he also introduced things like pep bands, spotlighted introductions and big-time recruiting to college basketball.

My first coach here, Norm Sloan, played a huge role in the development of the sport, including the integration of men's basketball and winning the school's first NCAA Championship. Had it not been for the success of his teams, the NCAA Tournament might still be limited to just one team per conference, the dunk might still be outlawed and UCLA might still be winning national titles.

Jim Valvano, who took over the program my sophomore year, brought an unbelievable amount of energy and excitement to Wolfpack basketball. The first time he met with the team, he told us he was going to win the NCAA Championship. And that's exactly what we did in my final game as a player at NC State, thanks to Dereck Whittenburg's airball — um, pass — and Lorenzo Charles's dunk against Houston's Hall of Fame lineup of Akeem Olajuwon and Clyde Drexler.

We should all be thankful for the traditions Les Robinson and Herb Sendek helped continue. Coach Robinson, who played for and was an assistant to Coach Case, brought the wooden court back to Reynolds and reconnected the program to its roots, both as coach and athletics director. Coach Sendek was here when the school honored the jerseys of our most outstanding players and moved the program into our state-of-the-art homes, the RBC Center and the Dail Basketball Center. Like Reynolds when it opened in 1946, they are unmatched by any facilities in the country.

I am blessed every day to sit in the chair of the men who brought so many innovations to college basketball and so many championships to NC State. And I am proud to be the caretaker of the traditions they introduced.

As we begin the next century of Wolfpack basketball, I can't wait to see what happens next.

Sidney Lowe stood at midcourt at the RBC Center — NC State's plush, state-of-the-art basketball arena on the edge of campus — when he heard the surprisingly clear, strong voice.

The coach put his face in his hands and allowed the memories to wash over him.

The dozens of times he walked up the 23 steps from the locker rooms in the basement of Reynolds Coliseum onto the court. The loving, pulsating crowd that always embraced him and his teammates. The noise meter that crept slowly upwards to the red light at the top as the arena grew louder. The pep band that blared the "Red & White" song, the fight song and alma mater. The high-flying cheerleaders who seemed to linger in the air during timeouts.

Everything that happened during Lowe's four years as an NC State player flashed between his palms, from the tears of sadness he shed when Norm Sloan, the coach who recruited him to Raleigh from Washington, D.C., announced that he was leaving, to the tears of happiness he, his teammates and head coach Jim Valvano shared with a packed house the day after winning the 1983 NCAA Championship.

The mellow baritone that echoed in the coach's head belonged to C.A. Dillon, the longtime public address announcer at Thompson Gym, Reynolds Coliseum and the RBC Center, as he recited the same words he used for more than half a century to welcome Wolfpack fans and opponents to a home basketball game.

"Good afternoon, ladies and gentlemen, and welcome to the RBC Center," Dillon said on the afternoon of Jan. 16, 2010. "Today, North Carolina State University is pleased to have as its guest the basketball team from Clemson University."

Standing alone, in front of a crowd of nearly 19,000 spectators, Lowe silently wept tears of joy as he heard Dillon announce NC State's starting lineup one more time: "At guard, from Miami, Florida, Javi Gonzalez. At the other guard, from Boston, Massachusetts, senior Farnold Degand. At forward, from Marion, Indiana, freshman Scott Wood. At the other forward, from Fayetteville, North Carolina, C.J. Williams. And at center, from Detroit, Michigan, Tracy Smith.

"And the head coach of the Wolfpack . . . Sidney Lowe!"

The ovation that followed was as much for Dillon's silky voice as it was for the lineup of the 100th basketball team to represent NC State University.

That same voice, in February 1947, told an overflowing crowd at Thompson Gymnasium that the game against North Carolina had been canceled by Raleigh fire chief W.R. Butts. Essentially, from that day forward, North Carolina was transformed from a region ruled by football to a basketball hotbed, thanks primarily to the vision of Everett Case.

It was the same voice that announced the lineups for 16 of NC State's 17 conference championship teams, including the nine won in 10 years by Case (1947–56), the coach who put Dillon behind the microphone.

In a rare instance, just after the Wolfpack beat Duke for the 1965 ACC

PREFACE

Championship, the voice went silent as the players raced to the sidelines, lifted the ailing Case onto their shoulders and carried him to one of the baskets, so he could cut down the nets one last time.

The voice cracked on the afternoon of March 16, 1974, in the deathly silence of Reynolds Coliseum as superstar David Thompson was wheeled off the court after tripping over teammate Phil Spence's shoulder during the NCAA Tournament East Region championship game. And it boomed when he shared the great news that Thompson would be all right, causing an explosion of noise that has never been matched in the raucous arena.

Unless it was on April 5, 1983, when Lowe and his teammates were welcomed home by an arena full of Wolfpack fans the day after winning the school's second national title.

The only time the voice was ever too overcome to speak was on Feb. 21, 1993, when a dying Jim Valvano told the sell-out crowd at Reynolds to "Never Give Up" prior to a nationally televised game against Duke.

For more than 50 years, that voice bounced off the walls of the three permanent homes of NC State basketball, introducing nearly all the famous names that are remembered in this volume: Dickey, Ranzino, Molodet, Shavlik, Richter, Pucillo, Biedenbach, Burleson, Thompson, Towe, Carr, Whitney, Bailey, Whittenburg, Lowe, Charles, Gannon, "Errrrrrrrrr-nee Myers!", Webb, McMillan, Corchiani, Monroe, Gugliotta and Fuller.

And it correctly pronounced the names of not-so-famous Wolfpack teammates and opponents during the parts of eight decades Dillon sat behind the microphone, fulltime from 1946–1999 and on occasion during the 2000s.

That voice, Lowe knew, was the soul of NC State basketball. It had boomed through all but a few of the most important moments in the first 100 years of NC State basketball. And that sweet echo will reverberate for many years to come.

ACKNOWLEDGMENTS

Covering every single detail in a project that spans 100 years is impossible. That was not our intent. We hoped to relate the stories of NC State's champions and tell about the many innovations the school has added to the game of college basketball. Some of the stories here are familiar; some we didn't know about when we began putting this book together in the summer of 2009. But we hope it stands as a good record of what has been accomplished by the NC State basketball program since it played its first game against Wake Forest on Feb. 16, 1911.

Similarly, it would be impossible to thank everyone who has contributed to this project. Some of them are people we never met, like the unnamed students and reporters who wrote accounts of the earliest games, or the uncredited photographers from the thousands of pictures we sorted through to find just the right images for this book.

While a large portion of the images used had no photo credit nor copyright notice on the originals, we feel obligated to express our gratitude to those that we can give credit to for their creative efforts in recording the history of NC State basketball with their cameras: Burnie Bachelor, Bugs Barringer, Todd Bennett, Clayton Brinkley, Ed Caram, Patrick Chapman, Charles Cooper, Eddie Gontram, Simon Griffiths, Greg Hatem, Chris Hondros, Bryson Lewis, Mark McIntyre, Hugh Morton, Scott Rivenbark, Michael Russell, Phil Taylor, Taylor Templeton, Peyton Williams, Roger Winstead and Fred Woolard.

We would like to thank former NC State athletics director Lee Fowler for approving this project to honor the former coaches, players and staff members who helped bring success and distinction to NC State basketball. Associate athletics director Dick Christy helped guide the project from beginning to end and assistant athletics director Chris Alston was extremely understanding in allowing us the time we needed to research and write this volume.

We owe a huge debt of gratitude to our editor, Kathy Bryant. She caught us every time our tired fingers tripped on the keyboard and every time our tired eyes missed a word. She's a great basketball fan, whose knowledge of the game and the language improved our efforts tremendously. And to Hannah Thurman, we thank you for your diligent last-minute proofing.

The media relations staff, led by assistant athletics director Annabelle Myers, gave us great support in editing stories, helping with research and digging up old photos. Brian Reinhardt, Mark Kimmel, Brandon Yopp and Bruce Winkworth were generous with their time and talent, as was marketing assistant Meghan Brown.

Chris Richter of the *NC State Alumni Magazine* has been generous with his help in tracking down the whereabouts of former players and coaches and allowing Tim use of the Alumni Association's library and archives.

The staff at the NC State Library Special Collections has done a terrific job in preserving old photos through the years, and we made liberal use of their digital collection. The recently completed project to digitize every *Agromeck* and put them online was an invaluable research tool.

Tim would like to thank his wife, Elizabeth, and his sons, Michael and Benjamin, for their support during this project. They have been extremely patient in his absence and grumpiness these last 18 months. They are the reason he spent so many hours early in the morning and late at night trying to make this book something they would be proud of.

Roger appreciates the support of his wife, Sarah, and his sons, Ridge and Dylan, while he toiled away countless nights and weekends poring over stacks of photos and hunched over the computer. He'd also like to acknowledge his parents, Dottie and Harold, to whom he owes so much — especially the gentle nudge to attend college in Raleigh from his NC State alumnus father.

We would like to thank everyone at UNC Press, which produced this book for the NC State Athletics Department, especially Mark Simpson-Vos, who helped us navigate through a short turnaround in the publication of this book.

Most important, we'd like to thank men like Gus Tebell, Everett Case, Press Maravich, Norman Sloan, Jim Valvano and all the other coaches and players who brought championships and glory to NC State basketball.

INNOVATIONS:
THE EARLIEST YEARS

The group of students sat in a corner of the auditorium of Pullen Hall, the large Greek Revival assembly building at the front door of the North Carolina School for Agriculture and Mechanic Arts. It was Feb. 21, 1911, and the eight young men were gathered here this Tuesday evening for a diversion in the building that had served as the center of student life since its doors were opened in 1903.

The large open room was ill-suited for its current purpose — the first college basketball game ever played in Raleigh, N.C. There were support columns in the middle of the wooden floor and a large stage on one end. It was, after all, designed to host mandatory assemblies, chapel services and other events for the fledgling school's enrollment of 450 students, not athletic competitions.

Fortunately, the game being played that night was just a blip on the school's social calendar.

The big event of the week had been three nights earlier at the annual midwinter dance of the Thalarian German Club, a social organization that hosted various dances throughout the academic year. For the students at the all-male A&M College, the dance was an opportunity to bring dates from one of the three neighboring girls' schools, Peace Institute, Meredith College and St. Mary's School for Girls.

That dance, however, caused major problems for the basketball teams from A&M and neighboring Wake Forest College. In preparation for the big dance, the wooden floor had been waxed and polished, allowing the awkward farmers and engineers to glide as gracefully as they could to the music provided by the school orchestra.

Unfortunately, the floor was still quite slick during the first half of the basketball game. Players from both teams had trouble standing upright. Perhaps that was a good thing for A&M: five nights earlier, on Wake Forest's campus 10 miles north of Raleigh, the teams had met for the first time and the more experienced Baptists whipped their neighbors, 33-6.

In the rematch, however, the Aggies scooted out to a 15-11 lead in the first half, thanks to the play of center Percy Bell Ferebee. With victory in their sights, they needed a small advantage if they were going to pull off an upset against Wake Forest, which had sponsored an intercollegiate basketball team since 1906.

So when Professor Howard Satterfield walked into the team huddle carrying a bucket of kerosene, the eight players and team manager thought it was strange, especially when he told them to take off their rubber-soled canvas shoes and dip them in the bucket. But they dutifully did what the longtime mechanical engineering professor told them to do. When the players put their shoes back on, they found the soles to be just sticky enough to gain traction on the slickened floor.

The tactic worked: A&M pulled off a stunning upset, 19-18, in front of an estimated 550 people, the first recorded basketball victory in school history.

"The A&M boys have had a hard fight to establish the sport in the college," wrote *The News & Observer* in its account of the school's initial victory. "But it has come to stay, and the crowds witnessing the game last night proved that the game will be quite as poplar [sic] as other college games."

From its beginnings, NC State basketball has been defined by forward-thinkers who changed the way the game is played and perceived. The first was YMCA general secretary John W. Bergthold, who, like so many other YMCA men around the globe, introduced basketball to young men who had little knowledge of the game invented 20 years before by Dr. James Naismith at Springfield (Mass.) College.

In the first 35 years of competition at NC State, there were some advances and a few successes on

Conference tournament, he turned the advantage of having the biggest and best arena in the region into championships, just as he had done at Frankfort (Ind.) High School, which he led to an unprecedented four state titles.

While popular among the members of the YMCA, basketball was not an immediate success at the school, which was basking in the glory of wildly successful football and baseball seasons in 1910. So there wasn't much notice paid when Bergthold organized five campus teams — one each representing the senior, junior, sophomore and freshman classes and one representing the

the hardwoods. But the landscape changed dramatically in 1946, when an innovative, veteran high school coach named Everett Case arrived in Raleigh, hired by school administrators who were desperate to find the success in basketball that they had found elusive on the football field.

Case turned basketball from a game to a celebration, introducing traditions he remembered from his days as Indiana's most successful high school coach. His teams were the first in college to cut down the nets after winning a championship. He had the nation's first pep band. Case was the first coach in college to turn the spotlight on his players during pregame introductions. He turned the skeleton of the basketball arena that had stood untouched for more than half a decade into the palatial Reynolds Coliseum. With the Dixie Classic, he introduced the importance of holiday tournaments. By hosting the Atlantic Coast

agricultural short course — to begin class-against-class play in the fall.

Despite the early difficulties in the program's beginnings, it is not exactly accurate to say NC State did not have basketball success until Case's arrival. But, in the earliest days, the class teams had no place to practice or play games, other than two makeshift outdoor courts, scratched out on the gravel-covered military drill fields on the site of present-day Pullen Park.

Development of the sport wasn't exactly smooth, Bergthold remembered years later.

"Many students and faculty members at first considered basketball a girl's game, because Meredith [College] played it," Bergthold wrote in a 1939 edition of the *NC State Alumni News*. "We inveigled [a] half-dozen innocents to go out on the old drill field and there, with some temporary goal posts, practiced throwing baskets and laying the foundation of basketball which has become such a factor in the sports of the college."

The YMCA organized a varsity squad from the five class team to represent A&M in intercollegiate competition in the fall of 1910. A game was scheduled against Virginia Tech in Norfolk, the night before the two schools' traditional Thanksgiving Day football game in the same city. But two weeks of rain prevented A&M from using its outdoor practice fields and the school's first scheduled game was cancelled. Another game, to be played against the University of North Carolina at Pullen Hall, was cancelled because the two schools, who were feuding over eligibility standards in other sports, could not agree on the terms of the game.

So the first season was made up of those first two games against Wake Forest.

Not until the campus YMCA building was completed in 1913, thanks to a generous gift from philanthropist John D. Rockefeller, did the school have a consistent place to practice indoors. For more than a decade, until Frank Thompson Gymnasium was opened in 1925, all home games were played in downtown Raleigh, in the 2,000-seat Raleigh Municipal Auditorium, which regularly attracted large crowds when the Farmers hosted local teams like Wake Forest and Trinity College, both of which began their programs earlier than A&M, but were not particularly successful either.

A&M played the University of North Carolina only once in the first decade of the program, because of the feud over eligibility. For that same reason, the two schools did not face each other in football from 1906-1918. Still, it was an amazing feat for the Farmers to beat UNC so thoroughly, 26-18, on the afternoon of Feb. 22, 1913. "There wasn't a department of the game in which the Techs of Raleigh did not outshine the classicists

of Carolina," *The News & Observer* reported. "The teamwork was infinitely better. It was no uncommon thing to see the Carolina boys huddled together under their own goal while the Farmers were complacently watching their discomfiture as a member of the home team laid, unmolested, the ball into the big pocket."

That teamwork was amazing, considering A&M's administration was still not fully supportive of the sport. Team members were not awarded monograms and were not excused from military drills for practice and games. In the first year after the Athletics Association took over administration of basketball in 1912, football and baseball players were not allowed to participate in basketball because school officials did not want them to be overinvolved. And school rules prevented the team from beginning its practices until after Christmas break, while other schools in the state began drills in the late fall.

In the early days, the Farmers were organized, drilled and managed by coaches and managers culled from the faculty or the student body. In 1916, coached by dairying and animal husbandry professor Chuck Sanborn, the Farmers posted the first winning season in school history.

In 1917, the same year the school's name was changed to the North Carolina State College of Agriculture and Engineering, former four-sport athlete Harry Hartsell was hired in the off-season to become its first real athletics director. He was also charged with coaching football, baseball, basketball and track. He matched Sanborn's feat of producing a winning record, 10-8.

But that was nothing compared to what happened in the winter of 1918, when Hartsell's team claimed the championship of the Carolinas, based on its 12-2 record. There was no play-off in determining these championships, but the team, captained by Elbert Lewis, lost only once in its 11 games against teams from the two states. The only setback was an early loss to Trinity College that was later avenged.

The 1918–19 basketball season was one of the most critical times in the 30-year history of the school. At the outset of the Great War, NC State had been converted into a military training ground, with all 590 students being automatically enlisted into the Student Army Training Corps. More than 30 of the school's most experienced students, including seven starters from the 1917 state championship football team, were shipped out to Army camps across the country for final training before they were sent overseas.

Frank Thompson, one of the school's most beloved athletes on the football and baseball fields from 1907–10 and the head coach of both programs after his graduation, was killed on a battlefield in France.

At the same time, a worldwide outbreak of Spanish influenza — which killed 10 times more people around the globe than all the casualties of the world war — swept through the campus, claiming the lives of 13 students and two nurses at the campus infirmary. One of the nurses was the daughter of beloved school president W.C. Riddick, for whom Riddick Stadium was named.

In the fall of 1918, all extracurricular activi-ties, including football games and practices, were cancelled for five weeks. When play resumed, the flu-stricken and outnumbered football Farmers lost to John Heisman's Golden Hurricane of Georgia Tech, 128-0, by far the worst defeat in school history.

So, when the basketball team gathered to begin practice after Christmas, the school was desperate for something good to happen. First-year coach Tal Stafford, a former NC State football and baseball player, had taken over both the football squad and the basketball squad after Hartsell was drafted into the Army.

While the football team was decimated, the basketball quintet actually had good prospects for the winter because, amazingly, most of the players from the 1918 Carolinas championship team returned. Guided by captain Franklin Cline and Raleigh's own Thomas Park, A&M raced through the season with an 11-3 record, playing and beating every team in the state except Davidson and North Carolina.

Davidson and NC State could not agree on a date to play, but the Wildcats made no claim on the state championship. That was not the case with North Carolina, which was also undefeated against opponents within the state.

With both teams claiming the state basketball title, administrators and students from the rival institutions were eager for a resolution. They put aside their differences to schedule a one-game playoff at the Raleigh Municipal Auditorium. So,

Harry Hartsell

5

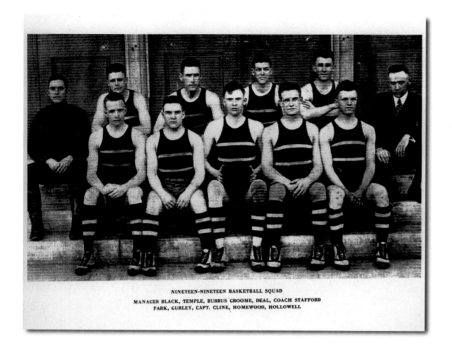

NINETEEN-NINETEEN BASKETBALL SQUAD

MANAGER BLACK, TEMPLE, BURRUS GROOME, DEAL, COACH STAFFORD
PARK, GURLEY, CAPT. CLINE, HOMEWOOD, HOLLOWELL

That game did much to ease the strain between the two teams and bring some liveliness back to the moribund NC State campus. The two teams scheduled a football game in the fall of 1919 and a basketball game in 1920. They have met at least once in each sport every year since.

Stafford coached his alma mater's football and basketball teams for only one season. He gave up the positions, which didn't offer much salary, to become the primary sports reporter and editor of the school's alumni magazine, which began publishing again after taking a hiatus during the Great War.

Dr. Richard Crozier, who introduced the game of basketball to Southern colleges in 1906 when he moved from Indiana to Wake Forest and was the opposing coach in the first two games in NC State history, had moved to the Raleigh school in 1918 as the Farmers' team trainer. He took over for Stafford and led the team back into position to win its second consecutive state championship. But a player from Trinity hit a shot from midcourt at the end of the game, giving the Methodists a 25-24 win and the state title.

on March 15, 1919, "madness" officially started in the state of North Carolina.

The two teams were not that evenly matched. North Carolina had a height advantage in its center, over NC State's J.D. Groome, but the Aggies liked playing a fast style of basketball. Stafford's "tossers" jumped out to a 15-7 lead early in the game. North Carolina slowed the pace by closely guarding the Farmer forwards and managed to cut their deficit to just 17-14 at the half.

But NC State resumed its speedy play in the first seven minutes of the second half, forcing North Carolina to call a time-out just to catch its breath. Trailing 23-17, the White Phantoms of the University had little hope of catching the Aggies, who finished strong by outscoring their new rival 12-8 over the final five minutes of the game to secure a 39-29 victory and the state championship.

The News & Observer described the game like this: "Witnessed by an auditorium that nearly packed the big place, the exhibition was hotly contested from beginning to end and full of thrills and pretty plays."

NC State had a private celebration a few weeks later, when almost the entire student body gathered to cheer on Riddick as he presented each member of the team with a small gold basketball in honor of their accomplishment.

Neither Crozier nor Hartsell, who returned as head coach for the 1921–22 season, had much success as A&M suffered through four consecutive losing seasons. But the game was growing in the South. The Atlanta Athletic Club hosted the

nation's first postseason basketball tournament in 1921, the same year NC State became a charter member of the Southern Conference. The tournament was open to any member of the Southern Intercollegiate Athletic Association, a loose organization of schools from the South that was a forerunner to the Southern Conference. NC State, however, chose not to participate in the Atlanta tournament until 1925, when the field was limited to only Southern Conference members.

Not long after NC State joined the league, school administrators began to change the way the entire institution operated, as they tried to cope with the increased postwar enrollment. There were major shake-ups in every department, as the school made a turbulent change from a technical institute to a more rounded college, with the establishment of the School of Engineering, the School of Agriculture and the School of Science and Business. Eugene Clyde Brooks replaced Riddick as the school president. Liberal arts were introduced. The athletics council — chaired for more than a decade by Satterfield, the mechanical engineering professor whose bucket of kerosene assisted in the school's first win — was reorganized, with Graduate School dean Carl C. Taylor taking over as its chairman.

In 1924, the school hired John F. Miller, a former University of Missouri standout athlete and major league baseball player, from Albion College in Michigan to revamp athletics and to establish the school's first physical education department. The timing was important, since the school was in the midst of the biggest building boom until after World War II.

Enrollment doubled after World War I, reaching more than 1,200 students. To accommodate the growth, the North Carolina legislature gave NC State an unprecedented appropriation of $2.4 million to build a new library, named for former school president D.H. Hill; a new physics and electrical engineering building, named in honor of Josephus Daniels; a new animal husbandry building, named for Leonidas Polk; a liberal arts building, named in honor of Joseph Peele; and a new power plant that featured a distinctive smokestack that advertised "State College."

But, most important of all to students and the athletics department, the school broke ground in 1923 on its first full-sized gymnasium, a state-of-the-art, $245,000 multi-purpose facility to be named in honor of Thompson, the early athletics hero who died in the war. After doing away with required military drills, a gym was thought to be a major necessity, not only for intercollegiate activities, but also to keep students physically fit. All freshmen and sophomores were required to participate in physical fitness classes, and juniors and seniors had the option of doing so.

The gym, which had living quarters in the basement for basketball and football players, was ready for the 1924–25 season, which coincided with the arrival of new basketball coach and assistant football coach Gus Tebell. He was one of the first coaches hired by Miller, under the strict new guidelines that prohibited the athletics department from hiring any NC State alumni. Tebell, a four-sport standout at Wisconsin, had just completed one season as a player-coach of the Columbus Tigers of the American Professional Football League. A pupil of eventual Naismith Basketball Hall of Fame member Dr. Walter Meanwell, Tebell was young, energetic and full of ideas.

His first basketball team, led by Rochelle "Red" Johnson and G.C. "Red" Lassiter, made its debut in Thompson Gym wearing bright red wool uniforms. They played the "Meanwell System" of short passes and zone defenses to perfection and became known on campus as "The Red Terrors," a nickname that stuck to all athletics teams other than football for more than 20 years.

Tebell took his Terrors to the Southern Conference Tournament in Atlanta for the first time in 1925, beating Maryland in the opening round but falling to Tulane in the second. Still, it was an auspicious start in Tebell's successful tenure.

With Thompson Gymnasium, NC State was finally able to offer gymnastics classes, develop intramural programs and host outside activities. It also became the first school in the South to offer physical education classes for credit. One of Miller's many innovations — some of which didn't go over so well — was starting an open high school basketball tournament. A total of 39 teams from across the state accepted his invitation

Gus Tebell

to play in the inaugural three-day tournament, which quickly became one of the most popular of its kind, a prep precursor to Everett Case's Dixie Classic. The tournament died after seven years, only because the school could no longer accommodate the 72 teams and more than 800 players who flooded the campus.

But Miller's time as the athletics director was short-lived. The school, after several poor seasons in football, separated intercollegiate athletics from the physical education department in 1927. Miller remained at the school as the head of the department, developing its first full-time degree in physical education.

Tal Stafford, who coached football and basketball for one season each during World War I, returned to become the graduate manager of athletics, an equivalent of athletics director.

Thompson Gym — "one of the largest and best equipped in the south," bragged the student newspaper — was dedicated on June 8, 1925. The next season, Tebell led NC State to its first (and only) 20-win season before Case took over the program. The Terrors won 19 consecutive home games from the end of 1925 until the fourth game of 1927, when old rival Wake Forest eked out a 20-18 victory.

Tebell, who also took over the NC State football team in 1925 after the departure of future Hall of Fame coach Buck Shaw, was a rising star in the coaching ranks, leading the football Wolfpack to the 1927 Southern Conference championship. And in 1929, Tebell reached the pinnacle of his coaching success, when he led the NC State basketball team to the Southern Conference Championship, becoming the only coach in league history to win both major titles.

Tebell, under pressure from influential alumnus David Clark to be more successful in football, resigned from NC State following the 1929–30 basketball season to become an assistant football coach and head basketball coach at Virginia, a position he held for 21 seasons. He also spent three seasons as head football coach and was the school's athletics director from 1953 until 1964.

Dr. R.R. Sermon, one of many head college basketball coaches who learned the game under legendary Kansas coach Forrest "Phog" Allen, took over Tebell's duties as basketball coach and Stafford's duties as athletics director in 1930. But he faced many insurmountable challenges during his decade in charge of the athletics department.

His tenure began not long after NC State, the University of North Carolina, and the North Carolina College for Women in Greensboro were brought together into the Consolidated University, a move that made NC State alumni, faculty and students wary but was considered a necessity during the turbulent financial times following the stock market crash of 1929. State appropriations were cut by nearly 50 percent, the school slashed professors' salaries by as much as 25 percent for three consecutive years and popular sports wrestling and track were dropped to save money.

Not surprisingly, the basketball program was relatively stagnant throughout the Great Depres-sion, as Sermon juggled his multiple duties within the department, tried to keep finances in line with a shrinking budget and watched as the Consolidated University bickered with the rest of the Southern Conference schools over eligibility standards.

Throughout most of the 1930s, NC State continued to rely on multisport athletes for whatever success it had on the basketball court, in effect saving scholarship money by making do with the best players from the football and baseball teams. The three all-conference members of the 1929 championship team — Bob Warren, Maurice "Johnny" Johnson and leading scorer Frank Goodwin — all won letters in football. Connie Mack Berry, who led the Southern Conference in scoring in both 1936 and '37, might have been the best multisport star in school history. He ended up playing professionally in football, basketball and baseball, twice winning the championship in the National Basketball League, a forerunner of the NBA, and once winning the championship of the National Football League.

In 1932, the 22-team Southern Conference split into two separate leagues along geographic lines. The 10 schools from Maryland, Virginia and the Carolinas remained in the Southern Conference and the 12 schools in the southernmost states formed the Southeastern Conference. The SEC kept its tournament in Atlanta, but the Southern Conference tournament needed a new home.

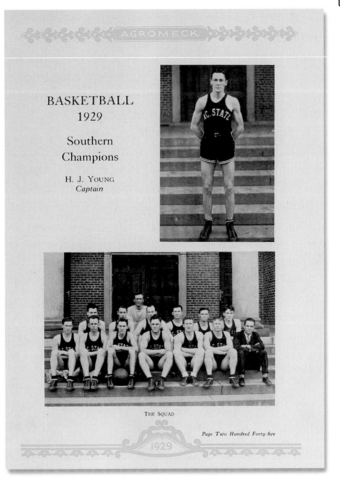

AGROMECK

BASKETBALL
1929

Southern
Champions

H. J. YOUNG
Captain

THE SQUAD

Page Two Hundred Forty-five

1929

At the same time, the city of Raleigh opened a new 2,500-seat downtown auditorium and was eager to attract the Southern Conference's popular postseason event to North Carolina in 1933, to be near the four league schools that were within 25 miles of the arena. But, unlike in years to come, NC State could not exploit its hometown advantage. Only once in Sermon's 10 seasons as head coach did the Red Terrors advance as far as the semifinals in the eight-team tournament.

In 1934, Sermon's Terrors pulled off the biggest upset of the college basketball season, beating South Carolina in the first round of the Southern Conference Tournament to end USC's 31-game winning streak, which at the time was the longest in the NCAA. But NC State lost in the second round to Washington & Lee.

In 1935, UNC System president Frank Porter Graham introduced a plan for intercollegiate athletics at all Southern Conference schools that prohibited giving athletic scholarships, required all athletes to sit out for one season before they were allowed to participate and limited the income coaches could make. Though initially approved, the entire plan was scrapped within four months after an uproar from alumni across the conference. A modified set of eligibility require-

ments for Graham's two institutions, NC State and North Carolina, took effect in 1936, but they were largely ignored until the NCAA adopted a uniform set of eligibility requirements in 1948.

The Southern Conference added six new teams in 1936, making the league too big to have round-robin regular-season play. Only eight teams qualified for the postseason tournament, and members squabbled over the selection process right up until the seven strongest members of the league formed the Atlantic Coast Conference in the summer of 1953.

In the Terrors' best season under Bob Warren, NC State was 15-4 in 1936, but another outbreak of the flu forced several games to be canceled. Unfortunately, the flu didn't wipe out the games against UNC, which accounted for three of the team's four losses that season, including a 36-28 setback in the second round of the Southern Conference Tournament.

As the economy began to recover, basketball began to grow in popularity. Warren's 1936 team drew praise for a potent offense that averaged 41 points in its 15 wins. But it was still far different than the game that is played today. Because of the rule that required a jump ball after every made basket and a narrow free-throw lane,

centers dominated the games, even though few of them were taller than 6-4.

"If you had a center tall enough to control the tip-off, why you had the game won, because that is where all the games were won," remembered former NC State basketball letterman Sam Womble in a 2005 interview at the age of 92. "Back then, the hook shot was what won games for everybody. And when you would go to the free-throw line, you would hold the ball between your legs and lob it up real soft towards the basket.

"Law, I don't even recognize what basketball is nowadays. It's just entirely too rough. If we had played like that back when I played, we wouldn't have lasted one quarter."

One of his teammates, Neal Mack Dalrymple, echoed those thoughts that same year, remembering his all-star career some 70 years before.

"Today's basketball is so different from the game I played," said Dalrymple, who was 90 at the time. "Somebody asked me a while back if we ever dunked. I told them, 'Good gracious, if the net ever got caught up in the rim, we had to throw a ball up there to dislodge it.'

"Players are so gifted today. There is no comparison in the type of basketball we played."

Sermon's tenure as athletics director and basketball coach was filled with turbulent times. He had an ongoing feud with Clark, the booster who helped force Tebell out as football coach. Clark twice went to the athletics council and the board of trustees to get Sermon removed from his various positions. Primarily, Clark didn't like Sermon's attitude toward the football program and the head coach, Hunk Anderson, whom

Doc Sermon

Clark helped hire. Clark wanted Anderson to be the basketball coach as well, and spent three years trying to have Sermon relieved of his duties, accusing him of using school funds for a variety of personal gains. It didn't work, and Clark, a prominent businessman in Charlotte, withdrew for awhile his support of State College athletics.

Big-time basketball was on the horizon. In 1938, when the NCAA eliminated the center-jump rule after each basket, Raleigh expanded its Memorial Auditorium to 4,700 seats and the Southern Conference Tournament drew a standing-room only crowd of 5,000 for that year's semifinals. The newspapers reported it to be the largest crowd to ever witness an indoor sporting event in the South. Both Duke and North Carolina were pursuing new basketball homes. UNC built 6,000-seat Woollen Gym to replace the Tin Can in 1938. That same year Duke designed its 9,500-seat Duke Indoor Stadium in Durham. Construction began in 1939, thanks in part to funds the school received for hosting the 1939 Rose Bowl. Thus inspired, Clark took advantage of a summer rainstorm in 1940 that disrupted the annual Farmer's Week meeting to convince the board of trustees that NC State needed an indoor gathering place bigger than the now-crumbling Thompson Gym. He envisioned this facility would serve as an on-campus armory and an indoor gathering place for large meetings during inclement weather. And, the big booster explained, it might be a good opportunity to improve the school's basketball facilities.

In the fall of 1940, Clark bought the first load of structural steel and oversaw the start of construction on a coliseum based on modified drawings of Duke's mammoth arena. No one at the time envisioned that the new arena wouldn't be nearly big enough to contain the excitement that was on the way.

Meanwhile, Sermon finally stepped aside in 1940, after his final team failed to qualify for the Southern Conference Tournament, ending his tumultuous relationship with Clark and the school. He handed the reins over to Warren, his long-time freshman coach and a member of the school's 1929 championship team.

Warren found some success in his two seasons as head coach, thanks primarily to a lanky young center from Durham named Horace "Bones" McKinney. In 1942, McKinney, Bernie Mock and "Buckwheat" Carvalho helped lead the Red Terrors to a 13-6 regular-season record and a fourth-place finish in the league. In the team's best postseason showing ever in Raleigh, the Terrors beat South Carolina and William & Mary to qualify for the title game for the first time since 1929. But Duke, led by three of McKinney's former Durham High School teammates, beat the

Terrors for its second consecutive conference title.

Warren was forced to step down as head coach when he received his commission in the U.S. Navy at the outset of World War II. McKinney was also drafted into the U.S. Army. The war decimated not only the basketball program, but also the school. While the campus swelled with incoming military recruits who were being trained in various technical fields, they were not eligible for intercollegiate play under Army regulations. Regular enrollment at the college dwindled from approximately 2,500 in 1943 to about 700 in 1945.

From early 1943 until the war's end in August 1945, NC State trained 23,628 men and women in preflight training, Navy diesel engineering and other valuable subjects necessary for the war effort. More than 5,000 alumni and regularly en-

rolled students served in the war, and 206 current or former NC State students gave their lives in the conflict.

Construction on the grand coliseum being built adjacent to Thompson Gym was halted in 1944 because of wartime appropriations cutbacks, leaving a stark skeleton of steel girders standing on a concrete foundation for more than four years.

Not surprisingly, Warren's replacement as basketball coach, Leroy Jay, found little success as the head coach of the team he played for during his four years as a student, suffering double-digit losses during his three losing seasons.

Jay, who worked full-time for the North Carolina Highway Commission, was simply a wartime fill-in as the Terrors' basketball coach, making just $600 a year.

When the war ended, enrollment at NC State exploded, topping out at nearly 5,000 students in the fall of 1946. Jay knew that would be his last

season, and he limped through the regular season with a 6-11 record. The Terrors still qualified for the Southern Conference tournament, drawing second-seeded Duke in the first round. The Terrors led the entire game, but lost in overtime after the team's leading scorer, Hotdog Herzog, fouled out in the final minute of regulation.

But the days of relying on part-time coaches and multi-sport players were done. The school — bursting in all directions from the influx of thousands of GI Bill veterans, many of whom were already married — was ready for its biggest and best innovation yet.

"The school plans to sign a fulltime basketball coach of high caliber and hopes to produce teams capable of holding its own against any competition," *The News & Observer* reported after the loss to Duke.

The relatively calm world of college basketball in the South had no idea what was in store.

A. & M. 19, WAKE FOREST 18

The Teams Appeared to be Evenly Matched

First Basket-ball Game Ever Played at A. & M. College Was Witnessed Last Night By Large Crowd and Resulted in a Victory For the Farmers the Score Being 19 to 18.

The first basket-ball game ever played at the A. & M. College was played in Pullen Hall last night between the A. & M. and Wake Forest teams, resulting in the score of 19 to 18 in favor of A. & M.

A similar contest between these two teams at Wake Forest last Thursday night resulted in a decided score against the farmer boys, owing largely to the lack of coaching and of a floor on which to play.

The teams last night seemed almost evenly matched, neither of them doing brilliant team work, although A. & M. showed some flashes of good team work at times.

The A. & M. boys have had a hard fight to establish this sport in the college, but it has come to stay, and the crowds witnessing the game last night proved that the game will be quite as popular as other college games.

A. and M.—Cool, left forward; Chambers, right forward; Ferebee, Robinson, center; Phillips, Small, left guard; Seifert, Legrand, right guard.

Wake Forest—Holding, R., left forward; McCutcheon, Beam, right forward; Holding, B., center; Dowd, left guard; Utley, right guard.

Referee—Crozier of Wake Forest. Umpire—Freeman of Wake Forest. Scorer—Davis of A. and M. Timekeeper—Stafford of A. and M. Time of halves—30 minutes. Attendance 350.

HERMIT OF LAKE DRUMMOND.

Mr. B. E. Lee, of This City, Was a Kinsman of This Unique Person.

A news item from Suffolk, Va., in this issue tells of the death of Mr. Lassiter, known for nearly "Hermit of Lake

First team...

No cheerleaders. No pep band.
No Mr. or Ms. Wuf.
Just eight young men at
the start of something special

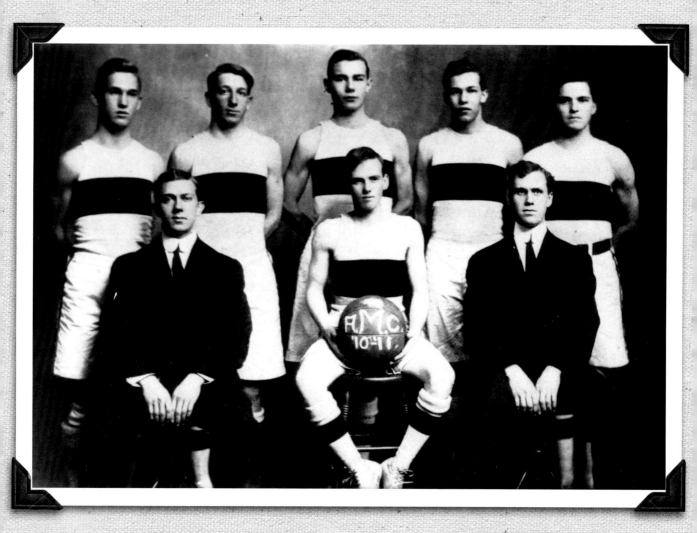

Pullen Hall

Basketball was introduced to the North Carolina School for Agriculture and Mechanic Arts in the fall of 1908, when John W. Bergthold became the general secretary of the Young Men's Christian Association (YMCA). He helped the students at the campus YMCA learn the rules of the game on the unpaved gravel drill fields on the grounds of present-day Pullen Park.

He borrowed a set of uniforms from the football team and sent a team representing the A&M YMCA to face Bingham Military School, a game that was played outdoors and was delayed while players and students swept snow off the dirt court, and to face the Guilford College varsity team in a game that was played indoors. The A&M team won the first contest, but lost the second.

According to school records, that first non-varsity team included Percy Bell Ferebee of Elizabeth City, N.C.; John W. Bradfield of Charlotte; Frank Lee Crowell of Concord; Davis A. Robertson of Portsmouth, Va.; J.C. Small of Elizabeth City; Harry Hartsell of Asheville; Henry Spooner Harrison of Enfield, N.C.; and J.R. Mullen of Charlotte.

Bergthold appointed senior Guy Kader Bryan to head a committee made up of Ferebee, several faculty members and representatives of the Athletics Association to study the possibility of adding basketball as a varsity sport. Though the committee couldn't assure that basketball would be a profitable sport, it continued to gain popularity on campus, as each of the school's four classes and the agricultural short course each had teams that played a round-robin schedule in the fall of 1910.

A handful of players were chosen from those teams to represent A&M in the school's first intercollegiate game, scheduled against Virginia Tech for Wednesday, Nov. 23, 1910, the night before the two schools met in their traditional Thanksgiving Day football game in Norfolk, Va. But that game had to be cancelled because two weeks of rain leading up to the inaugural game prevented A&M's team from practicing on its outdoor courts.

On Jan. 17, 1911, the faculty approved a single game to be played in Pullen Hall against the University of North Carolina, which was also just starting its program. But the game never developed, as the teams could not agree on the terms of the game. Instead, the basketball team scheduled two contests against the much more experienced Baptists of neighboring Wake Forest.

Richard "Red" Crozier came from Evansville, Ind., in 1904 to become the baseball coach at Wake Forest College. Two years later he organized the first college basketball team in the South at the school. By the time the Baptists hosted A&M's first game on Feb. 16, 1911, the Wake Forest players were far more experienced at playing the game. So it's not surprising that the Baptists won the initial contest in the unbroken rivalry, played in its own gymnasium, by an overwhelming score of 33-6.

The first game of the series garnered little attention. However, the teams played again two nights later at Pullen Hall on the A&M campus. And the outcome was vastly different, as the below account shows.

From Red & White (March 1911)

In the first game of college basketball ever played in Raleigh, A&M turned the tables on Wake Forest for its defeat of last Thursday night (February 16) in Wake Forest, by a score of 33 to 6, and came back strong, defeating the Baptists 19 to 18.

The game was hotly contested throughout, but owing to a slippery floor both teams were at a disadvantage. The score at the end of the first half stood 15 to 11 in favor of A&M. The Baptists played hard in the second half, keeping the Red and White on the jump. Every man on the A&M team did good work, while for Wake Forest, B. Holding and McCutcheon and Dowd did particularly good work.

The lineup

A&M	Position	Wake Forest
Cool	R.F.	McCutcheon (Beam)
Chambers	L.F.	R. Holding
Ferebee (Robertson)	C.	B. Holding
Siefert (Legrand)	R.G.	Utley
Phillips (Small)	L.G.	Dowd

Time of halves – 20 minutes. Referee – Crozier of Wake Forest. Umpire – Freeman of Wake Forest. Timekeeper – Stafford of A&M. Goals from field – A&M 9; Wake Forest 8. Goals from foul – A&M 1, Wake Forest 3. Attendance – 550.

More important, the game made money. Special street cars were arranged to deliver girls from Meredith, Peace and St. Mary's and the temporary stands that were set up in Pullen Hall were filled. The spectacle certainly caught the eye of school administrators, who quickly agreed to take over sponsorship of the sport.

"At the beginning, the Athletic Association would not recognize the basketball team and would not allow us to state that we represented the college but rather that we represented the YMCA of the college," Ferebee wrote in the April 1948 issue of the *State College News*. "After the Wake Forest game, however, Dr. Riddick called me over and stated that the Athletic Association had decided to sponsor the basketball team and would finance it from then on. We were to turn over to the Athletic Association the funds that we had on hand which amounted to two or three hundred dollars, net proceeds from the Wake Forest game."

For their work, both Ferebee and Bryan earned the praise of Bergthold and their fellow members of the campus YMCA.

"Ever since the spring of 1909 we have been trying to establish basketball as one of the college sports, but not until just recently have we met with any encouragement. Last fall, the association [YMCA] appointed an Athletic Committee, with Guy Bryan as chairman, and through his efforts and those of his committee and P.B. Ferebee, all of whom have worked cheerfully and with dogged determination in face of the most discouraging conditions till their efforts were finally crowned with success in the recent magnificent game with Wake Forest, the first game on our own floor, which disproves the claims of some of our number that the game would never be successful, financial or otherwise. Never was there a more enthusiastic crowd, and never was a crowd more highly entertained.

"Basketball, thanks to Ferebee and Bryan, has come to A&M to stay; and after long years the history of this great college sport at A&M shall have been written, the names of G.K. Bryan and P.B. Ferebee will stand out in glaring letters as the pioneers on the frontier of this form of athletics at their Alma Mater. To the able manager of this year's team, W.H. Davis, will be given the credit of the financial success of this, the opening of basketball."

Ferebee was born in Elizabeth City, N.C., in 1891 and became a prominent banker in the western part of the state following his graduation from A&M with a degree in electrical engineering. He was on the board of directors for the North Carolina Department of Conservation and Development, the State Highway Patrol Commission and a member of the Consolidated UNC System board of trustees. College scholarships are still given in his name to deserving students from Cherokee, Clay, Graham, Jackson, Macon and Swain Counties and the Cherokee Indian Reservation pursuing studies at a North Carolina university or college.

Tampa native Bryan, the drum major in the college band and a pole vaulter on the A&M track team, earned a degree in civil engineering in 1912 and returned to Florida. What exactly happened afterwards is not known, but he was admitted into the Florida State Hospital for the Insane in Chattahoochee, Fla., prior to World War I and died there in 1920.

A century later, their names still stand in glaring letters for their efforts in bringing the sport to NC State.

For just a few minutes, the players in the 1929 Southern Conference Tournament Championship game became spectators.

Upstart Duke was leading NC State College 11-10 in the first half of the title game, when a plank on the floor of the Atlanta Municipal Auditorium came loose. The players retreated to their benches while a carpenter was summoned to fix the broken board. When he arrived with tool belt and hammer, both the Red Terrors and Demons hovered around him, as the guards made a mental note to forget about using that particular dead spot in the floor to their advantage for the rest of the game.

The 10-minute break was apparently an inspiration for NC State coach Gus Tebell's team, an experienced group of underdogs who had pulled off three consecutive upsets to get in this position. Despite the late starting time — 9:30 p.m. — and the long delay, the Red Terrors weren't about to lose focus in their golden chance to win the league tournament for the first time since the Atlanta Athletic Club began having a postseason tournament in 1921. (The inaugural event was open to any team in the South; the Southern Conference took over the tournament in 1924 and it was open only to the league's membership.)

Tebell's Terrors were a mediocre 6-5 in the Southern Conference regular-season race, finishing 11th in the 22-team league. That was good enough to qualify them for the nation's only postseason tournament at the time, which invited the top 16 teams from the Southern Conference regular-season standings. But it also left them as the underdogs against their first three opponents. Duke, in its first year in the league, was also a surprise participant in the title game, thanks to its semifinal upset of Georgia the day before.

But Duke seemed a little bored after the incident

with the board, and NC State reeled off an 11-1 scoring run to take control of the game.

NC State center Frank Goodwin of Greensboro did most of the damage, as he had in the Terrors' wins over Tennessee, Clemson and defending tournament championship Mississippi. Though there was no official Most Valuable Player named in the tournament, Goodwin surely would have been the overwhelming choice.

In four games, the lanky 6-2 center scored 63 points, including 23 points in the opener against the Volunteers; he had a pair of game-winning free throws in the semifinals against Ole Miss; and was the top scorer with 14 points in the title game against Durham's Demons.

NC State increased its lead over Duke with a four-point play by Larry Haar of Wilmington, who was fouled on a made shot and awarded two additional free throws, which was the rule of the day. Haar had been the hero of the semifinals against Ole Miss, scoring four consecutive baskets in the second half to erase an eight-point deficit against the Rebels and setting up Goodwin's game-winning free throws.

Against Duke, the Terrors led 25-18 at intermission.

The second half was played at an unusual pace. Duke, coached by Eddie Cameron, liked to use its speed to score quickly. NC State, thanks to experienced guards Bob Warren of Mooresville and Hank Young of Raleigh and Tebell's "Meanwell System" of short passes and layups, preferred a leisurely pace. They spent much of the second half dribbling the ball in wide circles in the backcourt in order to kill the clock.

The game hardly resembled the fast-paced, physical play of modern times. The rules were still evolving. There was still a jump ball after every made field goal and free throw. Because of that, talented centers

GAME...

like Goodwin could dominate a game. Players were expelled after four fouls. That same year, a proposal to outlaw dribbling was passed by the National Basketball Committee, but it was repealed before the next season began.

Duke never managed to get within nine points of the Terrors in the second half, and when the buzzer sounded, Tebell's team began a wild celebration on the court.

"We had a big time," said Tebell, who had also led the NC State football team to the 1927 Southern Conference championship, with a 9-1 overall and a 4-0 Southern Conference record. "Our boys played well, better than I could have asked of them, and every one of them fulfilled his duties supremely."

The team's celebration wasn't nearly as wild as the one in Raleigh, however, as some 100 students followed the action on the Associated Press teletype machine in *The News & Observer* sports department and relayed the news of the great victory back to campus.

When the game ended, they all rushed back down Hillsboro Street, as it was called then, to join 500 more students in a bonfire celebration on campus that lasted late into the night.

Two days later, the students were ready to party again. Nearly the entire student body, including the 750 uniformed members of the school's ROTC and the full college band, joined college president E.C. Brooks at Raleigh's Union Station to greet the triumphant team's train.

The players stepped off the train platform, near the corner of Dawson and West Martin

Streets, straight onto the shoulders of their schoolmates, who carried them down Fayetteville Street to the state capitol. There, they were greeted by the state's newly inaugurated governor, O. Max Gardner, who had been the captain of A&M's 1907 championship football team during his undergraduate days.

"If I could roll back the pages of time for 20 years to the days when I was a student at State, I'd rather be captain of this championship team than to be Governor of North Carolina," Gardner told the thousands who joined in the celebration.

It was an excellent harbinger of what would come many years later, when students refined their celebration skills and Hillsborough Street became the city's party destination. It was also the first glimpse into the excitement that championship basketball could bring to the school, the community and the state, as Raleigh officials clamored to organize the makeshift parade and a banquet to honor the returning champions.

"Tebell has produced a team that has brought honor to the State, the college and to themselves," Dr. Brooks told them. "The entire administration is proud of every one of them."

RED TERRORS

FARMERS
TECHS
AGGIES
NORTH STATERS
CARDINALS
HORNETS
CULTIVATORS
COTTON PICKERS
PINE-ROOTERS
AUCTIONEERS
CALUMETS

WOLFPACK

Before the Wolfpack, NC State's athletic teams were known as the Farmers, or the Techs, or the Aggies, or whatever other fanciful agrarian/technical names newspaper writers of the time could come up with.

The football team was given the name "Wolfpack" in 1921, after an angry letter writer complained that "as long as State's players behave on and off the field like a wolfpack, the school could never have a winning record." Students, particularly those at the campus-run newspaper, liked the pejorative nickname, and the NC State gridiron team has been known as the Wolfpack ever since.

But there was also a time, for nearly a quarter century, that all other athletic teams were known as "Red Terrors" thanks to a combination of things, including the Bolshevik Revolution in Russia, a three-sport athlete named Rochelle Johnson of Chalybeate Springs, N.C., and a bright red set of new wool basketball uniforms.

Red and white had been the State College school colors since 1896, after an early dalliance with pink and blue (1891–94) and a one-year experiment with brown and white (1895).

Students and alumni embraced the fiery colors. The first student newspaper was called "The Red and White," until it ended publication in 1918 after a flu outbreak and World War I halted most extracurricular activities on campus.

That same year, shortly after an attempted assassination of leader Vladimir Lenin, the Russian Bolsheviks began a campaign of arrests and executions — in which hundreds of thousands of citizens in targeted social classes were systemically eliminated — known as "The Red Terror." It was a phrase that for four years struck worldwide fear, until the revolution ended in 1922.

Johnson, a strapping Irishman from Chalybeate Springs, N.C., had strawberry blonde hair that made him a distinctive figure as he played football, basketball and baseball for NC State. He was a popular man on campus, twice named the school's athlete of the year. He was known to all as "Red" Johnson.

The 1925 basketball season was filled with excitement, as the team began playing in its new home, Frank Thompson Gymnasium, and for a new head coach, Gus Tebell. Johnson's spirited aggression on the court and Tebell's fast-paced passing game gave birth to the new nickname, "The Red Terrors."

The name stuck until the Everett Case years.

In 1946, Chancellor J.W. Harrelson decided that all the school's teams should be called the same thing. He was actually trying to get rid of the Wolfpack nickname, since that was what German U-boats were called during World War II. His opinion was that "the only thing lower than a wolf is a snake in the grass."

But his plan backfired. After running a campuswide contest to come up with a new nickname — some suggestions included North Staters, the Cardinals, the Hornets, the Cultivators, the Cotton Pickers, Pine-rooters, the Auctioneers and the Calumets — students and alumni rallied around the name Wolfpack and overwhelmingly voted to keep that name over Harrelson's objections.

Since then, all NC State teams have been called the Wolfpack, and other than Nevada's similar Wolf Pack, no other NCAA school uses the one-word nickname.

THE HERO

FROM ATHLETIC FIELD TO BATTLEFIELD, FRANK THOMPSON LEFT A LEGACY FOR THE AGES

The second lieutenant who picked up his pen to write a letter home that afternoon in August 1918 was filled with fatigue and perhaps a little false bravado. He was hunkered down in a trench on a battlefield in France, dodging German artillery shells and fighting off field rats the size of housecats.

He vowed to dig his foxhole down to 30 feet, just to stay safe, even though he tried to suggest that he was not in fear of his life.

"I have had a taste of the rifle bullets and the artillery fire," he wrote. "It isn't bad. Am to take a night patrol out tonight to inspect the wires. Am anxious to keep going and get into the Boche trenches and bring back a few souvenirs."

He had, however, encountered the horrors of war, and many of the inconveniences.

"The cooties are here all right and bite like blazes," he wrote. "The other pets are rats, and they are all kinds and sizes. They will run over you, nibble at your fingers, and make a regular playhouse out of your bunk. Guess it is a good thing I stay up at nights and manage to get a few hours of sleep in the daytime."

Not long after his lengthy letter was published in the *NC State Alumni News*, Frank Thompson's parents received a telegram from the United States Army informing them that their son had died in action on Sept. 13, 1918, just a few weeks before the fighting ended on the Western Front.

It was a loss that reverberated throughout the campuses of A&M College and Wake Forest.

Thompson, born in west Raleigh, N.C., was one of the top athletes in the early history of A&M. He was the captain of the baseball team in 1906 and '07 and the captain of the football team that won the championship of the South in 1907.

Immediately after he graduated, he was hired as an instructor, a baseball coach and eventually head football coach at his alma mater. For three years, he had one of the state's best baseball programs and claimed the championship of the South again for the football team in 1910.

Abruptly, in 1912, he switched allegiances, becoming the head football and baseball coach at A&M's biggest rival, Wake Forest, and causing tension between the two neighbors. In the spring of 1917, at the age of 32, Thompson enlisted in the

U.S. Army for service in the Great War, becoming a second lieutenant in the 15th Machine Gun Battalion.

However, both campuses mourned when the news of Thompson's death spread throughout the state.

"No young man from Raleigh has gone to the front richer in friends than Frank Thompson, and the death of none could bring more widespread grief and deep regret," read his obituary in the Oct. 1, 1918, edition of the *Alumni News*. "As an athlete, [he] was known from one end of the State to the other. He was a graduate of State College, where, as a student, he made a record, in both

football and baseball. He was later athletic coach at his alma mater and at Wake Forest College. He was liked by all who knew him, for he had those fine qualities of character that won the love and esteem of all."

Interestingly, Thompson had no association with basketball at either school. However, when the state legislature approved the largest construction initiative (at the time) in A&M's history, the board of trustees approved naming a proposed gymnasium in Thompson's honor, long before it had been designed or construction actually began.

The building was designed by renowned

church architect Hobart Upchurch of New York. It was initially praised for its aesthetic beauty, thanks to the prominent Romanesque columns facing the railroad tracks. It was also praised for its versatility, at least in the early days.

The only previous building for athletic competition was the YMCA building, which opened in 1912 with the school's first swimming pool and open auditorium for athletic activities. But it wasn't built for basketball.

Thompson Gym, on the other hand, was open year-round and featured polished wooden floors that made it just right for basketball, gymnastics,

intramural sports, physical education classes, commencement and frequent school dances.

It also had a 35 x 75-foot swimming pool in the basement and an indoor running track suspended around the interior perimeter above the playing floor.

When Thompson Gym was designed, the school barely had 1,200 students and the 2,500-seat facility was thought to be of ample size to serve the campus for many years to come.

But not long after the Red Terrors won the 1929 Southern Conference Championship and enrollment at the college began to swell, the basketball team began to outdraw Thompson's capac-

ity, thanks to the play of early stars like Maurice "Johnny" Johnson, Bud Rose, Connie Mack Berry and Horace "Bones" McKinney.

In 1940, with a push from influential alumnus David Clark, plans were made to replace Thompson as NC State's multipurpose auditorium. Using plans borrowed from Duke Indoor Stadium, the school purchased structural steel and poured a concrete foundation.

But the start of World War II halted construction for nearly seven years, and Thompson remained the home of the Red Terrors until the end of the decade, much to the displeasure of head coach Everett Case, who was attracted to NC State on the promise of a new auditorium, not the continued use of the old one.

Case had immediate success after he was hired in May 1946, and Thompson did not fit into his plans for building a nationally prominent program. On a postwar campus with a swelling enrollment of more than 5,000 students, there was simply no way for Thompson to contain all the people who wanted to see Case's team play.

Though the building was only 22 years old, athletics director Roy Clogston called Thompson "a disgrace to the college."

"The lighting is

inadequate and unsafe," he reported to the athletics council. "The showers plugged, and one moment a shower is well-adjusted, and the next the temperature changes from cold to scalding hot. . . . The general overall condition of the building and the quality of the janitorial service requires immediate attention."

On Jan. 17, 1947, Case's team was scheduled to play North Carolina in the gym, but Raleigh fire marshal W.R. Butts canceled the game because more than 5,000 spectators were jammed into the seats, the aisles and the doorways of the old gym.

The next year, Thompson Gym was condemned by city building inspectors for having inadequate exits.

As much as he wanted a new building to play in, Case had reason to love Thompson, which he dubbed "The Lion's Den." In the two seasons it

was his home, the Red Terrors never lost a game there, going 18-0 in parts of two seasons. After the basketball team moved to Reynolds Coliseum in December, 1949, Thompson was still used as a multipurpose facility, at least until Carmichael Gymnasium was built behind Reynolds in 1966. Thompson was converted to a theater and arts center in the early 1970s and recently went through a $15 million renovation that will keep the doors open — and Frank Thompson's memory alive — for many years to come.

The First Big Time Pro

One of the reserves on the first basketball team was Dave Robertson, a sophomore from Norfolk, Va. Robertson played only a few moments as a backup center in the two games against Wake Forest's Baptists, but he eventually became the first accomplished professional athlete in the early history of North Carolina A&M.

Davis Aydelotte Robertson was a four-sport letterman during his college days, whose speed in football, basketball and baseball was rivaled only by teammate Harry Hartsell. On the track, he excelled at the 100-yard dash, the broad jump and the high hurdles.

It was on the baseball diamond, where he played third base and pitched, that Robertson was a superstar, in an era when every school did its basketball recruiting from its other sports on campus.

Robertson was a terror at the plate, and he and future football and basketball coach Tal Stafford gave the Farmers a 1-2 pitching punch that was second to none in the southeast. In Robertson's final year, A&M lost only two games all season.

His greatest achievement in college came on April 15, 1911, when the sophomore lefthander struck out 23 batters in a 5-2 victory over Guilford College. The *Agromeck* breathlessly proclaimed it to be "the world's college strike-out record" and "the greatest performance of its kind ever to fall to the lot of an amateur pitcher." In fact, it is a record that no individual NC State pitcher has matched in the 100 years since. It wasn't until the spring of 2009, in an 18-inning game against Akron, that a Wolfpack team surpassed Robertson's single-game total, as the staff combined to strike out an NCAA-record 31 batters in the longest game in NC State history.

A local scout who saw the game recommended Robertson to legendary New York Giants manager John McGraw, whose team was in the midst of winning three consecutive National League pennants. McGraw agreed to sign the young pitcher if he agreed not to play football the following fall. Robertson talked the crusty manager into letting him play in three games for the Farmers during the 1911 season.

But against Bucknell in the season's second game, Robertson suffered a career-altering shoulder injury in a mass pileup of players.

"He had the shoulder strapped up and went back into the game. But he was speedily put out of commission with another damaged shoulder, and as that exhausted his supply of shoulders, he quit," said a 1916 story in *The Baseball Magazine*. "Later it came to light that both shoulders were broken, although he didn't realize it in the heat of battle."

The football injuries cost Robertson his pinpoint control on the mound, but not McGraw's commitment to signing him to a professional contract. He became an excellent outfielder, known for his combination of speed and power. Less than three months after leaving A&M (and only seven weeks after the *Titanic* sank), Robertson made his major league debut for McGraw on June 5, 1912, in a 22-10 blowout against the Cincinnati Reds. The Giants, en route to an NL-leading 103 wins and 828 runs, didn't really need Robertson's power and speed that season, so he played in only three games.

He spent all of 1913 with the Mobile Sea Gulls in the South Atlantic League, where he batted .335

Dave Robertson

Jim Thorpe

and smacked a whopping (during the dead-ball era) 11 home runs. He returned to the Giants in 1914 as a utility player. In 1916 and '17, Robertson tied for the National League home run championship, with 12 in each season.

Robertson, known as the "National League Ty Cobb," loved to tell the story of how one of his homers in 1915 cost him the unheard-of sum of $100.

"We were playing the Chicago Cubs in the Polo Grounds in 1915. We had a man on base and John McGraw instructed me to bunt," Robertson once told *The Virginian-Pilot* newspaper. "A fat pitch came over and I couldn't resist. I slammed the ball into the right field bleachers for a homer, winning the game 3-2.

"But instead of receiving congratulations for my feat, McGraw said the homer would cost me $100 for disobeying orders."

He was a starting outfielder for the Giants in the 1917 World Series against "Shoeless" Joe Jackson and the Chicago White Sox. Robertson had 11 hits in 22 at-bats against the White Sox, a World Series batting average record that stood for 36 years until it was broken by New York Yankees outfielder Billy Martin.

His major league career ended after nine seasons with New York, the Chicago Cubs and the Pittsburgh Pirates.

Robertson served as state game warden for 28 years after his baseball career ended and successfully operated a sporting goods store. He died at the age of 89 on Nov. 5, 1970, in Virginia Beach, Va.

The Ace

He was the most famous "Opie" from North Carolina until Andy Griffith's television son came along.

Though at 6-1 he was one of the tallest students on campus and an accomplished early basketball player at North Carolina School for Agriculture and Mechanic Arts, Robert "Opie" Lindsay didn't gain fame on the hardwoods.

Instead he became a hero in two world wars.

Lindsay's classmates knew this textiles major from Madison, N.C., would one day be wildly successful. While on campus, he not only played center for the basketball team, he was the business manager of the student newspaper and associate editor of the yearbook.

The 1916 edition of the *Agromeck* said, "We predict a great future for this boy."

Yet Lindsay failed in the first thing he tried to do after his graduation in 1916 — he was medically disqualified when he tried to enlist in the U.S. Army's Officers Training Corps in Oglethorpe, Ga., at the outset of World War I because of appendicitis. After an appendectomy in Greensboro, Lindsay went to Washington to join the U.S. Signal Corps, becoming one of a handful of the 1,897 A&M students who served during World War I as an aviator.

He learned to fly a French-made biplane, the SPAD VIII, and quickly became one of the top American pursuit pilots. On Oct. 27, 1918, in his first aerial engagement, Lindsay was credited with two kills over Saint Mihiel, France. His heroic performance in that initial aerial dogfight earned him the Distinguished Service

The Booster

Few names in the history of North Carolina political power carry more weight than the descendants of David Clark II, a brigadier general in the North Carolina militia during the Civil War. His son, Walter McKenzie Clark, was the Chief Justice of the North Carolina Supreme Court and married the daughter of Governor William A. Graham.

It's little wonder that the power couple's five sons chose to be active in the affairs of their alma mater, the North Carolina School for Agriculture and Mechanic Arts.

The oldest of the quintet, named David in honor of his grandfather, graduated with three

engineering degrees from the A&M by the time he was 21. He earned another engineering degree from Cornell. And he served in the Spanish-American War.

He opened his first textile mill shortly after he left the Raleigh school, and watched it go bankrupt during the bankers' panic of 1907. He rebounded after founding the Southern Textile Association and publishing the *Southern Textile Bulletin*, wielding considerable influence in North Carolina's largest industry with his ultra-conservative, pro-business editorials. Adamantly opposed to child-labor laws, Clark twice took his cause all the way to the United States Supreme Court.

At times, "Uncle Dave" was accused of having a hard heart, but there was a definite soft spot for athletics at his alma mater. He played both football and baseball at the school at the turn of the century and became the most influential booster in the history of NC State, long before names like Abernethy, Carter, Finley, Gunter, Murphy and Dail became prominent in the construction of athletics facilities.

Without Clark, the school would not have hired and fired five football coaches and two athletics directors from 1931–44. Many student-athletes would not have received the loosely defined grants Clark handed out through his Delaware Student's Loan Fund.

And Reynolds Coliseum would never have been built.

Cross, the Army's second highest combat decoration. Later, Lindsay shot down four more German aircraft over the Argonne Forest.

After 20 aerial battles, Lindsay was officially credited with shooting down six German planes, making him the only North Carolina native among the 63 American aces during the war. But it was hazardous duty. He was twice shot down from more than 20,000 feet, once behind enemy lines.

Lindsay survived the war and returned to the United States as a hero. He held several positions in the civil air service, including four years as the director of aeronautics for the state of Tennessee. When World War II began, he organized a National Guard Squadron in Oklahoma and served as the commanding officer at Fort Sill.

Promoted to Lt. Colonel, he finished the war as the

Air Liaison Officer for the Third Army. Afterward he was a founding member of the Civil Aeronautics Administration, a forerunner of the Federal Aviation Administration.

Born on Christmas Day, 1894, Lindsay died in Houston, Texas, on Aug. 1, 1952.

Clark served as the president of the Alumni Association — an organization for which his younger brother John was the general secretary for more than two decades — and was a member of the Board of Trustees for the consolidated University of North Carolina.

But nothing affected Clark — or the future of the university — quite like the annual statewide gathering for Farmer's Week in the summer of 1940. A daylong rain storm prevented the 5,000 farmers from gathering at Riddick Field, and there was no other place on campus for such a large group to hold its meeting.

From that day forward, Clark made it his mission to build a replacement for decaying Thompson Gymnasium, the multipurpose home of NC State basketball and physical education classes. He envisioned an arena that could double as an armory for the school's ROTC programs and as a gathering spot for students, faculty, alumni and events of all kinds.

He also suggested that the arena should have the ice-making capability to turn it into the South's first and only ice rink, to generate income for the athletics department, an idea that ultimately failed because the humidity caused by the eight miles of ice-making pipes in the floor of the arena caused the ceiling tiles to disintegrate and fall to the floor.

The idea was considered outlandish at the time, but Clark's foresight was remembered when the NHL's Carolina Hurricanes brought the

Stanley Cup to Raleigh in 2006.

In 1940, Clark purchased the first load of structural steel for an on-campus arena/armory and suggested the school make use of the Depression-era Works Progress Administration (WPA) to get the project started. When World War II broke out in Europe, Clark encouraged the school to begin the construction, even though there were no funds to proceed, so that the steel would not be recalled for war purposes.

Clark was also instrumental in suggesting that UNC consolidated university comptroller W.D. Carmichael go to Greenwich, Conn., to visit Mary Katherine Reynolds Babcock, an heiress to the Reynolds tobacco fortune.

Mrs. Babcock not only contributed $100,000 to the project prior to the outbreak of World War II, she kicked in another $52,000 after the war to purchase the ice-making equipment. For those contributions, Mrs. Babcock was allowed to name the arena in honor of her uncle, William Neal Reynolds.

The Clark family name still adorns the Clark Chemistry Labs, Clark Hall (the former home of Student Health Services) and Clark Avenue, which runs parallel to Hillsborough Street, just north of the main campus. But the basketball arena, known for years as "The House that Case Built" and now home to "Kay Yow Court," is as much a tribute to Clark's ornery persistence and devotion to his alma mater as it is to any other individual.

The All-Star Coach

Much like Everett Case years later, Gus Tebell was an early innovator and master marketer as the head football and basketball coach at North Carolina State College.

During his tenure in Raleigh (1924–30), Tebell became the only coach in the history of the Southern Conference to win championships in both sports. He also launched the career of the most famous shoe salesman basketball has ever known, Chuck Taylor, whose signature is on the Converse All-Star. And he offered many ideas that helped create interest in both sports as the school began to grow in the years following World War I.

At the age of 19, Gustave Kenneth Tebell enlisted as a second lieutenant in the U.S. Army for service in World War I in 1917. Immediately after he was discharged following the war, he enrolled at the University of Wisconsin, where he played football, basketball and baseball. On the hardwoods, Tebell

learned the game under
Naismith Hall of Fame coach Dr. Walter Meanwell, who brought order to the sometimes rough-and-tumble game of college basketball. The "Meanwell System" relied on short passes, fancy dribbling and zone defenses, and was later adopted by one of Meanwell's other pupils, Everett Case of Frankfort (Ind.) High School.

As a basketball player, Tebell was a three-time All–Big Ten performer who helped the Badgers win conference championships in 1921 and '23.

Following his college career, Tebell spent one season as a player-coach for the Columbus Tigers of the American Professional Football League, a predecessor of the NFL. He was an all-pro end who also alternated head coaching duties with Pete Stinchcomb, while also scoring a team-high 37 points on three touchdowns, seven extra points and four field goals.

Besides Meanwell, Tebell became friendly with some influential people in basketball's early days, including an Indiana-born player named Charlie Taylor. Tebell gave the kid a boost by inviting him to Raleigh in 1925 to conduct a basketball clinic for the grand opening of Thompson Gymnasium.

By then, Taylor was known to everyone as "Chuck" and he had taken a job as a salesman for the Converse Rubber Shoe Company. Thousands of similar clinics later, Taylor was known as basketball's biggest ambassador, and Converse rewarded him by naming a pair of high-top basketball shoes with a patch on the ankle in his honor.

As a coach at North Carolina State College, Tebell introduced such advances as bright red uniforms in basketball, the annual spring football game and the first basketball game programs.

It was under his guidance that all NC State teams other than football were named the "Red Terrors," because of those brightly colored uniforms and the fast-paced play led by forward Rochelle "Red" Johnson.

In 1927, he led the football team to a perfect 4-0 Southern Conference record and a 9-1 overall mark, for NC State's only conference championship on the gridiron until Earle Edwards arrived in 1953.

Two years later, Tebell took the basketball team to Atlanta for the Southern Conference tournament, beating Tennessee, Clemson, Mississippi and Duke for the school's only league basketball title until Case arrived in 1946.

But in the spring of 1930, after compiling a 21-25-2 record in football and a 76-39 record in basketball, Tebell announced that he would leave NC State to became an assistant football coach and head basketball coach at the University of Virginia. He still owns the second-best winning percentage (.687) of any NC State basketball coach who coached at least 100 games, after Everett Case (.738).

In 21 seasons at Virginia, Tebell compiled a 240-190 record on the hardwoods, which still ranks as third all-time in career wins. He led the team to its first appearance in a postseason tournament, losing in the first round of the 1941 National Invitation Tournament to City College

of New York. He also spent three years as football head coach from 1934–36.

A colorful, popular character, Tebell was twice elected mayor of Charlottesville, Va.

Even after he left, Tebell still had an impact on NC State athletics. He helped fuel the fire between longtime rivals Case and Kentucky coach Adolph Rupp. In 1950, both the Wolfpack and the Wildcats were among the best teams in the nation, with Case's Southern Conference champions ranked No. 5 with a 24-5 record and Rupp's SEC champions ranked No. 3 with a 25-4 record.

Tebell, the chairman of the Region 3 selection committee, suggested that the two teams decide the NCAA bid with a one-game playoff. Case agreed to play "any time, any place." But Rupp, whose team had won the previous two NCAA titles, didn't believe his team needed to prove itself and refused to participate in a playoff game.

The committee voted to take NC State over the Wildcats, infuriating Rupp and furthering the divide between him and Case.

When Virginia athletics director Norton Pritchett died in the summer of 1951, Tebell gave up his job as basketball coach to take over that position. In 1953, despite opposition from Virginia president Colgate Darden, he convinced the school's Board of Visitors to accept an invitation to join the newly formed Atlantic Coast Conference. Some six months after the other charter members committed to breaking away from the old Southern Conference, Virginia became the eighth school to officially join the ACC.

Tebell was one of two candidates considered to become the ACC's first commissioner, losing a 6-2 vote to Wake Forest athletics director Jim Weaver.

Tebell remained at Virginia as athletics director until his retirement in 1962. He died in Charlottesville, Va., on May 28, 1969.

The Y-Factor

John W. Bergthold likely had no idea what he would unleash.

A slight, energetic man of great faith, Bergthold just knew that the campus of North Carolina School for Agriculture and Mechanic Arts needed some other diversions to keep its growing population of farmers and engineers occupied during their time out of class.

As the general secretary of the campus Young Men's Christian Association, Bergthold was at the center of social and religious life on campus. His little room in Holladay Hall had a single flashing light on the outside that drew students into a common area, where they could read national magazines, play cards, get a haircut or perhaps participate in a discussion about news of the day.

In the fall and spring, football and baseball were always favorite topics. But Bergthold believed that A&M students needed something

Our New Y. M. C. A. Building

more during the dreary winter months. When the Minnesota native and graduate of Oklahoma A&M College arrived to become the second full-time general secretary of the YMCA, the campus was embroiled in a hazing controversy that caused North Carolina governor Robert Broadnax Glenn to threaten to cut off state funding for the school.

Bergthold's mission was to engage more students through the Y, which had been an integral part of the campus since the first class of students arrived in 1889. In Bergthold's first year, membership grew from 125 to 243 members. That was more than half of the entire enrollment of the college.

Like all YMCA men of the time, Bergthold began pushing "basket-ball" as a good means of indoor exercise. It was a game that had been invented by YMCA instructor Dr. James Naismith some 20 years before in Springfield, Mass., and had rapidly spread across the globe, thanks to YMCA instructors, just like volleyball, another game that was invented by a YMCA man.

Though only 25 when he arrived, Bergthold made important friends quickly. Gov. Glenn was the speaker at his first weekly meeting. Newspaper publisher Josephus Daniels was also a frequent visitor and speaker to the YMCA membership. Only two years after he arrived, he procured a $20,000 commitment from philanthropist John D. Rockefeller for A&M to build its first permanent YMCA building — as long as the school and its students could raise a similar amount. The state legislature kicked in $10,000 and Bergthold began a successful fundraising campaign on campus for the other half.

The YMCA building, completed in 1913 near Holladay Hall, included the school's first gymnasium and swimming pool.

After he built momentum, Bergthold turned the organization of the basketball team over to two students, Percy Bell Ferebee of Elizabeth City and Guy K. Bryan of Tampa, Fla. After just one year, the YMCA team was a financial success and the school agreed to make it a permanent varsity sport, sponsored by the athletic association.

Bergthold stayed on campus through 1914, long enough to marry the first of his three wives, before leaving for a similar post at Alabama Polytechnic Institution (now Auburn University). He traveled the world during his career, participating in the 1922 American Pilgrimage of Friendship to Europe. During his full life, he lived in Chicago, Tampa, West Virginia and Washington, D.C.

He retired in 1946 and settled in Black Mountain, N.C., where he founded the High Top Colony and became one of the state's first all-organic farmers. He died at the age of 73 on July 18, 1955, and is buried in a Buncombe County cemetery.

Bergthold said in a 1939 article in the *NC State Alumni News* that one of his favorite students during his time at A&M was a football player named John Von Glahn, hero of the 1907 football championship and a striking figure on campus at the time.

In 1946, Von Glahn was the business manager of the athletics association, who joined faculty athletics chairman Dr. H.A. Fisher on a trip to an Atlanta hotel to interview a basketball coach.

His name? Everett Case.

INNOVATIONS:
A CASE STUDY

CASE

for *Success*

The first official meeting of the Raleigh Touchdown Club was held March 2, 1946, at the Sir Walter Hotel during the Southern Conference basketball tournament. The idea was to promote all athletics in North Carolina's growing capital, so the organization was looking for a big-name speaker at its initial meeting.

At the time, there were few public speakers bigger than Chuck Taylor, the vagabond shoe salesman for the Converse Rubber Shoe Company and unofficial ambassador for the game of basketball. Taylor, an Indiana schoolboy legend who played briefly for several semi-pro teams, had been given his start some two decades earlier by former NC State coach Gus Tebell, who asked his young friend to give a short clinic to the Red Terror basketball team, just after the opening of Thompson Gymnasium.

It was the first of thousands of clinics Taylor would give around the globe over the next half century. The longtime bachelor made frequent trips to Wilson, N.C., to visit his surrogate family, and never forgot his ties to NC State. He was also eager to see the game he loved — and profited from — grow in the region. During his introduction to the club, Taylor was described as an "ex-professional basketball player who probably sees more basketball than any other person in the country and who is one of the best qualified observers of the game."

Tebell, who moved on to become the basketball coach and then athletics director at Virginia, was on hand to introduce Taylor to the luncheon's guests, which included Lt. Gov. L.Y. Ballentine and Dr. Hilbert A. Fisher, president of the Southern Conference.

Dr. Fisher also happened to be a longtime professor of mathematics at NC State and faculty chairman of the school's athletics council. He spoke with *The News & Observer* sports editor Dick Herbert, a former publicity director at NC State, and Taylor about the school's vacant basketball position. Taylor immediately recommended that Fisher hire a middle-aged bachelor from Indiana who had no college experience, but was one of basketball-crazed Indiana's most accomplished coaches.

"The best coach in America is a Lieutenant Commander in the U.S. Navy. His name is Everett Case," said Taylor, who was a frequent instructor before the war at Case's annual Indiana High School Coaches Training School. "If you want him, you'd better not waste any time because some other colleges have been after him to coach for them when he gets out."

Fisher, a North Carolina native and a graduate of the U.S. Naval Academy, traveled to Atlanta with athletics business manager John Von Glahn to interview Case. They told him how the school was revamping the athletics department, replacing its part-time war coaches with accomplished veterans in football, baseball and basketball, in an attempt to become more competitive. They told him of Raleigh's association with the Southern Conference basketball tournament, and how the event regularly drew sellout crowds. They may not have mentioned that the downtown municipal auditorium was smaller than the high school gym where Case coached for 23 years, but who knows for sure? They portrayed a school that was eager for success.

And, perhaps most important, they told him of the steel skeleton of a building erected prior to World War II that would eventually become the school's new 9,000-seat multipurpose coliseum/armory/meeting hall.

Case was intrigued, especially by the large arena. His experiences as an Indiana high school coach taught him that the school with the best gym hosted all the big games. Fisher took an immediate liking to the fellow Navy officer. They began talking terms, even though Case had never stepped foot on NC State's railroad-bisected campus.

Case was a shrewd businessman. During his high school coaching career, he not only ran a lucrative coaches' training school in the summer, he also owned a chain of drive-in restaurants, including one just down the street from his school called the Campus Castle. He obsessed over his investments. By the time he took the job at NC State, he was wealthy enough not to worry about a significant salary or multiple-year contract.

In fact, he insisted that he not have one. When Dr. Fisher asked him what terms he wanted in his contract, Case suggested the school pay him $5,000 a year. But he was against a multiyear contract. "Oh, that is not important," Case said. "I've been fortunate in my investments. Money isn't a big consideration. I don't want any contract. Then, if I find out I don't like it here, I'll be free to leave. And if you find you don't want me, you'll be free to replace me."

Dr. Fisher, who had been involved with athletics at the school since he first arrived as an assistant professor in 1921, had never heard of such a thing.

NEVER PLAYED THE GAME

Case was indeed an excellent coach, though he never actually played the game, even in high school. He won his first championship—coaching the 75-pound division entry for a Methodist church in Anderson, Ind.—at the age of 15. He listed his future occupation under his senior portrait in the 1919 Anderson High yearbook as "basketball coach."

Case was so busy chasing that dream he never stopped long enough to become a full-time college student. After graduating high school, Case completed a 12-week summer course to receive a teaching certificate, which the state of Indiana allowed to reduce a postwar teacher's shortage.

At the age of 19, he was hired at Connersville High School to coach basketball and track. In his first season, he became one of the youngest coaches ever to lead a school into the 16-team state finals. Once, a security guard prevented him from entering the coaches' area at the state finals because he didn't think Case looked old enough to be a coach.

In 1922, Case was hired for the tidy sum of $1,800 to coach basketball and track at Frankfort High. In his second year at Frankfort, the school opened 3,500-seat Howard Hall, one of the biggest high school gyms in the area and a frequent host of high school sectional and regional events. In 1925, he won his first state championship, accepting the trophy afterward from none other than Dr.

James Naismith, the inventor of the game. It was the only time Naismith ever witnessed the spectacle of the Indiana state finals. Case won his second title in 1929.

Instead of attending college classes in the fall, winter and spring, Case spent some 14 summers pursuing his bachelor's degree in physical education, taking classes at schools all over the Midwest. While he did (most likely) take summer school classes, he spent almost as much time learning basketball from the great coaches at the schools where he studied, like Ralph R. Jones of Illinois in 1919, Dr. Walter Meanwell of Wisconsin in 1920 and '23 and Sam Barry of Iowa from 1924–26.

Case left Frankfort in 1931 for his hometown of Anderson, where he was paid, with bonuses, the enormous Depression-era sum of $12,000 a year, which was not only more than the head coach of the Chicago Bears, but it was also more than twice his initial salary at NC State some 15 years later. Case finally earned his P.E. degree, with a minor in English, from Central Normal College in Danville, Ind., in 1933, one year before Indiana required all high school coaches to have a college degree. From 1933–34, he left Indiana to enter graduate school at Southern California and serve as an assistant coach for Barry, who had moved from Iowa to the West Coast in 1929. Case's thesis? "An Analysis of the Effects of Various Factors on the Accuracy of Free Throws."

Case returned to Frankfort in 1934 to tend to his ailing mother and to take his old job back. He picked up right where he left off, winning two more titles in 1936 and '39, becoming the first coach in the storied history of the Indiana state play-offs to win four titles. While he was adored by the people of the town, Case was reviled by opposing fans, coaches and the media, who gave him the derisive nickname "Slick." Not only did his success rub them the wrong way, they also accused him of illegally recruiting players from other parts of the state to move to Frankfort. Twice, his teams were suspended by the Indiana High School Athletic Association for flaunting eligibility rules.

His final victory as a high school coach came in the semifinals of the 1942 state tournament, when his Hot Dogs beat South Bend Central, which was coached by young Johnny Wooden. Long before he was known as the "Wizard of Westwood,"

Wooden faced Case as a high school player and as an opposing coach.

Case, along with former player and longtime friend Carl "Buttercup" Anderson, finally left Indiana for good when he enlisted in the Navy in 1942, shortly after the United States entered World War II. Neither Case nor Anderson ever came close to combat service. Case spent his active duty coaching several Navy service basketball teams, winning the 1946 all-service championship as the coach of the Iowa Preflight Seahawks with a 25-2 record.

QUIET ARRIVAL, LOUD RESULTS

Case's arrival at NC State got scant attention in the local media, making the page 11 headline in the April 19, 1946, edition of *The News & Observer*. But he was a welcomed addition to an athletics department that had already scored big hires in football coach Beattie Feathers, a one-time professional player who was the first running back in NFL history to rush for 1,000 yards in a single season, and baseball coach Vic Sorrell, who had just concluded his 10-year career as a pitcher for the Detroit Tigers.

Feathers made Case happy when he agreed to hire Anderson, the Frankfort High graduate who had played both football and basketball at Southern Cal, as an assistant football coach, adding to

43

ABOVE: Everett Case (left) and Lou Pucillo coach from the sidelines.
BELOW: Vic Bubas (left) and John Wooden visit Everett Case.

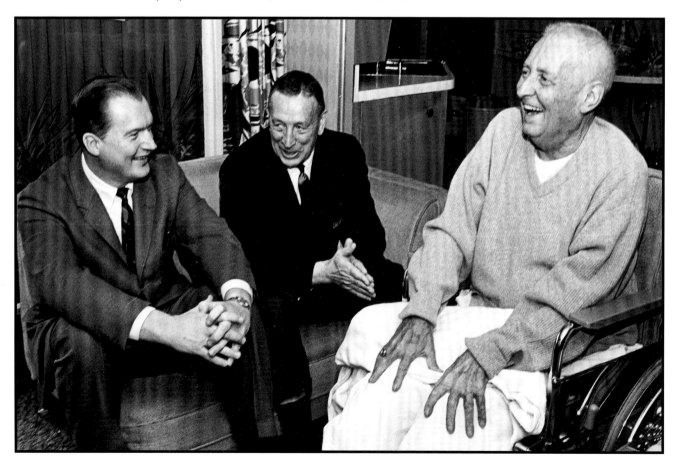

the duties Case gave Anderson, now known as just "Butter," as an assistant basketball coach. In his first season, Feathers took the Wolfpack to its first postseason game when it played Oklahoma in the Gator Bowl. It was easily the best news in years for a school whose programs had languished during the war.

At least until basketball season began to roll.

On a campus that swelled with nearly 5,000 students, Case had plenty of talent to choose from. In his first called tryouts, more than 60 prospective players showed up, including nearly every starter from the previous year's team. But it was just a smokescreen. Case had already brought to campus some of the best players he coached in the service and others he remembered from his prewar high school days in Indiana. The only former player Case kept on his roster was Leo Katkavek, who had played for the Red Terrors in 1942 before going to war. Every other roster spot was taken by players from Case's nationwide recruiting efforts. Because of the six players from Case's home state, the media dubbed his first team the "Hoosier Hotshots."

"When we came here, people in this part of the country were basketball illiterates," said Norm Sloan, a native of Indianapolis and a World War II veteran who was a member of Case's first recruiting class.

In the winter of 1947, basketball fever had swept through campus like earlier versions of the Spanish flu. The thousands of war veterans and their wives, looking for cheap entertainment, were captivated by the Hotshots, especially after Case took his team on a post-Christmas Midwest barnstorming tour. One of the Red Terrors' victims on that tour was Holy Cross, the team that would go on to win the 1947 NCAA championship. Students took notice of their team's success and loved going to home games. Trouble was, Thompson Gym was far too small to accommodate even half of the swelled enrollment of just about 5,000 students. Demand for tickets was so high, the school had no seats to sell to the faculty, staff or general public.

After Case's team beat New York University at home and Duke and North Carolina on the road, the Red Terrors were the darlings of campus. In late February, when NC State was supposed to host North Carolina, nobody on campus wanted to be left out. Tiny Thompson Gym was so packed with fans Raleigh fire marshal W.R. Butts canceled the game.

That might have been the moment Raleigh officially became the "Basketball Capital of the South." The first edition of the "Hotshots" roared through the Southern Conference regular season and the postseason tournament, which had to be moved to Durham to accommodate the requests for tickets. When the Red Terrors beat UNC's White Phantoms in the championship game, it was the school's first league title since 1929.

Case won nine conference championships in his first 10 seasons at NC State, and a total of 10 in his 18-year career. He took the school to its first eight appearances in the National Invitation Tournament and the NCAA Tournament. And, more important, he made every school in the area scramble to catch up.

"You have to understand that at the time he came here, there were a lot of schools that were just made up mostly of football players, who played both sports," said Vic Bubas, who spent 10 years as an assistant under Case before becoming the head coach at Duke. "There were no scholarships then. It was really back in the days when there was no such thing as a basketball program.

"He envisioned when he came to North Carolina State a whole basketball program that involved recruiting, coaching and promoting. I think N.C. State, and ultimately the ACC, were blessed to have somebody who knew how to sell the game of basketball, in addition to putting a good team on the court. In the process, others were forced to change."

Particularly neighbors North Carolina and Duke. Case beat the Tar Heels the first 15 times he faced them, forcing the school to hire nationally known Frank McGuire of St. John's to take over its program. Wake Forest tried to stay competitive by replacing Murray Greason with former NBA player and head coach Horace "Bones" McKinney, a Durham, N.C., native who played for one year at NC State before the war. The Wolfpack won the first three of six consecutive Southern Conference tournaments at Duke Indoor Stadium. Eventually, the Blue Devils hired Bubas, who built one of the nation's top programs in the 1960s.

"You have to realize that Carolina and Duke and

others were forced to improve [because of Case],” said the late Jim Valvano in a 1982 interview. “Everett had beaten North Carolina something like 15 straight times at one point. I asked Frank McGuire once if it was true that he was hired at UNC to beat Case. He said yes, without question.”

NC State proved to its neighbors that basketball could be a viable, moneymaking option in the world of college athletics, if properly maintained and marketed. Despite Feathers's initial success, he did not build a strong football program. That didn't come to the school until 1953, in the wake of Case's phenomenal hardwood success, when coach Earle Edwards came to Raleigh and won five ACC titles in 18 years.

“The NC State story is one of the most vivid illustrations of a truth the colleges have been learning in recent years: Basketball offers a much quicker, easier and cheaper route to athletic prominence,” wrote *The Saturday Evening Post* in its March 10, 1951, issue. “Here is a school that for years has put money and effort into football — notably in the 1930s, when Hunk Anderson was the coach — and has very little to show for it. State has come up with good clubs from time to time, yet never became a magical name in football. And

now, in the space of five years, its basketball team is established as a national power.”

Over the years, the marketing-savvy Case was credited with many, many innovations to the game, like cutting down the nets after winning big games, having pep bands in the stands and turning down the lights during player introductions. But one of the more overlooked things he did early on at NC State was persuading — some might say demanding — that the school implement something akin to a physical education program. The school did have a P.E. curriculum in 1925, just after the opening of Thompson Gym, under the direction of athletics director and P.E department head John W. Miller. But it graduated exactly one class before NC State was consolidated with the University of North Carolina in Chapel Hill and the North Carolina Woman's College in Greensboro. In order to prevent duplication on the three campuses, each school was forced to give up certain programs. NC State maintained all of the agriculture and engineering programs, but one of the things it gave up was a degree in physical education.

Shortly after Case arrived, the school instituted a course called “rural and industrial recreation,” which has grown over the years into the highly

popular and successful Department of Parks, Recreation and Tourism.

Case always maintained the pipeline to his home state, bringing in Indiana boys like Dick Dickey, Norm Sloan, Sammy Ranzino, Vic Bubas, Vic Molodet and Pete Auksel, to name a few. But he also became one of the nation's first coaches to move from regional to national recruiting. Though he always tried to bring in a foundation of players from North Carolina, he sent his assistant coaches all over the country to find players from far-flung locations like New York City, Philadelphia, Chicago and (in the case of All-America center Ronnie Shavlik) Denver, Colo.

He had so many options that he turned away some players who did fairly well at other schools, like future All-Americas Lennie Rosenbluth of North Carolina, Dickie Hemric of Wake Forest, Hot Rod Hundley of West Virginia, Tom Gola of LaSalle and Tom Heinsohn of Holy Cross. Case couldn't take them all, but he was well acquainted with each of them.

One of the first things Case did when he took over was change the architectural plans of the on-campus arena, making it longer on each end so an additional 2,000 seats could be squeezed into each end zone. When the doors opened on Dec. 2, 1949, William Neal Reynolds Coliseum seated 12,400 fans—the largest basketball arena of any school in the South until North Carolina opened the doors of the Dean E. Smith Center in 1986.

Case carefully cultivated his home-court advantage, just as he had back in Indiana during the height of his high school success. He hired the same officials, Lou Eisenstein and Dr. Phil Fox, for most of the Wolfpack's home games, including the Dixie Classic, the Southern Conference Tournament and the ACC Tournament.

That didn't always sit well with opponents. LaSalle was leading the Wolfpack by 11 points during a 1951 regular-season game. But several controversial calls by Fox, all in favor of Case's team, allowed the Wolf-pack to roar back for a 76-74 victory. LaSalle coach Ken Loeffler stormed out of the Coliseum and walked along the railroad tracks all the way back to the downtown Sir Walter Hotel in a huff. Among the things he said before he left was, "This [was] one of the biggest steals since the Louisiana Purchase."

Billy Packer, veteran television announcer and a player for Wake Forest in the 1960s, remembers well how hard it was for a Wolfpack opponent to catch a break at Reynolds Coliseum.

"You have to realize, Case was the most powerful person in basketball at the time," Packer said. "He played 25 home games a year at Reynolds, when you counted the Dixie Classic and the ACC Tournament. And 22 of those games were called by the same two refs.

"If you played at NC State, you had everything working against you. They had the home court advantage every time."

Packer remembers watching the ball go out of bounds off a Wolfpack player and walking over to the sidelines to throw the ball back in play.

"The ref would say, 'No, it's our ball,' and give it to NC State," Packer said. "The NC State people had unbelievable advantages in the 1950s and '60s."

From what veteran opposition players remember, Packer's memories are only slightly exaggerated. But here's the key: No one other than Case had such an expansive arena to play in and no one other than Case could bring together the best teams in the country and put them in the spotlight they so desperately sought in an era before every game was televised.

Case was also a pleasant host, inviting opposing coaches, newspaper reporters, friends and players back to his home in Cameron Village to talk basketball and sip whiskey. Jesse Helms, long before he became North Carolina's longest serving senator, was a frequent guest at Case's home.

"The younger coaches always liked to go over and spend time with Coach Case," said C.A. Dillon, the longtime public address announcer at Reynolds Coliseum and friend of the coach. "He was always very hospitable to all of them — as long as he had won the game."

But, just like in Indiana, Case made some

enemies along the way. It wasn't long before other coaches — especially Kentucky's Adolph Rupp — began to wield their influence against him. There were rumors, confirmed as unfounded by the Federal Bureau of Investigation, that Wolfpack players were involved in the 1950–51 point-shaving scandals involving the City College of New York, Kentucky and Long Island University.

Case was also accused of illegally trying out players in Indiana, violating the state high school association's rule against off-season activities. The NCAA began looking into his program because the reports Case had offered full scholarships — including tuition, room and board, books and monthly spending money — violated the organization's Sanity Code of 1948, which eliminated athletics scholarships and off-campus recruiting.

When the unrealistic code was repealed in 1951, the NCAA established a Committee on Infractions to investigate reported abuses of on-campus tryouts and other accepted recruiting practices of the time. Within a year, the NCAA was looking into Case's recruitment of Hundley, Rosenbluth and Shavlik. Case was accused of holding an illegal on-campus scrimmage during the weekend of the annual spring football game. There were other allegations regarding Shavlik, an All-America high school center who chose the Wolfpack over Kentucky, but they were later disproven.

Nevertheless, in 1954, the school was placed on a one-year probation, prohibiting the Wolfpack from participating in the NCAA Tournament after it won the 1955 ACC championship in Reynolds Coliseum.

Less than a year after serving the probation, Ol' Joe Hayes — Case's fictional NCAA boogeyman — came calling again, after the organization decided to further crack down on illegal recruiting practices. The Wolfpack was fingered by an unnamed accuser for illegally recruiting Louisiana prep All-America Jackie Moreland, who, like Shavlik, had chosen NC State over Rupp's Wildcats.

Moreland was a talented young player from Minden, La., who was touted as the best college basketball player since Wilt Chamberlain. But, by all accounts, he buckled under the intense recruiting pressure that few players at that time had ever endured. As a result, Moreland's indecisiveness led him to sign nonbinding letters of intent with NC

ABOVE: Charlie Stine and Everett Case (right) look over a book about basketball.

State, Kentucky and Texas A&M as he tried to satisfy three legendary coaches: Case, Rupp and the Aggie athletics director and football coach, Paul "Bear" Bryant, who was handling Moreland's recruiting for his basketball staff.

The NCAA received a complaint against NC State and A&M, but not Kentucky. According to an investigative report by *Sport Magazine* reporter Furman Bisher, at the same time NCAA investigator A.J. Bergstrom showed up in Minden to look into the matter, a private investigator from Atlanta also began snooping into Moreland's recruitment. His client? The University of Kentucky.

The allegations of the report handed in by both the Infractions Committee, which was chaired by Kentucky Professor A.B. Kirwan, and the private investigator, were sensational, including the fact that Moreland had been whisked away from Louisiana to Raleigh by NC State assistant athletics director Willis Casey, assistant basketball coach Vic Bubas and Wolfpack Club executive secretary Harry Stewart. After long consideration and many accusations that included a seven-year medical school education for Moreland's girlfriend at Duke and a cash gift of $80, the NCAA handed down its harshest penalty ever, a four-year probation for all Wolfpack athletics teams. The NCAA explained that the penalty was so harsh because of previous infractions. The NCAA also upheld a previous two-year probation it had levied on Bryant's football program.

Case was unapologetic for his efforts in pursuing Moreland. NC State chancellor Carey Bostian supported the coach, in appeals to both the NCAA and the ACC, providing written testimony that no representative of NC State made any illicit offers to Moreland, his family or friends. But the penalty stood.

While it did not prevent the 1956 Wolfpack basketball team — perhaps the best Case ever assembled — from participating in the NCAA Tournament, it did prevent Earle Edwards's ACC champion football team from playing in the Orange Bowl in 1957 and Case's last ACC championship team in 1959 from participating in the NCAA Tournament.

Just as the Wolfpack began to put the lengthy probation in its rear-view mirror, another ordeal struck in 1961 that was even more devastating: players from NC State, North Carolina and several other southern schools were implicated in college basketball's second major point-shaving scandal in a decade.

Case had long been worried about gamblers affiliated with organized crime syndicates infiltrating his team. Many of his players were married, some with young families. Like all college students, they struggled to make ends meet. Every year in the preseason, Case invited representatives from the State Bureau of Investigation to address his team about the dangers of associating with gamblers.

But, in a Dec. 17, 1960, game against Georgia Tech, Case suspected at least one of his players might be trying to manipulate the score against the point spread. He called friends at the SBI to begin an investigation. Shortly after the end of the season, three Wolfpack players — team captain Stan Niewierowski, Anton Muehlbauer and Terry Litchfield — were arrested for illegal point-shaving. A fourth, Don Gallagher, was implicated in the scandal that eventually included 30 players from 15 different schools, NC State and North Carolina among them.

In a swift reaction to the scandal, the consolidated university made major changes at both schools to completely de-emphasize basketball. Coaches were not allowed to recruit off campus, players were no longer allowed to participate in summer leagues and teams were forced to play a limited number of nonconference games. Perhaps the most damning blow for NC State fans was the call by consolidated university president — and NC State alum — William Friday for an end to the Dixie Classic, Case's premier holiday event for 12 consecutive years.

"That had to be done because of gambling and the threats to human life," Dr. Friday said. "I was left with no option. By all odds, it was the most exciting basketball competition in the United States at the time. But it had to be done."

The point-shaving scandal did more than ruin the program Case had worked so hard to cultivate — it broke his heart. The coach everyone now called "The Old Gray Fox" loved the game and his players. He couldn't accept that either one would betray his trust. And, just like with Jim Valvano many years later, the stress of all Case had been through hastened his demise.

"There is no doubt that stress plays a role in a lot of illnesses," said Norm Sloan, one of Case's first recruits and a future head coach of the Wolfpack. "The scandals devastated him. For a man to whom basketball was his whole life and to whom loyalty meant everything, that scandal was just total devastation."

The limited schedule and limited recruiting prevented Case from continuing his success. He compiled a 377-134 record in 18 years at NC State. A total of 53 of those losses came in Case's final five years, as he experienced the only three losing seasons of his coaching career.

Irwin Smallwood, the sports editor of the *Greensboro (N.C.) Daily News* and a longtime friend of the coach, bumped into Case one day when Case was at his lowest.

"Irwin, I'm playing it straight and my team shows it," the sly coach said.

Just after the 1963 season ended, three of Case's players were involved in a car accident, and senior captain Jon Speaks died, sending the always joyful coach deeper into a state of depression. A year later, he was diagnosed with multiple myeloma, a rare form of bone cancer. Both of his parents developed cancer at the end of their lives, his mother dying of breast cancer and his father taking his own life after being diagnosed with inoperable brain cancer. When the coach took his final victory lap around

Reynolds Coliseum, snipping down the nets following the Wolfpack's unlikely win over Duke in the 1965 ACC Championship game, he knew it was the last taste of the feast he had spent his entire life preparing.

Case died quietly on April 30, 1966, at his home in Cameron Village.

"Basketball was his life," said veteran public address announcer C.A. Dillon, an NC State graduate who befriended Case soon after the coach arrived in 1946. "It had been from the time he was in Indiana, to the time he was in the military, to the time he was here, right up until the day he died."

Case had two final requests. Just before he died he divided his substantial estate between his sister, Blanche Jones, and all of his former players who had received their degrees from NC State. A total of 57 players were awarded one to three shares from a pot of $69,525.

Finally, he asked to be buried in a cemetery overlooking Highway 70 between Raleigh and Durham so he "could wave to the team when it goes to Durham to play Duke."

THE SOUTH'S GREATEST INNOVATOR

Case was not a great tactician of the game. But, before his arrival, schools in the South considered football to be the only moneymaking sport on campus. Case's fast-paced offense and pressing full-court defense brought unprecedented excitement to the overflowing campus and the basketball-savvy fans of Raleigh. And his accomplished skills as a promoter kept them coming back, even when he didn't win the championship every year.

"Coach Case wasn't a great game coach," said Bucky Waters, who played for Case in the 1950s and later became the head coach at West Virginia and Duke. "He attracted great people. He was more of a facilitator and a promoter. He was just ahead of his time in terms of putting on a show."

Indeed, Case transformed basketball from a game to an event. In turn, he made the game a highly profitable part of every athletic department in the area. He never won a national championship, but in the 45 years after he stepped down at NC State, teams from the Atlantic Coast Conference won 12 NCAA titles. One of those came in 1974, when Sloan led his alma mater to the school's first national championship. Another came in 1983,

when Valvano's Cardiac Pack beat Houston in one of the tournament's most memorable moments.

But, in Case's heyday, the two national tournaments were hardly the spectacle of today's March Madness. He was much more proud of winning his 10 Southern Conference and ACC titles and his seven Dixie Classic championships, because those were

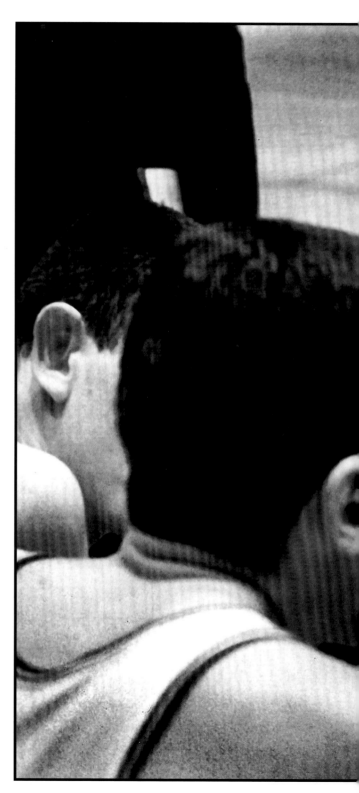

the things that turned the region on to basketball.

"He pushed basketball to a level that this area had never seen before. He was on the front edge of things like radio and television," Bubas said. "He knew the kind of exposure and money you could get from having a big arena.

"You can trace everything back to him. When you have a leader that is on top for a number of years, everybody else says 'Hey, what do we have to do to get our program headed in that direction?' Eventually, one by one, they did. They had some considerable ground to make up. Everett was indeed the founder of big-time basketball in the South."

THE CASE STUDY

OF **INNOVATION**

PLAYER INTRODUCTIONS: The coach had the lights dimmed and spotlights put on the players as their names were announced over the loud-speaker. It's a tradition that continues today at all Wolfpack games in the RBC.

THE 10-SECOND TIME LINE: In a reaction to Case's much despised full-court stalling tactic at the end of games, in 1932 the National Association of Basketball Coaches voted to place a time limit of 10 seconds for the offensive team to advance the ball past midcourt. The same year, the three-second rule was also established, in an attempt to de-emphasize the importance of the pivot player.

BASKETBALL CAMPS: In 1928, Case joined with longtime friend, rival and fellow inductee into the Naismith Memorial Basketball Hall of Fame Clifford Wells and Southern California coach Sam Barry to begin an instructional camp for Indiana high school coaches, which lasted through World War II. In 1934, while coaching in California, Case developed camps for young players. Soon after he arrived in Raleigh, he began conducting weeklong basketball camps for young players at Dorton Arena, which opened in 1952.

INDIANA ALL-STAR GAME: Case organized the profitable all-star game, in which players who had completed their eligibility from Frankfort High faced an elected group of all-stars from around the state. The game was banned by the Indiana High School Athletic Association after two years, but was morphed into the Indiana/Kentucky All-Star Game, which has been played continuously since 1942.

ELECTRONIC TIME CLOCK: For most of Case's high school coaching career, time was kept on a stop watch and only the timer knew how much time was left. In 1939, thanks to an electronic clock made by John Ewing and Abe Martin, Case made sure he knew, too.

BIG-TIME RECRUITING: Before Case arrived, most schools in the South recruited from their football and baseball teams. Case, however, scoured the country for the best players, beginning in Indiana. He spread to New York, Philadelphia, Chicago and Denver. His tactics, however, in the days just after the NCAA passed its Sanity Code of 1948, twice landed the school on probation.

THE DIXIE CLASSIC: The idea actually came from *News & Observer* sports editor Dick Herbert and the name was suggested by assistant coach Carl "Butter" Anderson. But, like the holiday basketball tournaments he used to host in Indiana, this was Case's event. It was a regular feature at Reynolds Coliseum from 1949–60, when it was killed after the point-shaving scandals of 1960–61.

IN-GAME MUSIC: Case equipped Reynolds with the largest organ produced by the Hammond Company. For years, Bob Yoder served as in-game entertainment. Case also filled some of Reynolds' seats with the region's first pep band, gleaned from the school's popular Redcoat Band.

CUTTING DOWN THE NETS: Case instructed his first team to clip the nets following its 50-48 victory over North Carolina in the 1947 Southern Conference Championship game, played at Duke Indoor Stadium in Durham, N.C.

SCOUTING FILMS: Case began filming his opponents in the Indiana State Tournament as early as 1938. Thanks to the bright lights in Reynolds Coliseum, Case was able to film, in color, nearly every game played during his career. He also had someone travel with the team on long road trips. Many of those films still exist.

"If you build it,

they will come."

The day William C. Friday received his bachelor's degree from NC State University in the fall of 1941, a brief announcement during the ceremonies was met with great cheers: Mary Reynolds Babcock of Greenwich, Conn., and Winston-Salem, N.C., had made a $100,000 donation to NC State to help build a multi-purpose gathering place on the southern side of the railroad tracks.

Influential alumnus David Clark had pushed for several years to get a replacement for outdated Frank Thompson Gymnasium, which could not hold all the attendees for the annual Farmer's Week activities. When a rainstorm prevented the 1940 meeting at Riddick Stadium, Clark began his fundraising push for a place where the meeting could be held indoors.

With additional funds from the North Carolina Legislature and a start-up grant from the Works Progress Administration, a Depression-era federal agency, the school was ready to begin construction of a 10,000-seat armory/coliseum that would, at the very least, be on par with similar buildings that had recently opened at the University of North Carolina (6,000-seat Woollen Gym in 1936) and Duke University (9,000-seat Duke Indoor Stadium in 1939).

The building was not just a necessity for athletics and for physical education classes, it was also to be the home for the school's Reserve Officers Training Corps and the host for special events.

"The old place has really been a good deal more than just a sports arena, which is what most people know it to be," Dr. Friday said. "It has participated in the inauguration of every governor since it was built. It is the home of NC State's ROTC program. There have been many, many different events there, which means it has given an enormous service to NC State."

The building's name is William Neal Reynolds Coliseum, and there has never been a better use of $2,461,741.78 in state funds and donations. That was the final price tag of a building that was originally supposed to cost just $300,000.

When Everett Case arrived in 1946, he made a quick inspection of the rusting steel structure and concrete foundation that had been sitting untended since before the war. School administrators were far

too busy trying to find housing for the nearly 5,000 students who showed up in the fall of 1946 to worry about the proposed coliseum.

Case's quick success, which included a game against North Carolina in his inaugural season that had to be canceled because of overcrowding at Thompson Gym, hastened the restart of construction, but not before the coach suggested a few changes. He asked that it be made longer in both directions, stretching the ends so the building could hold some 3,200 more spectators than the building it was modeled after, Duke Indoor Stadium, and giving the building its distinctive shoebox shape. The school's architecture department also drew up plans to retrofit the existing structure with a full basement for storage.

When the doors opened on the not-quite-finished building on Dec. 2, 1949—after nearly 10 years of planning, war-caused construction delays and multiple revisions—it was the largest on-campus facility in the nation and the biggest building of its type anywhere between Atlantic City and New Orleans.

For 50 years, it was the unrivaled home for the Wolfpack men's team. And it has been the home of the Wolfpack women since Kay Yow was hired as the first full-time women's coach in the state. Over the years, it hosted 16 conference championships, 12 Dixie Classics and a handful of NCAA Regionals.

In the more than six decades since NC State guard Vic Bubas made the first basket in the building, an estimated 20 million people have walked through the doors for various events. The multi-purpose venue has hosted sitting presidents Lyndon Johnson, Ronald Reagan and George H.W. Bush. Candidates John F. Kennedy and Barack Obama both gave campaign speeches there, and former president Bill Clinton gave the keynote address for the 2009 Millennium Speakers seminar after he left office.

Musical performers as diverse as jazz pioneer Louis Armstrong, the Rolling Stones and violinist Itzhak Perlman played in front of sold-out audiences. NC State students have graduated in Reynolds, stood in line during change day and camped outside its doors for football and basketball tickets.

The Namesake

The name William Neal Reynolds is etched in the memory of every old-time NC State basketball fan and alumnus. But relatively few know that much about the famous industrialist, philanthropist and sportsman whose name adorns "The House That Case Built."

Reynolds never attended the school, nor was he a big basketball fan. But his name is on the South's largest on-campus basketball facility because he raised the four children of his late brother, R.J. Reynolds, founder of the world's largest tobacco company.

R.J. Reynolds died in 1918, leaving four young heirs under the age of 13 and his much-younger wife, the former Mary Katherine Smith. When she died in 1923, the four underage children went to live with "Uncle Will" and his wife Kate, who had no children.

The oldest of the children, Richard J. "Dick" Reynolds Jr., enrolled at NC State shortly after his mother's death and graduated with a degree in mechanical engineering in 1927. He became one of the state's most prominent early aviators. His international airship pilot's license was signed by Orville Wright.

In 1941, while he was serving on a carrier escort in the Pacific Theater of World War II, the school began to seek funds to finance the grand new arena being built south of the railroad tracks. So they went to his younger sister, Mary Katherine Reynolds Babcock of Greenwich, Conn., who at the time was one of the wealthiest women in the world, thanks to her $30 million inheritance from the family estate.

She and husband Charles agreed to provide $100,000, or one-third of the projected construction cost, to build the arena, as long as her beloved uncle approved of the expenditure. His reply, in a letter to her on May 5, 1941, was, "I know of no more worthy cause in the state."

The Babcocks also provided an additional $52,000 following World War II to purchase the ice-making equipment needed to make Reynolds Coliseum the South's first ice rink.

"It is appropriate . . . that the Coliseum be named for William Neal Reynolds," wrote William D. Carmichael on the day the arena was dedicated. "No man in North Carolina is more deserving of recognition by the University—and, because of the wide variety of the significant activities that have characterized Mr. Reynolds' worthwhile life, it is a 'natural' that the Coliseum, with its varied usages, spiritual, cultural, scientific, agricultural, industrial and recreational, should be known forever as the William Neal Reynolds Coliseum."

After Reynolds opened in December 1949, William Neal Reynolds became a major benefactor to NC State's School of Agriculture. Since 1951, the top agricultural professor at the university has received the William Neal Reynolds Professorship.

Reynolds, a graduate of Trinity College (now Duke University), was an early benefactor to his alma mater. Later, his Z. Smith Reynolds Foundation, named in honor of a murdered nephew, provided the funds and land needed to move Wake Forest College from its original location 10 miles north of Raleigh to Reynolds's adopted hometown of Winston-Salem.

Reynolds was not much into basketball—his lifelong interest in sports was much more aristocratic. He was a successful harness racing horse breeder and trainer, and a personal friend of golf course designer Donald Ross. Reynolds was instrumental in hiring Ross to design the golf courses at the Forsyth Country Club and Roaring Gap Country Club.

When he died in 1951, he also left the grounds of his Tanglewood Farm to the city of Winston-Salem, which turned it into one of the country's largest municipal parks.

On the day the building was dedicated prior to an ice skating exhibition, *The News & Observer* quoted coliseum manager W.Z. Betts: "The coliseum is not a gymnasium, and will not be used as such. It will be used for the promotion of educational, professional and cultural affairs as well as for sports attractions and entertainment."

What few people remember, however, is that Reynolds nearly became a 371-foot-long, 180-foot-wide boondoggle. Despite Case's immediate success, the athletics department was in deep debt during the 1950s. Because there was no allowance made for upkeep of the arena when it first opened, many of the profits generated by popular events like the Ice Capades and the Friends of the College Series were poured right back into upkeep for the sprawling building. The ice-making equipment, for which Mrs. Babcock paid more than $55,000 above and beyond her original gift, turned out to be a disaster. Humidity from the eight miles of water pipes that chilled the ice rink caused the basketball court to warp and huge chunks of insulation to fall from the ceiling. It was removed after just five years, killing one of the arena's primary ways to make money: public skating sessions.

Because of the lack of funding, and the deep debt that the athletics department and the Wolfpack Club had incurred at the college dining hall, the administration considered dropping football in 1954, a sport where the Wolfpack had rarely had success other than the 1927 Southern Conference Championship. But the program was spared, the university business office took over management of the building long enough to improve its finances and

Reynolds continued to attract the biggest names in college athletics, entertainment and politics.

Not all of the people who spent time in the building were superstars. C.A. Dillon was the voice of the building, sitting behind the microphone for nearly every men's game ever played in the building. Duma Bledsoe was the official scorer from the day the building opened until he retired in 1985. Har-old Wall was the timekeeper on press row for nearly half a century. Assistant trainer Chester Grant guarded the back door for more than three decades. And Dorsey Poole and Brenda Keene oversaw the equipment room in the basement for the men's and women's programs based in Reynolds.

The building received a $1 million facelift in 2005, with the installation of a wall-to-wall wooden

floor and the construction of new locker room and player lounge facilities in the basement.

Since Feb. 16, 2007, the polished hardwood court at Reynolds has been named "Kay Yow Court," in honor of NC State's Hall of Fame women's basketball coach, who won more games than any other person in the building.

On the night it was renamed in her honor, Yow's team whipped second-ranked North Carolina, 72-65, an outcome that would have made Case break into a broad grin.

Of all the people who have passed through the doors of the "House That Case Built," NC State takes pride that both the Father of ACC basketball and the Mother of ACC women's basketball have called Reynolds home.

Hoosier

Everything about Everett Case's first season at NC State was magical.

From cobbling together a squad of "Hoosier Hotshots," as the media liked to call his newcomers, to beating eventual NCAA champion Holy Cross during a December barnstorming tour in Indianapolis, to taking the Southern Conference by storm, Case and his squad made a statement that NC State was destined to become a force in college basketball.

And nothing could have been sweeter than the way it ended in the postseason conference championship game.

After finishing the regular season with a 21-4 record — and exciting the masses with a thrilling 11-2 record in the league — Case's Red Terrors went to Durham for the league tournament riding a wave of emotion and momentum.

Fans were literally beating down the doors to see Case's team play, especially after it went to Chapel Hill and took a 48-46 overtime victory from North Carolina. They filled Thompson Gymnasium, the small, crumbling arena on NC State's campus, to see the Red Terrors beat Dolph Schayes and New York University in early February. And every seat, aisle and doorway of the team's home was taken for a Feb. 18 game against Duke. State won both games, taking over first place in the Southern Conference standings with an 83-57 victory in the latter game.

The regular season finale, scheduled to be against UNC's White Phantoms on Feb. 25, was canceled by Raleigh Fire Marshal W.R. Butts because NC State students stormed the doors at Thompson hours before the game in hopes of seeing the rematch between the long-time rivals.

Thompson clearly couldn't contain the excitement, but Duke Indoor Stadium could. Southern Conference officials, noting the passion the league tournament had developed in previous years, decided at a league meeting in December to move from Raleigh's 3,400-seat downtown arena, where the event had been played 14 consecutive years, to the gigantic stadium in Durham, which had a capacity of more than 9,000.

Every ticket was sold to the tournament, with fans waiting outside the doors looking to get in. But the action inside did not match the passion on the outside.

Hotshots

"Chief surprise has been the lack of interesting games," *The News & Observer* reported the day after NC State beat George Washington 70-47 in the first semifinal game and North Carolina won the second.

But the championship game was one to remember, a battle between two first-year coaches looking to establish a tone for their programs. North Carolina's Tom Scott inherited a team that had gone to the NCAA title game the year before under previous coach Ben Carnevale, who left for his alma mater Navy after the season. Scott had several stars returning, including forward Bob Paxton and guard Jim White.

Case, however, had built his contender completely from scratch. The year before, the Red Terrors were led by part-time coach Leroy Jay and lost in the first round of the league tournament to Duke, ending a pitiful 6-12 season. Not a single player from that squad was retained by Case, who held open tryouts for his inaugural squad. More than 60 aspirants showed up in hopes of making the team, including a Navy veteran who survived the Japanese attack on Pearl Harbor, but not Case's first round of cuts.

The only player who was not recruited by Case was Leo Katkavek, a native of Manchester, Conn., who had played for Jay's team in 1942 before entering the service for World War II, and returned as a junior for the 1946–47 season.

The rest of the team was made up of players Case recruited in his days as Indiana's most successful high school coach or the players he coached while serving in the U.S. Navy during World War II. Among the Hotshots he brought from Indiana were Dick Dickey of Alexandria, Pete Negley of Lawrence, Jack Mc-Comas of Shelbyville, Charlie Stine of Frankfort, Jack Snow of Anderson and Norman Sloan from Indianapolis. There were also recruits from other parts of the country, including Warren Cartier of Green Bay, Wis., who had played for Case at the Depauw Naval Training Station; Bob Hahn of Ann Arbor, Mich., and Eddie Bartels of Long Island, N.Y.

Dickey and Negley became the stars of that first squad, with Dickey earning the first of his four first-team All-Southern Conference honors. Case remembered

Dickey from St. Mary's (Calif.) Pre-Flight School, when the Case-coached Iowa Seahawks faced Dickey's team in a special two-game exhibition series. He was the coach's first recruiting target when he took over the program.

The first two games of the Southern tournament were no problem for Case and his squad. They beat Maryland 61-55 in a raggedly played game and George Washington 70-47. The action heated up considerably when the Red Terrors faced the White Phantoms in the title game. North Carolina had owned the series in recent years, winning 32 of the previous 48 meetings before Case led his team to the win in Chapel Hill.

This was the game that counted most, however, since the teams had been unable to play the rematch game in February.

The Phantoms, playing a deliberate, well-planned offense, jumped out to a 20-7 lead early in the title game's first nine minutes and seemed to be on their way to another league championship. But Case unveiled an old strategy that he had used many times during his three decades as a high school coach in Indiana: a full-court press.

It was an uncommon strategy at the time and it took Carolina by surprise. By halftime, UNC's lead was whittled down to four points. With Negley scoring 18 points and Bartels adding 14, the Wolfpack stormed back in the second half and took a six-point lead with 1:20 remaining.

Carolina drew within two points in the final minutes, thanks to a pair of baskets by White. It had the chance to tie the game a few moments later, when it elected to take the ball out of bounds instead of trying a pair of free throws (as the rules then allowed). But both John (Hook) Dillon and Dick Hartley missed shots to tie the game.

Bartels rebounded Hartley's miss and held the ball for the final 10 seconds, capping off the school's first tournament championship since Gus Tebell's Terrors won in Atlanta in 1929.

Immediately after the game, Case was lifted onto the shoulders of his players. He directed them to the basket, where he introduced them to the Indiana high school tradition of cutting down the nets after winning a championship. The prized twine was draped over the head of Negley, the star of the championship game, and explained by the NC State student newspaper like this: "The net around Negley's neck is the one cut down after the tourney and represents an old Indiana custom, seen in North Carolina for the first time, of cutting down the nets after winning the title."

Despite winning the crown, the Red Terrors did not have a chance to play in the 1947 NCAA Tournament. Before the league's event began, NC State's newly named athletic director John Von Glahn was offered the chance to play in the NCAA Tournament, contingent on Case's team winning the league tournament. Instead, he chose a spot in the more prestigious National Invitation Tournament. So the NCAA District 3 selection committee gave the area's bid to Carnevale's team from Navy.

Case's inaugural team became the first NC State team to be selected for national postseason play, earning a bid into the NIT in New York's Madison Square Garden, where they beat hometown favorite St. John's in the opening round in front of an awe-inspiring crowd of more than 18,000 spectators.

But in the second round, Case and his charges lost to defending NIT champion and top-ranked Kentucky, 60-42, in the only meeting ever between Case and his longtime coaching rival, Adolph Rupp.

The Red Terrors rebounded to win the third-place game over West Virginia, bringing home a trophy to a campus, city and state that were now enamored of basketball like never before.

Different name, same result

Everett Case's second team was called by a new name, as the school officially changed the nickname of all its athletics teams from the Red Terrors to match the longtime nickname of the football team, the Wolfpack. There were a few other changes. Pete Negley, the hero of the 1947 Southern Conference Tournament, transferred to American University.

Case replaced him with another strong recruiting class, featuring future All-America Sammy Ranzino and Vic Bubas. The coach was looking to maintain the momentum his team built in his first year and he did it by traveling to play the best teams in the nation.

In his second season, he went to play West Virginia in Morgantown. He returned to Madison Square Garden, the site of his loss to Kentucky in the previous National Invitation Tournament, for a rematch with St. John's. This time around, the coach on the opposing sidelines was Frank McGuire. It was the first time Case and the man who would become his greatest foe other than Kentucky's Adolph Rupp would ever face each other.

The coach took his team to New Orleans for a rematch against defending NCAA champion Holy Cross, whom the Terrors had beaten the year before in Indianapolis. The game was tied at the end of regulation, but the overtime period was marred by what Case later called "a bit of lousy officiating."

With the Crusaders leading 52-50, NC State created a turnover and was credited with possession of the ball. However, the game official mistakenly handed the ball to a Holy Cross player, who inbounded it to a teammate for an uncontested layup. After much arguing from Case and his players, the official refused to change the call, and Holy Cross went on to win the game, 56-51.

But that was the last loss of the regular season for Case's team, which rose to No. 1 in at least one of the national polls for the first time.

Students could not get enough of Case's team and continued to pack dilapidated Thompson Gym for Wolfpack home games — a little too much. On Jan. 17, 1948, Thompson was condemned by Raleigh City Building Inspector Pallie Mangum, postponing the long-anticipated Duke game and leaving the Wolfpack without a home.

The school and city came to a compromise after that game, allowing the Terrors to host High Point in Thompson with the doors locked and no spectators allowed. What was not seen that afternoon was the highest scoring game, to that point, in school history, a 110-40 victory. It was Case's final victory in the cozy building where he posted a perfect 18-0 record in a little more than one season there.

For the rest of its home games, the Wolfpack played in Raleigh's Memorial Auditorium, the downtown building that replaced NC State's one-time home, Municipal Auditorium, and the long-time home of the Southern Conference Tournament.

Case's team was dominant. It rolled over North Carolina 81-42 at the Auditorium, with students beginning a chant of "We want a coliseum!" Later on, the Wolfpack whipped North Carolina 69-45 as Case continued his dominance of his school's biggest rival.

Again, before the Southern Conference Tour-

Long Strange Trip

Every key player, except for pre–Everett Case holdover Leo Katkavek, returned to the squad for the 1948–49 season, building anticipation that the coach's third edition might actually have the opportunity to vie for the NCAA Championship.

Case, buoyed by the news that construction had restarted on the long-awaited on-campus coliseum, scheduled a long transcontinental road trip to show off his team to the rest of the country and to build the list of opponents he wanted to bring to Raleigh once the new arena opened. The coach later admitted that his 20-game road schedule was a mistake.

While on the west coast, Case was forced to suspend standout forward Eddie Bartels and All-America forward Dick Dickey was hampered by a thigh bruise.

After winning a pair of games over Nevada-Reno in Nevada, the Wolfpack lost, in succession, to San Francisco, Wyoming and Loyola of Los Angeles, with the latter two setbacks being in the Los Angeles Invitational Tournament.

The Wolfpack returned to the East Coast with the first three-game losing streak of Case's tenure. Things never really improved during the 12,000-mile road trip, which ended with losses to Long Island University in Madison Square Garden and Villanova in Philadelphia. In the final game, Dickey suffered a broken nose to go along with his nagging leg problem.

When the team returned to Raleigh, junior Norman Sloan, one of the original "Hoosier Hotshots," decided to leave the program, ostensibly to play football for Wolfpack coach Beattie Feathers. But Sloan admitted in later years that he was upset that sophomore Vic Bubas had taken over most of his playing time.

Dickey was still productive and the Wolfpack had another All-America candidate in Sammy Ranzino, but it lacked the chemistry that Case's previous teams had. Louisville came to Raleigh on Jan. 12 and handed Case his first ever home loss, 72-71, at Memorial Auditorium, thanks to poor free-throw shooting and a last-second layup by the Cardinals for the game-winning points.

The Wolfpack seemed glad to return to the familiar foes in the Southern Conference, where it owned a 23-game winning streak in the previous two seasons. The streak was finally snapped at 27 by Wake Forest, but the Wolfpack cruised through the rest of the regular season, including a gratifying 79-39 win over North Carolina in Chapel Hill, the largest margin of victory in the series for the Wolfpack.

nament even began at Duke Indoor Stadium, the NCAA District 3 selection committee chose its representative — Adolph Rupp's squad from Kentucky. Case was happy to accept his second consecutive bid to the NIT, before heading into the conference showdown.

The team had been led all season long by Dickey, who earned several All-America distinctions, but that changed in the postseason after the sophomore guard was hospitalized — diagnosed with the mumps the day after an opening-round win over William & Mary. In the semifinals, Warren Cartier filled in for Dickey and Leo Katkavek scored the game's final three points to lead the Wolfpack to a narrow 55-50 win over UNC,

the third of the season for Case's squad.

In the championship game, the Wolfpack faced Duke on its home court, but had little trouble dispensing the Blue Devils in a 58-50 win that stretched the team's winning streak to a record 19 games and gave Case his second consecutive Southern title.

But the winning streak ended in New York against DePaul, as the Wolfpack made its return appearance to the NIT with Dickey still ailing back in Raleigh. After a narrow first half, the Demons reeled off eight straight points in the opening moments of the second half and never gave up the lead, ending the most successful season in school history with a 29-3 record.

1949 **Southern Conference** Tournament Champions

Thanks to a win in Philadelphia over La Salle, the Wolfpack completed the regular-season schedule on an eight-game winning streak and hoped to continue its dominance of the Southern Conference at the tournament, which again was held at Duke Indoor Stadium.

A win over Wake Forest in the opening round was easy, but the Wolfpack had a difficult time over the same UNC team it had beaten by 40 in the regular season. A hook shot by Dickey with 1:20 remaining on the clock sealed a narrow 43-40 win, sending the Wolfpack to the title game for the third

consecutive year.

George Washington tried to slow the tempo, but the fast-breaking, pressing Wolfpack allowed its opponent to score just one point in the final 11 minutes of the contest. NC State raced away with a 55-39 victory and another set of nets for Case's personal collection.

But the late-season run — with wins in 17 of the team's last 18 games and a No. 13 national ranking — could not overcome the early season losses. Kentucky earned the NCAA's District 3 bid and also accepted an invitation to the NIT, becoming the first school to participate in both since the tournaments began in the late 1930s. When San Francisco, which had beaten the Wolfpack 54-47 in December, accepted a bid into the NIT, the Wolfpack was left at home for the postseason.

But change, in the form of the South's biggest home-court advantage, was on its way for Case's team.

When the doors opened on the gleaming new Reynolds Coliseum on Dec. 2, 1949, not all of the permanent seats were bolted to the floor. That was fine with a Wolfpack faithful that had waited for more than a decade for the 12,400-seat masterpiece to be completed. So they sat on the edges of the concrete foundation to watch the first game played in an arena that began in the innocent days before World War II.

The building — dubbed the largest sports facility between Atlantic City and New Orleans — was christened in a 67-47 victory over Washington & Lee, a game notable only because junior guard Vic Bubas worked so hard to make the building's first basket. That didn't outshine the performance of the Wolfpack's All-America forwards, senior Dick Dickey and junior Sammy Ranzino, who contributed 22 and 24 points in the game, respectively.

This was Case's finest team to date, with Dickey fully recovered from his injury-plagued junior campaign and Ranzino ready to step into a starring role. They were surrounded by Bubas at one guard, Joe Harand at the other, and 6-10 center Paul Horvath in the middle.

The Wolfpack made its first big statement by winning the inaugural Dixie Classic, the holiday showcase that became synonymous with big-time basketball in the South. The unique event, which featured four national opponents facing the Big Four schools from North Carolina in a three-day round robin, was one of Case's most successful innovations, even though he borrowed the idea from *News & Observer* sports editor Dick Herbert and the name from assistant coach Butter Anderson.

Ranzino established a new school record when he scored 33 points in an opening round victory over Rhode Island, and the Wolfpack cruised by Georgia Tech in the second round. Penn State offered some resistance in the championship game, but Case's team finished off a 50-40 victory for the

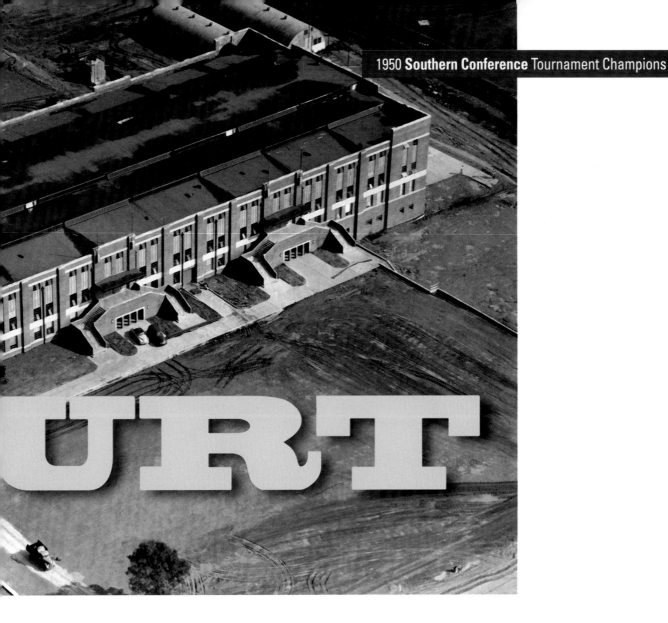

URT

first of seven titles in the 12-year history of the event.

But the big game of the season came just after New Year's Day, in the Wolfpack's ninth consecutive home game to start the season, when defending NIT champion San Francisco visited the new arena. In front of a sellout crowd of 12,014, Case's team scored the final 12 points of the game for a 69-54 win in front of a raucous home contingent.

The Wolfpack lost its first Southern Conference game of the new year, a 50-38 setback against Duke and star sophomore Dick Groat, and La Salle became the first team to win in Reynolds Coliseum a week later. But Case and his team returned to Madison Square Garden and pulled off an upset of No. 3-ranked Long Island, one of the biggest upsets of the coach's tenure.

His team also went to Louisville and broke the Cardinals' 23-game home winning streak, as Ranzino again carried the team with a 27-point performance.

The Southern Conference continued to pose little problem for Case and his squad, which lost only one more league game the rest of the season. They recorded their 9th and 10th straight wins over the Tar Heels during the season and won the regular-season championship for the fourth year in a row.

The only major setback came in the regular-season finale when Dickey suffered a leg injury after scoring 25 points in the final home game of his career, and Villanova forced the game into overtime. The Main Liners squeezed out a 65-64 win in the extra period.

Not only did Case and his team roll to three straight wins and another Southern Conference title — this time with a 67-47 win over Duke, led by Ranzino's 31-point performance — they also beat up a collection of the league's best players, 84-61, a week after the tournament concluded.

But this was a critical time in the national prominence of Case and his team. Both Kentucky and NC State made strong claims in the regular-season for the District 3 berth into the NCAA Tournament, and selection committee chairman Gus Tebell, the one-time coach at NC State who moved on to Virginia in 1930, delayed his until after both teams finished their respective tournaments.

Since both teams breezed to their respective league titles, Tebell decided that the berth into the national tournament would be decided by a one-game playoff, to be held at an undetermined location. Case, who had long tried to convince Rupp to schedule the Wolfpack in the regular season, readily agreed, telling *The News & Observer* that his 25-5 Wolfpack would face the 25-4 Wildcats "anytime, anywhere."

Rupp, whose team had won the previous two national titles, did not like the idea, pointing out that his team had beaten Villanova in Philadelphia while the Wolfpack had lost to the same team in Raleigh. He refused to participate in the one-game playoff. When Tebell awarded his former team the bid, Rupp called the decision "ridiculous," fanning the flames on the rivalry between The Baron and The Old Gray Fox.

Case and his fifth-ranked team had two full weeks to prepare for the first NCAA appearance in school history. The team received a big send-off from fans when it left for New York's Madison Square Garden to face an all-too-familiar foe, the fourth-ranked Crusaders of Holy Cross.

With Dickey guarding All-America point guard Bob Cousy — the country's top collegiate player — the Wolfpack duplicated its feat of 1947, beating the Crusaders 87-74 to advance to the national semifinals, the modern day equivalent of the Final Four. Dickey's defense limited Cousy to just two field goals on 17 shots. Meanwhile, Ranzino shattered the NCAA single-game scoring record with 32 points.

But Vic Bubas suffered a sprained ankle against Holy Cross and was hobbled in the semifinal game against the City College of New York, which had just won the NIT Championship in the same building the week before.

The game was close throughout, but Dickey, Ranzino and Paul Horvath all fouled out with less than a minute remaining and CCNY holding on to a 75-73 lead. Bubas's shot to tie the game in the closing seconds fell short, and CCNY went on to become the first team in college basketball history to win both the NIT and the NCAA Tournaments in the same season.

The Wolfpack played well, and Dickey concluded his spectacular career as the school's all-time leading scorer, with a 53-41 win in the consolation finals, the start of a five-game Final Four winning streak that was extended as the Wolfpack won NCAA titles in 1974 and '83.

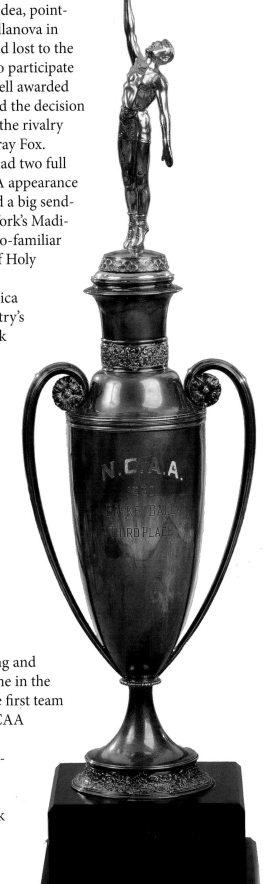

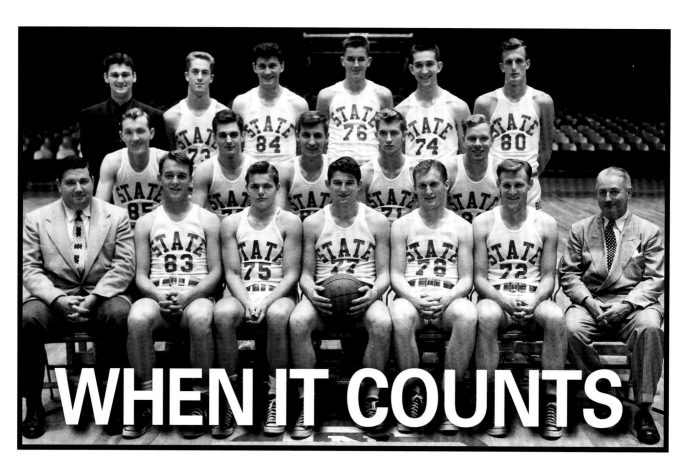

WHEN IT COUNTS

Without All-America forward Dick Dickey, Everett Case needed a slight restructuring in 1950–51, following the third-place finish in the national semifinals the year before.

Case still had All-America forward Sammy Ranzino on the team and the coach was counting on "The Kid," as Wolfpack fans called him, to carry the offensive load for the four-time defending Southern Conference champions.

Ranzino had experienced help in seniors Vic Bubas and Paul Horvath, a rising star in junior Lee Terrill and five newcomers who included future All-America Bobby Speight. The Wolfpack swept to its second consecutive Dixie Classic title and was recognized among the best teams in the nation.

Early in the season, the Wolfpack was ranked as high as No. 3 in the nation, after nemesis Kentucky and Bradley. Villanova became the first team to beat a Case-coached team twice in the same season, handing the Wolfpack its first loss in late December in Reynolds Coliseum and a second in Philadelphia in mid-January. It was the Main Liners' fourth consecutive win over Case in three years of competition.

William & Mary handed Case's team its only loss in Southern Conference play, but the Wolfpack continued to dominate league competition. Against Virginia Tech, Ranzino led his team to a 60-26 halftime lead, personally outscoring the Hokies 27-26. At the final buzzer, the Wolfpack owned a record-setting 114-66 victory and Ranzino reset the school scoring record one more time with 47 points.

The celebration over such marks, however, was short-lived. The day after the win over Tech, it was reported in the local media that Ranzino, Bubas and Horvath had all been declared ineligible for the NCAA Tournament, should the Wolfpack earn a berth into the postseason.

The NCAA had relaxed its eligibility requirements during World War II to allow freshmen to compete in intercollegiate athletics. But, when it established its Sanity Code for Eligibility in 1947, it rescinded the freshman eligibility rule. The Southern Conference, however, did not, allowing freshmen — including Ranzino, Bubas and Horvath — to compete in 1947–48.

Not until the three players were nearing the end

of their college career, however, did the NCAA inform Case that they would only be allowed three years of varsity play. They were still allowed to play in the rest of the regular-season games, the Southern Conference Tournament and the National Invitation Tournament.

But Case was counting on them to carry his team into the postseason, since both the Southern Conference Tournament and the first round of the NCAA Tournament were being played, for the first time, at Reynolds Coliseum.

The well-oiled Wolfpack was the nation's top scoring team (78.9 points per game) and Ranzino was ranked in the top 10 among individuals, along with Duke's Dick Groat. But, on the same day the Wolfpack whipped South Carolina in the semifinals of the Southern Conference Tournament, the NCAA denied the school's appeal to allow the three seniors the opportunity to play in the postseason.

Case guided his team to a 67-63 win over Duke, in the final showdown between top-scorers Ranzino and Groat, for its fifth consecutive Southern Conference title. Case not only took the NCAA bid, but also a bid into the NIT, as Kentucky's Adolph Rupp had done the year before.

Just before the team left for the NIT in New York, news broke that federal investigators were looking into point-shaving allegations from the previous season and at least one newspaper, the William Randolph Hearst–owned tabloid *New York Daily Mirror*, implicated NC State in the scandal.

Case's top assistant, Butter Anderson, quickly told the NC State student newspaper, *Technician*, that no one on the team was under suspicion, which was quickly verified by the FBI office in Charlotte. But Case took no chances during his team's weeklong visit to the Big Apple.

He sequestered his team inside the New York Athletic Club, overlooking Central Park, to keep them away from gamblers. Instead of wandering around the city, the players were forced to take mid-semester exams that Case brought with him in a sealed envelope.

Even though the team was the No. 2 seed in the tournament, the Wolfpack players were in a foul frame of mind when they went out to face little-known Seton Hall. Their lackluster play included 18 percent shooting from the field in the second half of the 71-59 loss.

The Wolfpack returned to Raleigh for the first round of the NCAA Tournament at Reynolds Coliseum. Case was forced to share the spotlight with Kentucky, which was one of the other three teams in the event, and he wasn't looking forward to losing on his home court in front of nemesis Rupp.

To make matters worse, the Wolfpack drew as its opponent Villanova, the team that had already beaten Case's squad twice that season. Though the Wolfpack had the advantage of playing in its home arena, there seemed to be little chance of ending its four-game losing streak against the Main Liners without Ranzino, Bubas and Horvath, especially after the abysmal performance in New York.

But newcomers Bill Kukoy, Bernie Yurin and Bobby Goss stepped into the starting lineup, inspiring the home crowd. Kukoy scored State's first 11 points in the second half, leading the team to an emotional 67-62 win.

"I think one of the games that stands out most in my memory," Case said years later, "and the game so many State fans have said they remember the most, was the win over Villanova."

The Wolfpack headed back to New York for the next round of the NCAA Tournament. Case's team could not replicate the magic of its first round win, as Kukoy suffered a dislocated shoulder in the early moments of the game against Illinois and the Wolfpack's lack of depth led to an 84-71 loss. The next day, the Wolfpack lost again to St. John's, 71-59.

Though Case was disappointed in his team's lack of postseason success, he pointed out that the Wolfpack won the events that meant most to him.

"We won the Dixie Classic and our fifth straight Southern Conference Tournament," he said. "That's what counts."

Six Pack

The Wolfpack had a taste of what life would be like without Sammy Ranzino, Vic Bubas and Paul Horvath in the final three games of the previous season, after the trio of seniors was declared ineligible for NCAA Tournament play.

Coach Everett Case made do with sophomores Bill Kukoy, Bernie Yurin and Bobby Goss during the postseason. When the 1951–52 season began, Case had all three of them returning, plus one of the largest rosters in his tenure, with 21 players in the preseason team picture. So, even though highly touted freshman Dave Gotkin missed three quarters of his freshman season with a broken wrist, the coach had plenty of options to choose from in the team's quest for yet another Southern Conference title.

And it seemed like he used them all at some point during the season to maintain his six-year dominance of the Southern Conference. Junior Bobby Speight, a native of Raleigh who grew up just across the street from NC State's campus, was ready to step into Ranzino's role as the Wolfpack's top scorer.

Case tinkered with his lineup throughout the season, relying on sophomore forward Kim Buchanon early in the season before relegating him to the bench. Midway through December, he inserted undersized center Mel Thompson into the lineup. Kukoy and Terrill helped the Wolfpack win its third consecutive Dixie Classic title, with wins over Navy, North Carolina and Cornell.

Yet another contributor from the bench, Paul Brandenburg, hit a 16-foot jumper late in a double-overtime victory over Duke in Durham, but the Wolfpack suffered back-to-back losses to familiar nonconference foes, Louisville at home and Villanova on the road.

Pete Jackmowski came off the bench to help lead the Pack to another win over North Carolina, this one in overtime. The Wolfpack would beat the Tar Heels again later in the season, running Case's winning streak in the rivalry to 15 straight games.

No one could help the Pack, however, when it went to Norfolk, Va., to face William & Mary. Playing its third game in four days, the Wolfpack fell to the Southern Conference foe, 70-61. A week later, Duke came to Reynolds Coliseum to beat the Wolfpack, the first time Case ever lost to a league rival at home. In celebration, the Blue Devil players cut down the nets at Reynolds Coliseum, something they had seen Case's team do far too often when the Southern Conference Tournament was held at Duke Indoor Stadium.

For the first time in Case's tenure, the Wolfpack did not finish the season atop the Southern Conference standings. West Virginia, led by All-America center Mark Workman, finished with a near-perfect 15-1 mark in the league, though it did not face Case's team during the regular season because of the Southern Conference's unwieldy, unbalanced regular-season schedule. The Wolfpack finished 12-2 in the standings, just percentage points ahead of Duke's 13-3 record.

The Blue Devils, behind the scoring of senior Dick Groat, upset the Mountaineers in the semifinals, in a 90-88 thriller, setting up the third consecutive NC State–Duke championship game.

Case, remembering the Blue Devils' postgame antics in Raleigh in Reynolds, was not about to see another streak end this season, and his team easily topped Duke, 77-68, for his sixth straight conference title. Groat won the most valuable player award for the second year in a row, despite being on the losing team.

The NCAA East Regional was again played in Raleigh, with an all-star lineup of coaches on the sidelines. Besides Case, the four coaches consisted of Kentucky's Adolph Rupp, St. John's Frank McGuire and Penn State's Elmer Gross, who brought with him Solly Walker, the first African-American college player to participate in a college game in North Carolina.

The Wolfpack lost in the opening round to McGuire's team, 60-49, in another foreshadowing of the coaching rivalry that would blossom the following year when McGuire would be hired at North Carolina. The Johnnies advanced to the national title game, where they lost to Kansas.

The Wolfpack won its third-place consolation game over Penn State, finishing the season with a 24-10 record, its first double-digit loss total under Case.

BACK on TRACK

Look out, Everett Case: the rest of the world is gaining on you.

That was the story of the previous year, when the Wolfpack failed to win the Southern Conference title for the first time since Case's arrival in the summer of 1946. Several things happened that season to rock the Wolfpack, including Case's first loss to archrival North Carolina.

The Tar Heels had hired St. John's coach Frank McGuire, who had twice beaten Case in the NCAA Tournament, to become competitive with Case's juggernaut. In McGuire's first game against the Wolfpack, the Tar Heels pulled off a miracle when Jerry Vayda hit a jumper with 26 seconds remaining for a 70-69 win at Reynolds Coliseum. In celebration, McGuire led his team in cutting down the nets on the Wolfpack's home court.

The Pack entered what would be its last Southern Conference Tournament with a 24-5 record and a No. 8 ranking. It repaid the Tar Heels with a humiliating 85-54 win in the opening round and edged West Virginia in the semifinals.

But in the finals, Wake Forest's Billy Lyles helped his team score eight unanswered points in the final two minutes, and the Demon Deacons took a narrow 71-70 victory to end the longest string of championships the South has ever seen.

In a weak attempt to hide the Wolfpack's disappointment, fans murmured "at least the championship stayed in Wake County."

The winds of change were blowing hard. NC State chancellor John W. Harrellson retired and was replaced by long time faculty member Carey Bostian.

In May 1953, NC State joined six other schools in breaking away from the Southern Conference to form the Atlantic Coast Conference. The move was made because of football, and there was a long discussion about whether NC State should be included because of its lack of success on the gridiron. In the end, the new league knew it would be foolish to leave Case behind, so the school was included after it promised to upgrade its football squad. Earle Edwards was hired from Michigan State later that summer and, within four seasons, the Wolfpack won the 1957 ACC

football title, the first of five Edwards won at the school.

Among the things the ACC schools gave up with the move was freshman eligibility. At the time, the Southern Conference allowed all athletes to play four years, but the NCAA changed its standard in 1951 to just three years of varsity competition. Case was burned by the new rule in its initial year when three of his best players — Sammy Ranzino, Vic Bubas and Paul Horvath — were not allowed to compete in the NCAA Tournament during their senior season because they had played as freshmen.

Because of that, Case immediately began redshirting his freshmen players the next season, while other schools like Wake Forest and Duke allowed freshmen to compete. When the Wolfpack lost to Wake Forest in its final Southern Conference championship game, Case had future All-Americas Ronnie Shavlik and Vic Molodet sitting on the bench.

When they formed the new Atlantic Coast Conference, the breakaway schools decided to adopt the NCAA standard, though it grandfathered in everyone who entered school between 1951 and '53. The schools also agreed, at Case's insistence, to officially recognize the tournament champion as its representative in the NCAA Tournament.

But the big story of the 1954 season was not the new league — it was the war of words between Case and McGuire. The Wolfpack was loaded with talent, led by senior captain Mel Thompson and 6-10 transfer Cliff Dwyer. Shavlik and Molodet also moved up to the varsity, along with Whitey Bell.

Still, for the first time, the Wolfpack did not win the Dixie Classic title, losing games to Navy and Wake Forest. Case's team, which had been ranked as high as No. 5 in the nation, answered the wake-up call by beating Villanova for the first time in Philadelphia and beating Duke.

Case showed just how fine-tuned his team was in Chapel Hill, using a full-court press to beat North Carolina, 84-77, in a game that was apparently not as close as the score indicated. McGuire took offense at the 40 minutes of pressure the

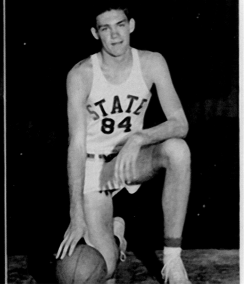

Wolfpack put on the Tar Heels. "It was ridiculous," said McGuire, who refused to shake hands with Case after the game. "He could beat us by 20 points without [pressing us] and he comes over here and tries to beat us by 40 points. If that's the way he wants it, I'll fight him right back when we get the boys to compete with him. I am declaring open war against Everett Case. And some day, perhaps a year or two, the shoe will be on the other foot."

Case's public retort fanned the flames even more: "That is the most childish thing I have ever heard of. Since when did he get to the place he could coach my ball club?"

Behind the scenes, this public feud may well have been a clever strategy by the two coaches to build even more interest in the new league. Case and McGuire were actually quite close, often having dinner together during the off-season or when they happened to be in the same town. McGuire's successor, Dean Smith, remembered years later: "They thought it was better to be rivals. Coach Case told us, 'Don't shake hands upstairs [on the arena floor]. We'll shake hands after the game, downstairs.'"

At the end of the season, the Wolfpack turned up the pressure, using its full-court press to finish the regular season with a 21-5 record, including

yet another win over the Tar Heels, 57-48, at Reynolds Coliseum. But Case's team finished fourth in the inaugural ACC season, with Duke earning the regular-season title and the top seed in the first tournament.

In a twist of fate that proved to be perfect for the fledgling league, the Wolfpack and Tar Heels squared off in the first round of the tournament, and fireworks quickly ensued. The Tar Heels led 33-32 at the intermission. In the second half, McGuire turned the tables on Case, slowing the tempo with the same kind of full-fledged stall that Case used to use as a high school coach. The strategy worked, but with 12 seconds remaining on the clock, the Wolfpack owned a slim one-point advantage.

That's when the rivalry that had always been heated turned nearly violent. With eight seconds on the clock, North Carolina's Tony Radovich knocked NC State's Dave Gotkin down with a hard foul. Gotkin grabbed the ball and hurled it at Radovich, and the game nearly turned into an all-out brawl.

Officials quickly called a flagrant foul on Radovich and ejected him from the game. Gotkin was assessed a technical foul, giving the Tar Heels a free-throw opportunity. Gotkin, a junior from New York City, made only one of his two

free-throw attempts and the Tar Heels answered by making its free throw, leaving the score at 52-51.

But the two coaches argued with the officials about possession of the ball. McGuire thought the Tar Heels deserved it, since Gotkin had been called for a technical foul, superseding Radovich's personal foul. After a lengthy consultation, the officials ruled that the multiple-foul situation required a jump ball.

In a crucial battle, sophomore Shavlik tipped the ball to teammate Molodet and the Wolfpack managed to run out the final seconds of the game.

The next two games were hardly as exciting, though Case and his squad avenged their two regular-season losses to the Blue Devils, behind the scoring of Thompson and Shavlik. In a rematch of the '53 Southern Conference championship game, the Wolfpack faced the Demon Deacons in the initial ACC title game.

NC State was leading comfortably going into the fourth quarter, but All-America Dickie Hemric brought the Deacons back to tie the game, 70-70, at the end of regulation. Case had a deeper bench and the Wolfpack won the game 82-80, starting a new streak of conference championships in its new league.

The NCAA Tournament fluctuated between 24 and 25 teams from 1953–74, with several neutral site games played in the opening round to determine what teams advanced to regional play. The Wolfpack played in such a game against Southern Conference champion George Washington for the right to go to Philadelphia for the NCAA East Regional. The game was held at Duke's Cameron Indoor Stadium.

Case maintained his dominance over the Southern Conference, thanks to Phil DiNardo's tip-in at the end of the game that gave the Wolfpack a 75-73 victory and DiNardo a free trip to his hometown of Philadelphia.

At the Palestra, Case's team faced LaSalle and its All-America forward Tom Gola in a rematch of a game from earlier in the season. Gola fouled out of that game, but the Explorers still managed an 88-78 win at Reynolds Coliseum.

The second game turned into a showdown between Gola and Shavlik. Gola had 26 points and 26 rebounds in the contest, while Shavlik nearly matched him with 24 points and 18 rebounds. But the Explorers were too much for the Wolfpack and every other opponent they faced in the tournament. They took an 88-81 win over State, then beat Navy for the right to advance to the national semifinals in Kansas City, where they beat both Penn State and Bradley to win the NCAA title.

Meet Joe Hays

The person, more than anyone else, who finally stopped Everett Case after his first 10 years of unprecedented success at NC State was Ol' Joe Hays. That was the nickname Case gave to the fictional boogeyman that was often found poking his nose into the coach's business.

Hays first showed up in 1953, looking into Case's recruiting practices and into the luring of Denver native Ronnie Shavlik, who had chosen the Wolfpack over Kentucky. For five years, the NCAA had tried to limit renegade recruiting, first adopting the Sanity Code in 1948 and then revamping its rules in 1951 to outlaw such common practices as on-campus tryouts.

In 1952, the NCAA looked into West Virginia native Hot Rod Hundley's visits to Raleigh, which were paid for by NC State booster Dave Clark, and Ohio native Jerry Weber's flight to Raleigh for a tryout. Southern Conference Commissioner Wallace Wade, the former Duke athletics director and football coach, had also received a complaint from a league member about Case trying out Lennie Rosenbluth.

The NCAA — after interviewing Weber, who had chosen to play for Adolph Rupp at Kentucky — ruled Case indeed broke its rules by trying out 14 high school players during the weekend of the school's 1952 spring football game. The ACC put Case's team on a one-year probation, from 1953–54, with the primary penalty being that none of the 14 players who tried out in Raleigh, including Rosenbluth and Indiana prep star Clyde Lovelette, could ever play for the Wolfpack.

The NCAA cleared Case of any wrongdoing in recruiting Shavlik, but slapped the program with a one-year probation from May 1954–55 for its illegal on-campus tryouts, barring the Wolfpack from the 1955 NCAA Tournament.

The limitations didn't seem to have an effect on Case's team during the season. The team, missing Mel Thompson (graduation) and Whitey Bell (military service) from the 1954 champions, was lacking in depth, but stacked with height. Case converted to a double-post offense to take advantage of 6-10 senior center Cliff Dwyer and 6-8 forward Ronnie Shavlik, with guard Vic Molodet running the show.

There were more new rules to adjust to, since the NCAA changed from four quarters to two 20-minute halves and implemented the one-and-one rule on free throws.

Shavlik had a breakthrough season, averaging 22.1 points and 18.2 rebounds per game and earning first-team All-America honors. His performance against Villanova in January, in which he scored 45 points and grabbed 35 rebounds, was one of the greatest by any player in school history, even though the Wolfpack lost, 107-96.

Case's team reclaimed the Dixie Classic title, its fifth in six years, thanks to a spectacular play by John Maglio, who drove the length of the court against Minnesota and hit a layup with six seconds to play, giving his team a 85-84 win.

The Wolfpack lost ACC games at Maryland

and at home again North Carolina, but Case was not upset: "Championships aren't won during the regular season in our conference. It's the tournament in March that counts."

His team won nine straight games to close out the regular season, including a win over the Tar Heels in Chapel Hill to clinch the top seed in the ACC Tournament. The Wolfpack cruised to its eighth conference title in nine years, recording three consecutive double-digit victories over Clemson, Wake Forest and Duke. Case won his second straight ACC Coach of the Year Award, but because of the probation, Duke represented

the ACC in its first-ever appearance in the NCAA Tournament.

Unable to play in the NCAA and barred by an ACC agreement that prevented it from playing in the National Invitation Tournament, Case circumvented the ACC's limit on non-NCAA postseason play by taking his team to Shavlik's hometown of Denver for the 25-team AAU National Championship, where it beat Wuthnow Furniture of Hope, Kan., and lost to the San Francisco Olympic Club, 70-60.

After the season, the ACC banned its teams from participating in the national AAU event.

EMPIRE FALLS

After serving its 1955 NCAA probation, the Wolfpack seemed poised for its best team in Everett Case's 10 years at NC State.

Seniors Ronnie Shavlik and Vic Molodet gave the Wolfpack two certified All-Americas in the lineup, along with talented players like John Maglio, Nick Pond, Phil DiNardo, Cliff Hafer, Bob Seitz and Lou Dickman. Case said it was the fastest team he had ever assembled, thanks to Molodet and Maglio, who were affectionately known as the M-Twins.

The team raced through the early season, winning another Dixie Classic title, and was just behind top-ranked San Francisco in the national polls. The only thing that slowed the Wolfpack down during the regular season was a viral infection that Molodet picked up while on a Christmas-break hunting trip.

With Molodet on the bench, the Wolfpack lost its first game of the season to Duke, snapping a school-record 23-game winning streak over two seasons. The team would lose twice more to ACC foes North Carolina and Maryland, but it still managed a tie for the regular-season title with the Tar Heels. The Pack did not lose to a team outside the ACC in the regular season.

In the finale against Wake Forest, however, Case's team suffered a major blow: Shavlik suffered what was expected to be a career-ending broken wrist. Case's dreams for his long-elusive national title seemed to disappear.

In the first round of the ACC Tournament, Shavlik made a surprising return to the lineup, playing 10 minutes as the Wolfpack pulled out a narrow 88-84 win over Clemson. Shavlik was still badly hampered by the injury, but NC State cruised in the semifinals with a 91-79 win over Duke and in the finals with a 76-64 win over Wake Forest.

Molodet was spectacular, scoring 79 points in three days to win MVP honors.

Limited by his cast, Shavlik still managed to collect eight points and 16 rebounds against the Blue Devils. He added eight points and 17 boards in the championship game against the Demon Deacons. He became a national celebrity for his three-day performance, appearing on "The Perry Como Show" once the Wolfpack arrived in New York for the NCAA Tournament.

It was Case's ninth league title in 10 years, an era of dominance in college basketball that was unmatched until former Indiana high school foe John Wooden built his dynasty at UCLA, with nine NCAA titles in 11 years, from 1965–75. Case clearly enjoyed the success.

"No," he answered when asked if he ever got tired of winning the conference title, "it's just like eating. You don't get tired of eating, do you?"

What the coach was tiring of, however, was his lack of success on the national level. His opponents suggested that Case's success was simply a factor of playing so many games at home, in front of the loud crowds that gave the Wolfpack a substantial advantage. Other coaches had begun to chafe at the fact that the Wolfpack always hosted the Dixie Classic and the ACC Tournament in Reynolds Coliseum. In the 12 years after Reynolds Coliseum opened, from 1949 until the death of the Dixie Classic after the 1960–61 season, only once did Case schedule more than 10 games away from his palatial home.

"State is 100 percent and two men better when they play at home," said outspoken Wake Forest star Dave Budd. "There ought to be a law against the home-court advantage they have. Every team has an advantage at home, but let's face it, it is beyond reasonable limits in Raleigh."

North Carolina coach Frank McGuire even took a little delight in seeing the Wolfpack struggle outside of Reynolds.

"Each time I go to New York, I rave and rave about State," McGuire said. "Then when they go north they never live up to expectations."

The Wolfpack had a full week after the ACC title to prepare for its first round NCAA Tournament game against Canisius at New York's Madison Square Garden. Case hoped the seven-day layoff

baskets by DiNardo and Maglio. When Maglio, a 73 percent free throw shooter on the year, was fouled with 14 seconds to play, it appeared that Case's team would break its Garden jinx. But the junior guard missed the front end of his one-and-one opportunity.

Canisius grabbed the rebound, raced down the court and found Frank Corcoran, a little-used player who had not scored a point in the game. Corcoran, who didn't even appear on the official NCAA Tournament program prior to the contest, had averaged less than one point per game during the regular season.

would give Shavlik even more time to heal and prepare for a tournament that everyone expected would end with a showdown between the Wolfpack and San Francisco.

The whole college basketball world hoped to see Shavlik play against the Dons' All-America Bill Russell, assuming both teams advanced all the way to the title game.

But tiny Canisius, a Roman Catholic school from Buffalo, N.Y., had other ideas. The Griffins had won 15 of their previous 16 games and shocked the fabled Wolfpack by taking an early lead. Case's squad had to scramble to keep up with Canisius, forcing a 65-65 tie at the end of regulation. Both teams opted to slow the tempo in overtime, eliciting boos and catcalls from the Garden crowd. They each scored four points in the first overtime, two points in the second overtime and no points in the third overtime.

Going into an unprecedented fourth overtime, the coaches decided to abandon the stalling strategy. The Wolfpack took a 78-77 lead, thanks to

But on this night, Corcoran lived the dream of every substitute who ever sat on the end of the bench. With five seconds to play, Corcoran hit the game-winning jumper to knock off the second-ranked Wolfpack.

"This was my greatest disappointment in 36 years of coaching," Case said afterwards.

"I just don't know what happens to us in New York," Shavlik added.

With just three losses on the season, it was still a wildly successful season, but Case's stranglehold on the ACC was waning. The next season, McGuire led his team to a perfect 31-0 record and the ACC's first national championship. The Wolfpack was hit with a four-year probation for the recruitment of Jackie Moreland. Case won just one more ACC title, in 1959, in his final eight years at NC State.

Case's Final Title

NC State had nowhere to go in March 1959. Just like the 1954–55 ACC champions, which were prohibited from playing in the NCAA Tournament because of recruiting violations, the 1958–59 Wolfpack was serving one of the harshest sentences ever doled out by the collegiate governing body.

The four-year probation over the recruiting of Louisiana high school legend Jackie Moreland prevented the Wolfpack from participating in any postseason event in any sport. That was particularly poignant for coach Earle Edwards's first ACC Championship football team, which was not allowed to go to the 1957 Orange Bowl because of the basketball penalty.

Still, the probation did not mean the Wolfpack had nothing to play for. Winning the ACC title was still Case's ultimate goal, with any postseason success that followed considered a bonus. He also was eager to win the Dixie Classic, which had the most challenging field in the event's history. Besides the No. 6 Wolfpack, the event included three other teams ranked in the top 10: No. 2 Cincinnati, featuring Oscar Robertson; No. 3 North Carolina, featuring Doug Moe, Lee Shaffer and York Larese and No. 7 Michigan State, featuring "Jumping" Johnny Green.

The Wolfpack, with a pair of All-Americas of its own in point guard Lou Pucillo and center John Richter, swept through the event for its seventh and final Dixie Classic title. A few days later, Kentucky suffered its first loss of the season, elevating the Wolfpack to the No. 1 spot in the Associated Press rankings for the first time in school history. But the day after the poll was released, North Carolina invaded Reynolds Coliseum to beat the Wolfpack, 72-68, in overtime. At the end of the contest, Tar Heel coach Frank McGuire called timeout to soak in the victory on the Wolfpack's home court, a moment no one in Reynolds Coliseum that evening ever forgot.

McGuire and his team celebrated even more after beating the Wolfpack in Woollen Gym a few weeks later, 74-67, a win that elevated the Tar Heels to the No. 1 spot in the AP poll. The Tar Heels suffered a pair of late losses though, and finished tied with the Wolfpack in the regular-season race.

The Wolfpack was eager to meet the Tar Heels for a third time, since it knew the ACC Tournament would be the end of its season. A little too eager, perhaps. The Pack struggled to beat South Carolina 75-72 in the quarterfinals and Virginia 66-63 in the semifinals.

The Tar Heels, secure in the knowledge they were headed to the NCAA Tournament, did not seem to be as motivated for the championship game as the Wolfpack. McGuire freely substituted for his starters, as the Wolfpack built a 35-27 advantage in the first half.

"Everett was not too happy that Frank McGuire wouldn't let his good guys play," said Vic Bubas, a longtime Case assistant who eventually became the head coach at Duke. "There was nothing illegal about what he did, so coach said let's play our best against who they put on the court. But he wasn't very happy about that."

In the second half, the game became a blowout. Pucillo, the flashy guard playing in his final collegiate game, scored 23 points, while Richter pumped in 15. George Stepanovich also played well enough to be voted on the first-team All-Tournament squad.

With the Pack leading 65-52 and 4:29 on the clock, McGuire pulled his starters for the last time.

An irate Wolfpack fan found the master switch in the expansive basement of Reynolds Coliseum and turned out all the lights, causing an eight-minute delay.

Pucillo begged Case to let him run out the final five minutes on the clock by dribbling on a darkened court. Case refused, perhaps because he wanted everyone in the building to see what happened in the final moments.

The Wolfpack poured on the points and eventually took an 80-56 victory, which still stands as the fourth most lopsided ACC Tournament championship result of all time. With four seconds to play, the Wolfpack called timeout to savor the win and to prepare to cut down the nets on what turned out to be Case's fourth and final ACC Tournament title.

"That was some of the boys' doing," Case said after the game. "I had nothing to do with it. In fact, I wished they hadn't done it. But you know how boys are."

He might have even winked as he said it.

McGuire got into a shouting match with a reporter who suggested that his team hadn't performed at its highest level.

"You always want to win the game you are playing," McGuire said. "That's basketball. We put the second string in there to rest our regulars. Don't forget, the game was lost when the regulars were in there. Not when the subs went in. The game was lost with about eight minutes to play."

Fatigue was definitely not a factor when the Tar Heels went to New York three days later for the NCAA Tournament's opening round. McGuire's well-rested team fell to Navy 76-63.

Case, "The Old Gray Fox," could only smile, especially when the AP ranked the Wolfpack No. 6 in its final poll and the Tar Heels No. 9.

Pucillo, voted the ACC Player of the Year and Athlete of the Year, accepted the tournament's most valuable player trophy with all the lights of the coliseum shining brightly on him.

"This is the greatest thrill of my college career," said the guard. "And my last."

End of a Legacy

Perhaps it was fitting that the only ACC Championship won by Press Maravich, the hand-picked successor to legendary coach Everett Case, began with a game at Clemson.

Maravich spent six seasons as the head coach of the Tigers, from 1956–62, before coming to NC State as Case's top assistant coach in 1963. An ailing Case knew he would retire following the 1964–65 season because of mandatory state retirement laws and his deteriorating health. The previous year, Case had been hospitalized for surgery prior to the season and took a 10-day leave of absence to treat gout and shingles while his team traveled to South Carolina and Virginia.

Case hoped to get through his final season, if only to help erase the painful memories of the previous five years, when the Wolfpack barely survived the point-shaving scandals of 1960–61 and struggled to remain competitive after the consolidated university system forced both NC State and UNC to de-emphasize basketball.

In early December 1964, Case was not feeling well, as the onset of the bone cancer that would eventually claim his life some 18 months later began to sap his vigor and once seemingly boundless energy. So, two games into the season, following a victory over Furman and a loss to Wake Forest, Case stepped down after more than 18 years as the ACC's most successful coach, turning the program over to Maravich.

Case left his successor with an excellent team, with a pair of accomplished senior forwards in Larry Lakins and Pete Coker and sophomore Eddie Biedenbach. Guards Billy Moffitt and Tommy Maddocks rounded out the starting lineup. Immediately after Maravich took over for Case, the Wolfpack reeled off 11 consecutive victories.

But Maravich knew, if the Wolfpack wanted to challenge Top-10 Duke, it would need a little more depth. When his team faced Clemson in early February, he was forced to find a little help when Lakins and Coker both got into foul trouble. He turned to junior forward Larry Worsley, a slow-talking, less-than-fleet country boy from Oak City, N.C.

Worsley came off the bench to score six points late in the 78-74 victory, bolstering the confidence he sometimes lacked during his career in Raleigh. The Wolfpack won four of its final five games in the regular season, with Worsley, a 6-5 forward, offering some much-needed perimeter scoring. The only setback during the season was a one-point home loss to North Carolina.

"Coach Maravich said many times he would rather see me shoot from 20 or 25 feet away from the basket than four or five feet away," Worsley said.

The Wolfpack went into the ACC Tournament inspired, not only by improved play all around, but by the hope of winning one more title for Case, who was in the advanced stages of bone cancer.

In the opening game, Worsley scored 12 points off the bench against Virginia, but that was hardly notable as the Wolfpack set a tournament scoring record in the 106-69 victory. In the semifinals, he led a second-half surge and finished with 15 points in the 76-67 win.

"Going into the tail end of the season, I just had all the confidence in the world," said Worsley, who averaged 7.4 points and 4.0 rebounds as a junior.

No one was prepared for what Worsley, who had never scored more than 18 points in a game during his two years on the varsity, did against No. 8 Duke in the championship game. The Blue Devils, who had played for the national championship against UCLA the year before and had gone to back-to-back national semifinals, had won 17 of 18 games at one point in the 1964–65 regular season. Behind the scoring of Jack Marin and Steve Vacendak and the leadership of sophomore point guard Bob Verga, the Blue Devils were the nation's highest-scoring team and used a relentless full-court press, like Case's teams of old.

In the title game, Moffitt picked up three fouls in

the first five minutes and the Devils seemed all but assured to win their third consecutive ACC title.

But Maravich turned to Worsley one more time. The forward shocked the roaring crowd at Reynolds Coliseum with a nearly unstoppable offensive performance. Playing against a variety of defenses, including a box-in-one that was intended to do nothing but slow him down, Worsley made 14 of his 19 field-goal attempts for a career-high 30 points. He also added eight rebounds.

"It was just too much Worsley for us," Bubas said after the game. "He was the difference. His shooting was fantastic."

In perhaps the most touching moment in the history of Reynolds Coliseum until Jim Valvano's farewell speech in 1993, after Maravich took his turn cutting down the nets, the Wolfpack players rushed over to the scorer's table, where the ailing Case was seated. The former coach had not been able to attend the tournament's first two rounds, but he made the short trip from his home on Daniels Street in Cameron Village to see his boys win one more title.

As the players hoisted the frail coach onto their shoulders, Case cut the final strand of the net from the rim, continuing the tradition he brought to college basketball.

"I have never been happier," Case said after the game. "The last taste is always the best."

A few minutes later, the coach presented the newly named Everett Case Award to Worsley as the tournament's most valuable player. He was the only nonstarter to ever win the award, until Duke's Daniel Ewing duplicated the feat in 2004.

Riding high upon the shoulders of his former players, an ailing and frail Everett Case heads to cut down the final strand of net after the Wolfpack's 1965 ACC championship. This would be Case's last celebration in Reynolds Coliseum.

The Math Man

John Richter was NC State basketball's mathematics engineering big man, an honor roll student who became an All-America performer on the basketball court.

The native of Philadelphia traveled south with Lou Pucillo, and the careers of the 6-8 center and the 5-9 point guard are forever connected.

They sat out as freshmen when the Wolfpack won its third consecutive ACC Championship in 1956. They played under the cloud of NCAA probation for the next two years, with the Wolfpack unable to participate in postseason play.

But Richter was a prolific player for three years, averaging a double-double in scoring and rebounding his entire career and earning second-team All-ACC honors as a sophomore and junior, and first-team honors as a senior. For his career, he contributed 15 points and 12.6 rebounds per season.

His best year, however, was as a senior, when he and Pucillo were the cornerstones of Everett Case's last great team. Richter rose to the top of an All-America crop of players in the 1958 Dixie Classic, outshining the likes of Oscar Robertson and Jumping Johnny Green to win Most Valuable Player honors as the Wolfpack won consecutive

The Hot Dog

Over the years, NC State had a handful of undersized guards with oversized hearts. Point guards Monte Towe and Anthony "Spud" Webb come to mind. Shooter Terry Gannon was another. But none was more accomplished than little Lou Pucillo, who led coach Everett Case to his last ACC Championship in 1959.

The 5-9 Pucillo was the shortest player Case ever recruited. And it took some serious convincing by assistant coach Vic Bubas to get the "Old Gray Fox" to bring Pucillo from Philadelphia to Raleigh.

Case's doubts had nothing to do with Pucillo's size. It had everything to do with the flashy player's behind-the-back passes, fancy dribbling and hot-dogging style.

Pucillo never started a high school basketball game, twice being cut from the varsity of Philadelphia's Southeast High by coach Jack Kraft as a freshman and sophomore. He didn't even try out as a junior, and as a senior he was an end-of-the-bench reserve, averaging a little more than four points a game.

How on earth did Pucillo become the 1959 ACC Player and Athlete of the Year and the winner of NC State's Alumni Athletic Trophy?

games over Louisville, Cincinnati and Michigan State to earn its seventh title in the holiday tournament.

The Wolfpack eventually rose to No. 1 in the Associated Press poll when Kentucky lost in January. Though the team was not allowed to participate in the NCAA Tournament, it still managed to give Case his final official ACC title, whipping North Carolina in the championship game. Pucillo edged Richter for the tournament MVP award.

Richter was the sixth overall pick of the 1959 NBA draft, and made the most of his only season in the league, contributing

4.3 points and 4.7 rebounds as a rookie as the Boston Celtics beat the St. Louis Blues for the 1960 NBA Championship. He sat out because of a blood clot in his arm the next season, and never returned to play in the NBA.

However, he continued to play for years in the East Basketball Association for the Sunbury (Pa.) Mercuries, where his hook shot and rebounding were hard to stop. Richter died in Collegeville, Pa., in March 1983, just before the Wolfpack won the school's second NCAA Championship.

His road to success began when he took his father's advice and enrolled at Temple Prep School in Philadelphia, where the elder Pucillo was a foreign language instructor. He was originally going to just take a Spanish class, but decided to enroll as a full-time, post-secondary student when he discovered the school had a basketball team.

Turns out, Pucillo was just a late bloomer. He led Temple to a 25-1 record, averaging 25 points a game. He also caught the eye of Bubas, who saw him play while in the Philadelphia area after signing future All-America John Richter.

But he was the antithesis of what Case wanted in his backcourt. The coach liked big guards who were disciplined and controlled. Pucillo played just like Bob Cousy, and never met a difficult or flashy pass he didn't like. Since no other school in the country offered Pucillo a scholarship, he jumped at the opportunity to play for a school that was dominating southern basketball. He eventually became one of Case's favorite players.

"He shows me something different every time I see him play," Case once said of Pucillo. "He's always thinking one step ahead of everyone else on the court."

Pucillo made his first big splash as a sophomore in the 1956 Dixie Classic, sparking the Wolfpack to a win over Iowa. Two years later, seniors Pucillo and Richter helped the Wolfpack beat Louisville, Cincinnati and Michigan State on three consecutive days to take the 1958 Dixie Classic.

After scoring 22 points in the Wolfpack's win over Michigan State, Pucillo ended his career with 23 points in the ACC championship game against a heavily favored North Carolina team, a victory that gave Case his 10th and final conference championship.

At season's end, both Pucillo and Richter were named first-team All-Americas. Pucillo, who never thought he would end up playing college basketball after his years of frustration in high school, won every possible award following his final season. But most important, he helped the Wolfpack win another ACC title.

"He is walking proof that there is still room for the little man in college basketball — if, as Lou was, you are willing to pay the price of practice," Case once said.

LIKE NO OTHER

Forward Dick Dickey stepped up to become the Wolfpack's first national star and NBA player

Of all the great players in NC State basketball history, no one ever matched the accomplishments of Dick Dickey, the 6-1 forward from Alexandria, Ind.: he was named first-team all-conference in each of his four seasons with the Wolfpack.

He also earned All-America honors three consecutive years, a feat matched only by Sammy Ranzino and David Thompson.

Dickey was an original "Hoosier Hotshot." Case first noticed him during World War II while serving in the U.S. Navy as the head coach of the Iowa Pre-Flight Seahawks. The war was the best thing that ever happened to Dickey, who was a 5-9, 150-pound guard when he enlisted in the Navy in 1942.

Within six months, the red-headed shooter grew four inches and added 35 pounds to his athletic frame. Working with basketball legend Hank Luisetti, his teammate at St. Mary's Pre-Flight School in San Francisco, Dickey perfected the one-handed jump shot that Luisetti used as a player at Stanford in the 1930s to revolutionize college basketball.

Both Case and Dickey were headed to Purdue after the war, but Case changed his mind and accepted the job at NC State. He immediately began recruiting Dickey to be the centerpiece of his first team. The decision was made easy because Case offered Dickey scholarship money, while Purdue did not. Case knew Dickey would be perfect for the fast-paced style the coach introduced to southern basketball.

"Case put some plays in for me because I could get that shot off," Dickey said in a 2004 interview. "It was one of the ways I could get open and I had fairly good jumping ability, so I could get over people."

The flashy forward was a part of the most dynamic transition in the basketball history of the school, winning four consecutive Southern Conference championships. He was on the 1947 team that introduced cutting down the nets as a college basketball tradition. He led the newly renamed Wolfpack to its first three postseason appearances, which included advancing to the national semifinals (the equivalent of the modern-day Final Four) in 1950. And he and Ranzino were the players everyone came to see when William Neal Reynolds Coliseum opened its doors during his senior season.

"I had a fair amount of ability," said Dickey, summing up his career. "Heck, I don't know if I could make the team now, but at the time I was pretty good and I played defense."

Despite the four league titles, the postseason was never kind to the Wolfpack. In 1947, Case's team was beaten badly by Kentucky in the first round of the NIT. In 1948, Dickey missed much of the postseason because of the mumps, which dramatically changed the way Case's team played in its first-round loss to DePaul. Dickey was hurt much of his junior year, suffering a thigh injury during a West Coast road trip in December and a broken nose against Villanova.

Dickey, whose No. 70 hangs among the honored jerseys at the RBC Center, briefly held the school scoring record with 1,644 points in his four years, but it was broken the next year by Ranzino.

Dickey was the first NC State player ever drafted into the NBA, going to the Baltimore Bullets in 1960 before being sold to the Boston Celtics during preseason training.

Even after graduating in 1950 with a degree in agriculture and life sciences, Dickey stayed close to the program, particularly when his former roommate, Norm Sloan, was named head coach in 1966. Among the many players he recommended to his old friend was an undersized point guard from Converse, Ind., named Monte Towe, a key figure in the Wolfpack's 1974 NCAA Championship season. Dickey was so sure that Towe would fit into Sloan's system, he drove the young player to Raleigh for his first recruiting visit. Sloan was convinced and the gritty guard was an integral part of the Wolfpack's 57-1 record from 1972–74, back-to-back ACC Championships and the school's first NCAA title in 1974.

Dickey, inducted into the Indiana Basketball Hall of Fame in 2005, died on July 3, 2006, at the age of 79.

The MVP

The storyline of the 1956 ACC Tournament concerned the health of NC State star Ronnie Shavlik, who suffered a broken wrist in the Wolfpack's regular-season finale against Wake Forest. The injury to the All-America big man certainly clouded the No. 2 Wolfpack's chances for winning Everett Case's long-elusive national championship.

But teammate Vic Molodet proved that the Wolfpack's high-powered offense, which scored 90 points on 10 occasions during the season, wasn't a one-act play. Shavlik, wearing a lace-up wrist guard, made a surprise return to the lineup for limited action, but Molodet stole the show.

The 5-11 guard went to his full repertoire of shots to score 21, 26 and 32 points in three days, leading his team to its third consecutive ACC

The First Shot

When Everett Case pulled the junior guard out of the game, the coach didn't let him go to the end of the bench with the rest of his teammates. It was unusually early for Case to bring out a starter anyway, so the player knew he was about to get some terse words of wisdom from "The Old Gray Fox."

"Damn," Case said. "You really wanted that first basket, didn't you?"

"Damned right I did," said Vic Bubas. "I don't care if people do call me selfish. It's something that nobody can take away from me."

Ever since he arrived on campus in the fall of 1947, Bubas had watched the interminable progress of construction of NC State's new basketball

home. He stopped by the building every single day on his way to practice at Thompson Gym, just to see how much progress had been made.

So on Dec. 2, 1949, when the Wolfpack hosted Washington & Lee in the first varsity game ever played at Reynolds Coliseum, Bubas wanted to etch his name into Wolfpack basketball lore forever, and if he had to fight, scrape and out-muscle everyone on the court — including All-America teammates Dick Dickey and Sammy Ranzino — to do it, he would.

The game was played even though construction was still under way. There were no locker rooms for the teams to go to. They dressed at Thompson Gym and walked over to the new arena. At halftime, both teams went to the ROTC classrooms in the outer hallways to talk strategy. Not all of the seats were yet in place and many of the spectators in attendance that night sat on bare concrete.

But when it came time for the opening tip, Bubas had done all the work he needed to make sure he title and winning the tournament's Most Valuable Player award.

With a week to prepare, the Wolfpack thought Shavlik would be closer to full strength by the NCAA Tournament, but the team, perhaps the best of Case's 18-year career, suffered a bitterly disappointing first-round loss at Madison Square Garden, a four-overtime defeat to unknown Canisius. Molodet was called for three early charging fouls and was out of the game before the first overtime started.

"That was a nightmare, that ball game," Molodet said in an interview more than 40 years later. "If that official was here today I believe I would kill him. He gave us a raw deal. It was a badly officiated ball game. I don't think I played two or three minutes of that game. Those three charging fouls were ridiculous.

"I can't get over that ball game, I really can't."

The loss ended the careers of Molodet and Shavlik, two of Case's most accomplished players.

Molodet came to NC State from East Chicago, Ind., part of the seemingly endless parade of Hoosier stars to play for Case. He had listened to the exploits of Wolfpack players like Sammy Ranzino on the radio, and joined the party just as NC State and seven other schools made the transition from the Southern Conference to the ACC.

And while Shavlik is still remembered for his scoring and rebounding prowess, memories of just how fast Molodet ran the Wolfpack offense have begun to fade.

"You look at the way these guys are running now and they are 6-5," Molodet said in 2010. "It makes me look like a midget. It's amazing how they run for the size they are. But they don't run any faster than we did. They are just bigger.

"What we did well was run and press, and that made us a really good team."

Molodet's brother, John, also had an impact on NC State athletics, as the coach of famed Washington High in East Chicago. He coached both Sam Esposito, the Wolfpack head baseball coach and assistant basketball coach during the 1970s, and Tim Stoddard, the pitcher-forward who played on the 1974 NCAA championship team.

was in the proper place. He had studied W&L film to see exactly how its players lined up for the start of the game. The ball came right to him on the opening tip and he headed straight for the basket.

Trouble was, he missed the first shot taken in the new gym. And the second. But on Bubas's third attempt, the ball went in the basket for the first points ever scored in the nation's largest on-campus arena.

"That was the one time in my life, maybe the only time, that I wasn't going to pass that ball to anybody," said Bubas, a two-time All-Southern Conference selection who helped the team win four straight league tournaments.

Maybe that wasn't the message that Bubas wanted to convey to his players while he spent eight years as an assistant and top recruiter for Case, or during his 10-year stint as the head coach at Duke — where he went to three Final Fours and had six consecutive 20-win seasons — but on Opening Night at Reynolds Coliseum, he didn't really care.

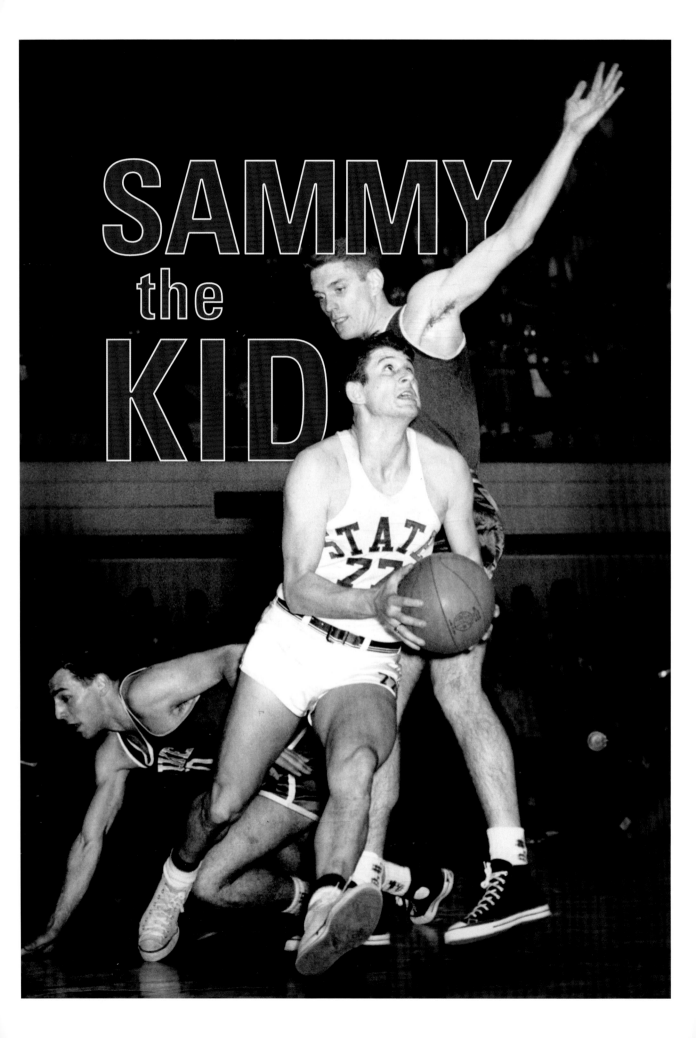

SAMMY
the
KID

On a team that was mostly made up of World War II veterans, Sammy Ranzino truly was a boy among men.

In the fall of 1947, "Sammy the Kid" Ranzino came straight to Raleigh from Emerson High School in Gary, Ind., but had no trouble fitting into Everett Case's second team at NC State as a 19-year-old freshman. By the time he left — all grown up — he was a three-time All-America, a three-time All-Southern Conference selection and NC State's all-time leading scorer with 1,967 points, a record that lasted until it was broken by David Thompson a quarter century later.

Though he had never heard of NC State before, Ranzino did know about legendary Frankfort, Ind., High School coach Everett Case, who had returned to his home state to look for a few more "Hoosier Hotshots." Ranzino heard that the coach, who had moved to some college down south, was holding an open tryout in the Indiana town of Pendleton and he wanted to show off his skills.

When he arrived, he found 300 hopefuls waiting to do the same thing for Case and assistant coach Carl "Butter" Anderson.

Like Dick Dickey, who was a year ahead by class but five years older in age, Ranzino perfected the running one-handed jumper. But, unlike Dickey, the young 6-2 forward could shoot it with either hand, making him NC State's first truly ambidextrous player.

He made his first splash as a freshman, coming off the bench to score 20 points in a controversial loss to defending NCAA champion Holy Cross in the Sugar Bowl Classic in New Orleans. It was one of the many times Ranzino led his team in scoring, including seven 30-point games during his career. As a junior, again playing against Holy Cross, Ranzino set the NCAA Tournament single-game scoring record with 32 points. Ranzino averaged 18.9 points for the season.

Truly a scoring machine, he once single-handedly beat Southern Conference foe Virginia Tech 47-46 in a 1951 game at Reynolds Coliseum. As a senior, he battled with Duke's Dick Groat for the Southern Conference scoring title in 1952. Groat did indeed finish with more points and the Southern Conference Tournament Outstanding Player Award, but Ranzino led the Wolfpack to its fifth consecutive title and another appearance in the NCAA Tournament.

However, Ranzino and teammates Vic Bubas and Paul Horvath were declared ineligible for the 1951 NCAA Tournament because they had played as freshmen in 1948. At the time, the NCAA allowed only three years of varsity competition, while the Southern Conference allowed four.

Ranzino earned first-team All-America honors as a senior, becoming the first player in school history to average more than 20 points a game.

During his career, the Wolfpack claimed 111 victories, four Southern Conference championships, two Dixie Classic titles and two NCAA Tournament appearances. Ranzino's No. 77 is among the jerseys honored in the rafters of the RBC Center.

"He would have scored a million points with the 3-pointer," long-time Everett Case assistant Carl "Butter" Anderson told *The News & Observer* in 1994. "I always said he had a rubber band in his wrist because he had such a soft shot. He was a great shooter, but was also good on the fake and

"OLD TIMES THERE ARE NOT FORGOTTEN"

Former *News & Observer* sports editor Dick Herbert came up with the idea and longtime NC State assistant Carl "Butter" Anderson came up with the name, but there is no doubt the Dixie Classic belonged to Everett Case. It was his vehicle to show off the South's biggest basketball arena and his nationally prominent program in the days before television.

Played 12 consecutive years between Christmas and New Year's Day, from 1949–60, the Classic featured a unique format that pitted a quartet of the best teams in the country against the Big Four of North Carolina: NC State, UNC, Duke and Wake Forest.

What made this event different — and so advantageous to Case and the Wolfpack — was that all the games were played at Reynolds Coliseum. Before the Southern Conference, the Atlantic Coast Conference or the NCAA hosted its tournaments there, the Classic turned the "House That Case Built" into one of the nation's premier basketball arenas.

Tickets to the Classic, which featured 12 games in three days, were the most popular stocking stuffers for every kid, no matter what age, in the Triangle.

"That was my Christmas present every year — two tickets to the Dixie Classic," said longtime NC State golf coach Richard Sykes. "And I was the most popular person in Wendell, N.C., because everybody wanted to go with me."

There were holiday tournaments before the Classic, and many others have followed, usually in exotic locales like New York, Hawaii or Alaska. But none have ever captured the fancy of the college basketball world quite like Case's showcase, with its unique format.

"The Dixie Classic turned out to be the Christmas tournament in the country," said former Wolfpack player and assistant coach Vic Bubas, who was later the head coach at Duke. "After it got started, Coach Case had teams calling him from all over the country asking when they could get in it. It became absolutely the thing to do between Christmas and New Year's."

Case, the ultimate promoter who wanted to see a basketball goal in every driveway as he traveled across North Carolina, invited great teams, guaranteeing what was considered big money at the time for basketball.

"As soon as he saw that a school signed a great player, he would immediately call the coach and invite that team to play in the Classic for that player's senior year," said Bucky Waters, a former Wolfpack player under Case.

Case made sure all visiting teams were smothered with Southern hospitality, from the time they arrived at the airport until they lost their last game in the tournament. The Old North State was gracious in every possible way, except on the court: all 12 Dixie Classics were won by a school from North Carolina. The Wolfpack won seven, North Carolina won three and Duke and Wake Forest won one apiece.

Dixie Classic Champions

Year	Championship Game Results	Most Outstanding Player
1949	**NC State** 50, Penn State 46	Dick Dickey, NC State
1950	**NC State** 85, Colgate 76	Sammy Ranzino, NC State
1951	**NC State** 51, Cornell 49	Lee Terrill, NC State
1952	**NC State** 75, Brigham Young 59	Ernie Beck, Penn
1953	Duke 98, Navy 83	Rudy D'Emilio, Duke
1954	**NC State** 85, Minnesota 54	Ronnie Shavlik, NC State
1955	**NC State** 82, North Carolina 60	Ronnie Shavlik, NC State
1956	North Carolina 63, Wake Forest 55	Lennie Rosenbluth, UNC
1957	North Carolina 39, **NC State** 30	Pete Brennan, UNC
1958	**NC State** 70, Michigan State 61	John Richter, NC State
1959	Wake Forest 53, North Carolina 50	Billy Packer, Wake Forest
1960	North Carolina 76, Duke 71	Doug Moe, UNC

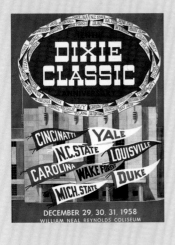

DIXIE CLASSIC

CINCINNATI · YALE
N.C. STATE · LOUISVILLE
CAROLINA · WAKE FOREST · DUKE
MICH. STATE

DECEMBER 29, 30, 31, 1958
WILLIAM NEAL REYNOLDS COLISEUM

Case also provided the same treatment to the best officials in the country, ensuring that the games were well-managed. And if an official's kinglike treatment helped Case get a favorable call somewhere down the line later, either in the Classic, a regular-season game or in the postseason, so be it.

Stars didn't just visit the Classic. Some of them were made there. All-America Ronnie Shavlik, the only player to ever win the Dixie Classic MVP twice, showed the nation that NC State was a national power in leading the Wolfpack to Classic titles in 1954 and '55. Wolfpack legends Dick Dickey, Sammy Ranzino, Lee Terrill and John Richter all won MVP awards during the course of the event.

Lou Pucillo remembers getting his first real chance to play for the Wolfpack during the 1956 Classic. With State struggling against Iowa, Case inserted Pucillo, the shortest player the coach ever recruited at NC State, into the lineup in the second half, and Pucillo helped spark a comeback against the unranked Hawkeyes.

Two years later, Pucillo and Richter led the Wolfpack to the championship in perhaps the greatest tournament held at Reynolds Coliseum. In three days, the Wolfpack beat Louisville in overtime, second-ranked Cincinnati with Oscar Robertson and seventh-ranked Michigan State with Jumping Johnny Green. That was the pinnacle of the Classic, with four of the eight teams ranked in the Top 10.

Some say the third-place game that year, between North Carolina and Cincinnati, may be the second greatest game ever played in the history of the state, eclipsed only by the 1974 ACC Tournament championship game at the Greensboro Coliseum.

"To this day, I could be in Asheville, or Wilmington or at a new Bible study class, and there is still nothing people ask me about more than the 1958 Dixie Classic," Pucillo said. "We were fortunate to win those games. I think it was the greatest tournament of all time."

drive. [He could] get a guy up in the air and go around him."

Ranzino was the No. 8 pick of the 1951 NBA draft, going to the Rochester Royals. But he averaged just 2.2 points in his 39 games in 1951–52, his only season of professional basketball. For three years, from 1958–61, Ranzino was the basketball coach at Frankfort, Ind., High School, where Everett Case won four Indiana state basketball championships. But the pupil did not match the record of the master, compiling a record of 34-38.

He returned to North Carolina in 1961, serving for six years on the Wake County Board of Education from 1972–77 and working as a lobbyist for the North Carolina Association of Educators.

"I ran for office so that I might be remembered for things other than basketball," said Ranzino, who died of brain cancer on March 13, 1994, in Long Beach, N.C., at the age of 65. "But it all started with basketball. If it weren't for athletics, I couldn't have ever paid my way out of Gary, Ind. The game brought me a lot of happiness."

"Sammy the Kid" did the same for Wolfpack fans.

Blue Chip Special

Big man Ronnie Shavlik ushers in the era of big-time recruiting for theWolfpack

When NC State assistant coach Vic Bubas traveled all the way to the Rocky Mountains to see a young basketball player who was making headlines for his play against older competition, it marked the beginning of transcontinental recruiting for NC State and the ACC.

The player, Ronnie Shavlik of Denver's East High School, had helped his team win back-to-back state championships as a sophomore and junior. But what really caught the eye of Bubas was when Shavlik was named the Most Promising Player in the 1952 national AAU tournament, which was held in his hometown.

Others noticed as well. Shavlik was being wooed by Kentucky's Adolph Rupp, UCLA's John Wooden and Oklahoma A&M's Hank Iba, just to name a few. In the end, he decided on the Wolfpack because he had family in Raleigh.

Shavlik sat out his freshman season, 1952–53, the only time NC State did not win the Southern Conference championship after Case's arrival in 1946. The next year, the Wolfpack broke off with seven other schools to form the Atlantic Coast Conference, and Shavlik ended up being the league's first great player.

Playing with the M-Twins, John Maglio and Vic Molodet, the 6-8 Shavlik raced up and down the court at speeds previously unseen in a big man. He scored at will against smaller opponents with his deadly hook shot, and ruled the boards like no one in Raleigh before or since.

In his three-year career, he grabbed 1,598 rebounds, more than a third more than second-place Tommy Burleson's 1,046. He owns 13 of the top 14 rebounding games in school history and still owns the single-season rebounding record for a sophomore, a junior and a senior.

"For his size, that boy moved up and down the court pretty well," said Molodet, who shared All-America honors with Shavlik as a senior. "He was always around the hole. He was always where the ball was."

He led the Wolfpack to championships in the first three ACC tournaments, all played in Reynolds Coliseum. Against Villanova as a senior, he had 49 points and 35 rebounds. He was the ACC Tournament's MVP in 1955 and the ACC Player of the Year in 1956, and first-team All-ACC both years. He was the only player in the history of the Dixie Classic to be named MVP twice.

But, in the end, his career ended with the ultimate disappointment: a four-overtime loss to Canisius in the NCAA Tournament. Shavlik had suffered a broken wrist in the regular-season finale against Wake Forest, and was hampered throughout the ACC Tournament.

Playing with a restrictive leather wrist guard, Shavlik still managed to dominate the game, scoring 25 points and grabbing 17 rebounds. But Molodet was whistled for three early fouls and the Wolfpack's high-powered offense never got out of the gate.

He was the fourth overall pick of the 1956 NBA draft, going to the New York Knicks. But he never had the same passion for professional basketball as he did for the college game.

He played only two years in the NBA, and spent three more seasons moonlighting with the Baltimore Bullets in the old Eastern Basketball League. Eventually, he stopped playing altogether and concentrated on his janitorial services business, which grew to three separate companies, worth as much as $250 million and covering 40 states.

"I didn't have much enthusiasm for pro ball," Shavlik said. "The adjustment was too big."

Shavlik began his lifelong outreach to those less fortunate than he while in school, as a Big Brother to an 8-year-old boy. He was also encouraged by Case to spend time at the Governor Morehead School for the Blind, which is across the street from the NC State campus. Eventually, Shavlik became one of the state's largest employers of the handicapped. In 1965, he was given the Meritorious Service Award by President Lyndon Johnson.

Shavlik accepted many honors and awards

throughout his life of civic service, and in 1979 he was inducted into the North Carolina Sports Hall of Fame. One of the awards he was most proud of was the 1981 NCAA Silver Anniversary Award, which is presented annually to five former athletes who achieved success in other fields after their college basket-ball careers were over. Shavlik and former Virginia standout Wally Walker are the only two ACC bas-ketball players to ever win the award.

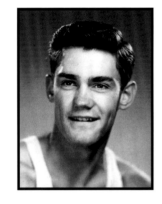

In 1983, about the time the Wolfpack began its miracu-lous run for the school's second NCAA championship, Shavlik was diagnosed with pancreatic cancer. He struggled to follow the Wolfpack from Raleigh to Atlanta for the ACC Tournament and later made the draining trip to Albuquerque, N.M., for the Final Four.

On the morning of the title game, sev-eral Wolfpack players and head coach Jim Valvano stopped by his room to visit before they headed over to the Pit for the game. Shavlik, who at the time was the president of the Wolfpack Club, knew that it would probably be the last NC State game he ever saw.

No one was happier than Shavlik when the Wolfpack pulled out its miracle win over heavily favored Houston, on Lorenzo Charles's last-second dunk.

"He was thrilled," said his wife, Beverly Shavlik. "It could not have ended any better than that."

Shavlik died on June 27, 1983, content to see the program he helped build with his All-America abilities win two national championships.

SEAT OF POWER

On Jan. 9, 1961, NC State basketball coach Everett Case arrived for his annual appearance at the Winston-Salem Tip-Off Club, with a crumpled chair in his arms and a solemn look in his eyes.

He held up the pieces of the chair, which had previously been seen on the sidelines of Reynolds Coliseum during the Wake Forest–NC State game a few weeks earlier, and began reading a letter from his boss, athletics direc-tor Roy Clogston, accusing Wake Forest coach Horace "Bones" McKinney of destruction of state property.

"During our Dixie Classic game, Mr. Mc-Kinney willfully and maliciously demolished this chair, which I produce as evidence," Case said, before breaking into his sly grin. "How-ever, since Bones is a former State player, the University is willing to settle for the damages as suggested by our athletics director … in this letter to Wake Forest President Dr. Harold Tribble."

With that, Case handed McKinney the pieces of the chair and an invoice for $14.33.

The room howled, knowing that Case and McKinney, two of the ACC's premier show-men, were going at it again, as they had many times when their teams faced one another.

McKinney, prepared to pounce on the pro-motional opportunity, claimed that his anger was caused by the game officials, all of whom were close friends of Case. So he refused to pay the bill. Instead ol' Bones suggested that the Wake Forest maintenance depart-ment piece the chair back together and from that game forward, the winner of the annual contests would get to keep the chair until the other team managed to win it back.

McKinney had the top half of the chair painted in Wake Forest's Old Gold and Black

and the bottom half painted in State's traditional Red and White.

The tradition of the Old Wicker Chair didn't last very long. Wake Forest, led by All-America center Len Chappell and guard Billy Packer, dominated the series, as NC State and North Carolina both de-emphasized basketball following the 1961 point-shaving scandal.

Wake won the first game for the chair, 76-66, on Jan. 14, 1961, and went on to win the first of its back-to-back ACC championships. The next season, the Deacons made their only trip to the NCAA Final Four.

McKinney's team won seven of the nine times the teams played for the chair.

On Dec. 5, 1964, Case and the Wolfpack traveled to Winston-Salem to face the Deacons in an early-season ACC contest. When McKinney shook Case's hand prior to the game, he thought something might be wrong.

"I asked him if he was feeling all right," McKinney told Frank Weedon in 1996. "Everett replied, 'I just feel so poorly. I don't think I can coach any longer.'"

The Deacons won the game 86-80, and the next day Case, citing health concerns, retired from coaching after 18 years at NC State. He turned the team over to his coach-in-waiting, Press Maravich. The Wolfpack beat the Deacons in Raleigh later that season, then honored Case by upsetting nationally-ranked Duke for the 1965 ACC Championship.

McKinney retired from coaching after the 1965 season as well, citing burnout. And the tradition of playing for a piece of broken furniture faded from memory.

The repaired chair is still around. It rests in a sealed trophy case at Wake Forest, adjacent to the two ACC Championship trophies McKinney's teams won not long after the coach destroyed it.

The Teacher

Few people have loved NC State more, and have done more to make the Wolfpack basketball program successful, than Eddie Biedenbach.

The quick-handed guard from Pittsburgh was the only player in the program's history to play for Everett Case, Press Maravich and Norm Sloan, twice earning first-team All-ACC honors. He was a little undisciplined when he arrived — Case called him "Wildhorse" — but he became the Wolfpack's best player during the 1960s.

He later became an integral part of Sloan's coaching staff and was the assistant coach primarily responsible for recruiting All-Americas Tommy Burleson, David Thompson and Kenny Carr.

He played a role in four ACC championships and the 1974 NCAA title. He was a sophomore on the 1965 championship team and a senior on the team that advanced to the 1968 ACC championship game. In Biedenbach's first year as an assistant to Sloan, the Wolfpack won the 1970 tournament. Three years later, the Wolfpack had its greatest sustained success, going 57-1 from 1972–74.

Biedenbach left NC State to become the head coach at Davidson, and had various coaching jobs throughout a successful career, including more than a decade and a half at UNC-Asheville.

"He loves the game of basketball," says Vann

The Recruiter

Bobby Speight grew up in New Jersey and Ohio, but he spent his summers at his grandparents' home on Raleigh's Hillsborough Street. For years during the late 1940s, he walked across NC State's campus to Frank Thompson Gym for classic pickup games with the current and former players who built Everett Case's program into one of the most feared in the nation.

There was no doubt where the 6-8 forward would play in college.

"Coach Case used to tell me, 'I don't know whether I recruited you or you recruited me,'" Speight said. "I think I locked up a scholarship by the time I was a junior in high school."

During his career, Speight helped the Wolfpack complete its six-year hold on the Southern Conference championship, leading the team to 1951 and '52 tournament titles as a sophomore and junior.

As a senior, Speight became just the third

Williford, who was a teammate of Biedenbach's for one season. "He was the best defensive player I can ever remember. He was never out of shape."

Biedenbach credits his career to the men who helped him develop as a player, from freshman coach Lou Pucillo to assistant Charlie Bryant to the three head coaches he played for.

"Those guys taught me if you play hard, if you listen and try to play together, you can be a good player," Biedenbach said. "They taught me to understand the game better. It wasn't anything astounding; they just worked hard at teaching me the mental and physical fundamentals of the game."

And Biedenbach taught those same lessons to generations of young players.

player in school history to score more than 500 points in a single season, averaging 16.9 points per game and earning All-America honors from several different outlets.

In three seasons, the two-time first-team All–Southern Conference selection scored 1,430 points and grabbed 1,057 rebounds, which still ranks as the fourth most in school history. His No. 80 is one of more than two dozen honored jerseys that hang in the rafters of the RBC Center.

Following two years of professional basketball and two years in the United States Army, Speight settled in Richmond, Va., where he founded the trucking company E&S Contract Carrier. He remained the company's president — and an ardent supporter of his alma mater — for 35 years.

In 1974, Speight's daughter, Elizabeth, became

NC State's first scholarship female athlete, signing with Kay Yow's fledgling program.

In 2006, Speight's three children donated the funds to name the lobby of the $2 million Dail Basketball Center in honor of their father. The sparkling facility — home to the Wolfpack's basketball offices, locker rooms and practice court — is something Speight knew his coach, the legendary Everett Case, would have thoroughly enjoyed.

"He'd probably spin over in his grave a couple of times if he saw this thing," Speight said. "But he always liked progress and new things, so I am sure he would have loved something like this that will be a big benefit to the basketball program."

Speight passed away at the age of 76 on March 1, 2007, after a long battle with cancer.

INNOVATIONS:
CONTINUING
CASE'S DREAM

CROSS

In his first 14 years as NC State's head coach, Everett Case won 10 conference championships and forced each school in the ACC to upgrade its program and facilities. But, by the beginning of the 1960s, the rest of the league had not only caught up to The Old Gray Fox — it had surpassed him.

Case knew he would be difficult to replace. So he made the decision for NC State athletics director Roy Clogston, hiring Clemson head coach Press Maravich to be his top assistant following the 1961–62 season. Case was impressed with the way Maravich guided the Tigers to the 1962 ACC Tournament championship game, something that didn't happen again until 2008 under Oliver Purnell.

But it was an extremely difficult time for NC State basketball. Case was heartbroken over the gambling scandals of 1961; the sport had been de-emphasized by the consolidated university system and he just wasn't feeling well, as the early stages of the bone cancer that would eventually take his life began to sap his energy. Maravich, who everyone knew was the coach in waiting, took over most of the day-to-day operations of the team and all of the tactical maneuvers, getting help from former All-America guard Lou Pucillo. Case had hoped to build one last championship team prior to his state-mandated retirement in 1965, but two games into what was to be his final season, he turned the reins over to his hand-picked successor.

The sad fact of the matter was that Case could no longer compete with his neighbors. Old nemesis Horace "Bones" McKinney won a pair of ACC

BIG FOUR COACHES: Dean Smith, Vic Bubas, Everett Case and Bones McKinney

ROADS

Tournaments and took Wake Forest to its only Final Four in school history. Case protégé Vic Bubas made Duke a fixture at the top of the ACC standings. Frank McGuire protégé Dean Smith was in the beginnings of his Hall of Fame career.

From 1962–69, the Demon Deacons, Blue Devils and Tar Heels went to the Final Four seven times, while the Wolfpack made the NCAA Tournament only once, after Maravich led his initial team to the emotional 1965 ACC title. But, as wonderful as it was for Maravich and his team to watch Case cut down the nets one last time at Reynolds Coliseum following the '65 tournament, the Wolfpack lost its first game in the NCAA East Regional semifinals to Princeton.

Maravich returned the Wolfpack to the ACC title game in 1966, but his days as Case's succes-

sor were numbered. On the same day Case died, Maravich signed a five-year contract to become the head coach at Louisiana State, primarily because the Southeastern Conference school could admit his All-America son, Pete, while NC State could not. The ACC had a strict policy requiring an 800 score on the SAT and the younger Maravich, despite all of his basketball talents, did not make the score, even after a year of prep school at Southwood College in Salemburg, N.C.

In May 1966, NC State basketball was at a major crossroads, mourning the loss of the coach who made the school a national power and trying to cope with the hasty departure of his replacement. It was time, once again, for something new. Even if it was an old, familiar face.

Press Maravich and his starting five

STORMIN'

Before coaching and the plaid jackets, Norm Sloan played for the Pack

Norm Sloan was an original "Hoosier Hotshot," a native of Indianapolis who followed Everett Case to North Carolina after a stint in the Navy during World War II. Even though he was an NC State graduate, he was hardly like the handful of alumni who had previously coached at the school, most of whom graduated, spent a few years at the school coaching the team they played for, and then moved on to other professions.

Sloan's profession was coaching. He had been successful at Presbyterian College, the Citadel and Florida, winning Coach of the Year honors at all three places. He was prepared to take over a major program, and jumped at the opportunity to take over the job once held by the coach he respected and loved.

Years earlier, during Sloan's junior year at NC State, the two had clashed. Sloan thought he should be playing instead of Bubas, who was a year younger and similarly talented. "But Norm," Case said, "we're winning with him." Sloan huffily replied, "Yeah, but if I were playing, we would be winning by more." He left basketball to join the football program for spring practice and did not return to the hardwoods.

Sloan didn't exactly mellow during his years away from Raleigh, but he clearly learned a few things about how to build a successful program. After a difficult first season, he took the Wolfpack to the ACC title game by beating Bubas-coached Duke in one of the most famous games in ACC history, the 12-10 slowdown game of 1968.

He lost badly to North Carolina in the title

game, but it set the stage for one of the most dominant periods for any school in the ACC. Sloan won three league titles in five years, recorded only the second undefeated season in league history and won the ACC's second national championship. In the best two-year run in school history, the Wolfpack was 57-1 from 1972–74.

Along the way, Sloan blew his gasket a few times. While in his first stint at Florida, his sideline antics practically forced sportswriters and opposing fans to refer to him as "Stormin' Norman," a nickname he despised. "You only call me that because it rhymes," he said.

He became one of the ACC's most colorful — if not tastefully dressed — characters, thanks to his frequent eruptions, his wild plaid jackets and, most of all, his team's success with Tommy Burleson, David Thompson, Monte Towe and others.

"Norm Sloan was a real friend who knew how to coach and recruit kids," said veteran radio announcer Wally Ausley before he retired in 1990. "And you hear all the talk about Stormin' Norman, but I would have to say that his bark was worse than his bite. He always instilled a lot of loyalty in his players and friends."

In the beginning, he won with scrappy, overachieving players. That allowed him to recruit coveted stars like Burleson and Thompson, both of whom were included in the Top 50 players of the first half-century of the ACC.

"I always thought Norm was an underrated coach," said Lefty Driesell, the former Maryland coach who was often Sloan's adversary on the

NORMAN

court. "He never had McDonald's All-Americas, but he knew how to coach and get the most out of his players. They always competed hard."

Perhaps Sloan's biggest innovation during his 13 years as head coach of the Wolfpack was putting a new face on the program. The three other members of the Big Four had already integrated by the time Sloan arrived, and the Wolfpack faced the proposition of falling even further behind the three more successful programs. So, just prior to the 1967–68 season, Sloan found Al Heartley of Clayton, N.C., through a campuswide tryout. Heartley made the freshman team to become the first black player in the history of the program. The next year, Heartley advanced to the varsity team. In 1970, he was on the team that surprised South Carolina in the ACC Tournament title game. As a senior, he was elected captain by his teammates, as well as winner of the Alumni Athletic Trophy, awarded annually to the school's best athlete by fellow students.

A year after Heartley arrived, Sloan offered his first scholarship to a black player, Ed Leftwich. Their arrival on campus, and their relatively smooth transition into the program, paved the way for future All-Americas like Thompson, Kenny

Carr and Charles "Hawkeye" Whitney. Before he left, Sloan recruited the core of Jim Valvano's 1983 NCAA championship team — Sidney Lowe, Dereck Whittenburg and Thurl Bailey — which few people remember was the first team with five black starters to win the ACC Tournament.

NC State, even though it trailed its neighbors in desegregating basketball and football, was a pioneer in integrating college athletics in the South. In 1956, four African American students, all from North Carolina, enrolled at NC State, making front-page headlines. What was unique was that three of the new students — Irwin Holmes, Walter Holmes (no relation) and Manual Crockett — participated in intercollegiate athletics while at State. On Feb. 9, 1957, Irwin Holmes and Crockett became the first black athletes to represent NC State, with both running the 60-yard dash in a track meet against North Carolina. Holmes later switched to tennis, and in 1960 he had the distinction of being the first African American graduate of the university and the first black athlete at an ACC school to be elected captain of his team.

"The atmosphere at NC State was nothing like what I had read about at other Southern universities," Holmes said years later.

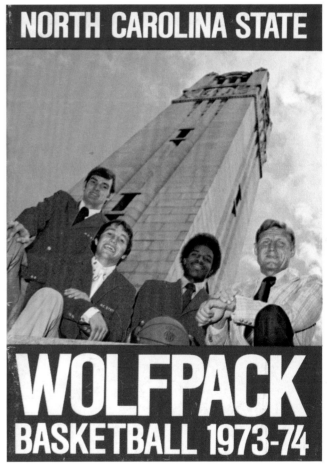

Case had often toyed with the possibility of recruiting black players, especially after Reynolds Coliseum opened in 1949. Case knew if he was going to invite the best teams in the country to his palatial home for the Dixie Classic, he would need approval for black players to compete in the coliseum, a practice that was generally not accepted in the pre–Civil Rights South. In 1949, athletics director Roy Clogston convinced the Faculty Athletics Council to grant permission for teams with black players to participate at Reynolds Coliseum, but it was at least three years before it happened. Penn State, a participant in the first Classic in 1949, had just integrated its roster with Hardy Williams, but Nittany Lions coach Elmer Gross chose not to bring the sophomore on the trip to the South. In 1951, African American player Chuck Cooper of the Boston Celtics played against the Rochester Royals in an NBA exhibition game. That same night, the Harlem Globetrotters played at Reynolds. In 1952, during the NCAA East Regional at Reynolds, St. John's coach Frank McGuire brought his great African American guard Solly Walker to face the Wolfpack in a first-round game, topping Case's team 60-49.

In 1958, Case sent representatives from the school, including three-sport athlete Bob Kennel, to New Bern, N.C., to talk to Walt Bellamy. But that was during the school's four-year probation and Bellamy was eventually steered to Indiana. Later that year, when Cincinnati brought All-America Oscar Robertson and Michigan State brought Johnny Green to Raleigh for the Dixie Classic, arrangements were made for their teams to stay at the old Colonial Pines, a former hotel near campus that was eventually converted into the Delta Sigma Phi fraternity house.

Sloan was one of three former Case players who integrated programs at their schools, along with Bubas at Duke and Bucky Waters at West Virginia. In 1975, the same year athletics director Willis Casey hired Kay Yow as the first full-time women's coach in the state of North Carolina, Sloan hired Wilbert Johnson to become the school's first black assistant coach.

The advent of integration was a big help for Sloan in 1972, when he landed Thompson, the remarkably talented forward from Shelby, N.C., who became a three-time selection as ACC Player of the Year and two-time pick as National Player of the Year. The coach strongly believed that Thompson might not have chosen to play for the Wolfpack had Heartley not given the program a strong recommendation. And the coach was certain that Thompson would not have had the temperament to be the first African American at any school.

While Sloan was working hard to rebuild the program to the same level of dominance as his mentor's, Casey was busy trying to effect change in the game of basketball on the national level. Casey, an extremely successful swimming coach who had spent nearly 20 years as Clogston's only assistant athletics director, was named the ailing Clogston's replacement in April 1969. Sloan claimed in his autobiography *Confessions of a Coach* that he and Casey were both up for the job. Sloan was offered and accepted the position, but reconsidered after he was told that he would have to give up his job as basketball coach.

Casey had run 19 consecutive conference basketball tournaments at Reynolds Coliseum and all 12 Dixie Classics, and was named the business manager of the athletic department in 1967, so he was prepared to take the job. But he and Sloan had a cool relationship from that day forward.

Casey had a reputation for being a tight-fisted miser during his 17-year tenure as athletics director, keeping costs down with a skeletal staff, low salaries and minimal upkeep on facilities. But he really had no choice. He inherited a department that had an operating budget of just $700,000 and was nearly $100,000 in debt. Even more remarkable, from 1966–79, his department received no funds from football ticket sales,

revenue stream that these days accounts for about two-thirds of the annual budget. When Carter Stadium was built in 1966, the school took out a 10-year bond to pay for it. As part of the agreement on the bond, all football ticket revenue was required to go towards repayment of the debt. But, thanks to the school's success on the field and on the basketball court, the bond debt was retired at the beginning of the 1979 football season.

"To me, that's as impressive an achievement as anything an athletic director can have," said Frank Weedon, who was a senior assistant athletics director under Casey at the time.

Casey ran a department without frills. No fancy promotions. No full-color media brochures. No plush weight rooms or locker rooms.

"I think the old axiom that you have to go first-class is a bunch of malarkey," he once told a newspaper reporter. "When we weren't getting the money (from football), we stayed in the black and we have been competitive with any team in the conference."

Not just competitive. In 1973–74, the Wolfpack became the first ACC school to win league titles in football, basketball and baseball in the same academic year. The 1970s, in fact, were the golden age of Wolfpack athletics, mainly because of Casey's eye for identifying up-and-coming coaches and letting them build successful programs — as long as they made their budget.

Soon after Sloan landed Burleson and his greatest single recruiting class of Thompson, Towe and Tim Stoddard, Casey hired a skinny, bespectacled football coach from William & Mary named Lou Holtz, who led his squad to four consecutive bowl games. He hired two more great ones before he retired in 1986, Bo Rein and Dick Sheridan.

Even before Title IX of the Educational Amendments of 1972 was signed into law, Casey began building a women's athletics program. He hired a part-time women's basketball coach, Peanut Doak, paying him $700 for the initial season; then he began a yearlong search for a permanent coach, whom he found at Elon College. Her name was Kay Yow and Casey hired her to be the basketball coach, softball coach and volleyball coach, as well as the women's athletics administrator. She gave up most of those titles shortly after she arrived in 1975, but she coached basketball, the game she loved since her father brought her to see Dixie

Classic games when she was a little girl, until almost the day she died, on Jan. 24, 2009. Like Case, Yow was inducted into the Naismith Memorial Basketball Hall of Fame.

Casey became one of the ACC's most influential administrators. Almost single-handedly, he negotiated the league's first basketball television contract with Castleman D. Chesley. From 1973 until 1981, when Chesley was outbid for the league's broadcast rights, television revenues went from $1 million to more than $30 million. He worked with Chesley to put together a network to broadcast a Super Bowl Sunday game between NC State and Maryland in 1973, the first nationally televised regular-season college basketball game in more than six years. Ratings soared as curious basketball fans around the country wanted to see Thompson, the sensational sophomore forward. He did his part, rebounding a missed Burleson shot in the final seconds and tipping it in to give the Wolfpack its most dramatic win in the 27-0 season.

Casey could be crafty in his business dealings. In a made-for-television game against UCLA in December 1973, in St. Louis, Casey had the choice of taking the money earned from the television contract or the money made from the sale of tickets. The amounts were nearly equal, so Casey offered to take the gate and let UCLA have the slightly larger television guarantee. The difference was, under ACC agreements at the time, NC State kept all money received from ticket sales. It would have been required to share any television revenues with the other six members of the ACC.

Casey was also involved with several important NCAA committees, during a time when the organization was making major changes to college athletics. In 1972, the year after Thompson wowed sellout crowds while playing for the Wolfpack freshman team, the NCAA ended freshman ineligibility, which had been the standard since the end of the Korean War.

The biggest decision facing college basketball was the expansion of the 25-team NCAA Tournament, which was growing in popularity even though only one team per conference was allowed in the field.

The power-

ful NCAA Basketball Committee, which was chaired by UCLA athletics director J.D. Morgan, considered the possibility of adding more total teams and multiple teams per league. The committee agreed to increase the number of teams in the field to 32, but Morgan was steadfastly against allowing more than one team per league.

The Bruins ruled the world of college basketball. Under one-time Case high school coaching foe John Wooden, the Bruins won nine NCAA titles in 10 years from 1964–73. While that is a remarkable achievement that will likely never be matched, it was hardly good for the rest of college basketball to have such a dynasty. When Morgan's term expired in 1974, he was replaced by Casey, who became the ACC's first representative on the powerful committee. Casey, and the rest of the ACC, supported a larger tournament with more than one team per conference. With the help of Tom Scott, who was the athletics director at Davidson and the one-time coach at North Carolina when Case arrived at NC State, Casey pushed through the rule change. A couple of years later, with the help of Bubas, who was then the commissioner of the Sun Belt Conference, Casey helped remove all limits to the number of teams per conference, creating the NCAA Tournament as we know it today.

So, when the Wolfpack ended the Bruins' streak of seven consecutive NCAA titles in the 1974 national semifinals, it was a victory for Sloan, his team, Casey and the rest of college basketball.

The year after Thompson left NC State, the Basketball Committee reinstated the dunk, which had been outlawed in 1967, just before

Willis Casey

Lew Alcindor enrolled at UCLA. It didn't help Thompson. By then, Thompson was playing for the American Basketball Association's Denver Nuggets, wowing fans in the Mile High City with his two-mile leaping ability. When the ABA held its All-Star game in Denver, Thompson won professional basketball's first dunk contest.

In the end, Casey's tight-fisted frugality and his gruff personality cost NC State two legendary coaches. First, in 1975, Holtz bolted for the NFL's New York Jets after he and Casey went head-to-head on several occasions. And in 1980, in another fit of stubbornness, Sloan left his alma mater and returned to Florida, primarily because he and his assistants were the lowest-paid staff in the ACC. The Gators were not only offering Sloan more money, but also significant raises for assistants Monte Towe, Marty Fletcher and Gary Stokan.

Sloan never had the same success after Thompson, Towe, Stoddard and Mo Rivers left following the 1974–75 season. In 1978, he took the Wolfpack to the NIT Championship game, but lost to Texas, 101-93. The only time the Wolfpack returned to the NCAA Tournament was in 1980, after he accepted the job to return to Florida.

"Personally, I wish he could have stayed and created a legacy like Dean Smith did at North Carolina and Mike Krzyzewski has done at Duke," Burleson said, not long after Sloan died of pulmonary fibrosis on Dec. 9, 2003. "But that was something between Coach Sloan and Willis Casey. I don't know why they didn't see eye-to-eye more."

The 1970s were over and the golden age of NC State had waned. What the program needed was an injection of excitement and energy.

What it got was an overdose, by the name of Jim Valvano.

STALL
TACTICS

Two stubborn, uncompromising men squared off in a war of wills on that fateful evening, neither willing to cede control of the game to the other.

It was Jan. 15, 1927. Everett Case's Frankfort (Ind.) High was hosting Clifford Wells's team from Logansport High. Both coaches were veterans of Indiana high school basketball and future inductees into the Naismith Memorial Hall of Fame. Wells had the better team. It was, in fact, dominant, beating its opponents by more than 20 points a game. He was also the more established coach, having spent a dozen years at various schools in the state.

He was also the guy, some eight years earlier, who gave 19-year-old Case some friendly advice on how to enter the coaching profession, despite his young age. Wells had won the prestigious Indiana state high school championship as a coach at the age of 22.

But there was no friendly chatter between the two coaches that night. Logansport was one of the best teams in the state, coming into the game with an 11-0 record. Case vowed that he would do whatever necessary to prevent an embarrassing loss when Wells and his squad came to Frankfort to play that evening.

And that's what he did. When Frankfort controlled the opening tip, Case had his team dribble away from its goal and set up his infuriating full-court, four-corner offense. Wells was dumbfounded. Case had used the full-court stall before, to kill the clock at the end of the game. But the only time he had tried it this early in the game, in the previous season against Bedford High, a riot ensued and Frankfort ended up losing the game.

Wells told his zone defense to sit back on the opposite end of the court and wait for Frankfort to attack. For the first 10 minutes of the half, the teams traded a few points until Logansport grabbed a 7-6 lead. When Frankfort won the next tip-off, Case sent his team back to its own end of the court. Logansport, with the lead, did not press and for the next 10 minutes the Frankfort guards dribbled the ball undefended. At the time, there were no rules that forced the offense to advance the ball and the defense was under no obligation to press.

It was the longest stall anyone had ever seen.

When the second half started, Logansport won the tip and retreated under the Frankfort basket, killing off four minutes before turning the ball over on a traveling violation. Frankfort took possession and held the ball for 11 full minutes, as the stopwatch that kept the official time slowly wound down. In more than 25 minutes of game time, neither team had so much as taken a shot.

With five minutes to go, Case crossed his legs, signaling his team to advance the ball. After a 15-foot basket, Frankfort had an 8-7 lead. On its last offensive possession, Logansport had five missed shots to take the lead. Frankfort finally grabbed a rebound and scored on an uncontested jumper.

The Frankfort Fighting Five won the tap and held onto the ball for a 10-7 victory over the superior opponent.

"The stall game caused quite a stir locally, regionally and perhaps nationally as time went on," wrote Roger Robison in *Everett Case and the Frankfort Hotdogs* (Hot Dog Press, 1998). "Holding the ball this long was indeed unique and the tactic spread nationally. The high scores of 1926 would gradually plummet. In the meantime,

Logansport was incensed and canceled the return game."

Less than five years later, after Case and others began to overuse the highly unpopular stall tactics, the National Association of Basketball Coaches considered several rules to outlaw the practice, including the game's first shot clock, the forfeiting of any game in which the defense did not press a stalling offense, and limiting the offense to just one dribble in the backcourt.

Instead, the Joint Basketball Rules Committee decided to draw a line at midcourt and require the offense to advance the ball over the line within 10 seconds or lose possession. It's a rule that remains in men's basketball today.

But it did not eliminate stalling tactics. Some 40 years later, two more stubborn, uncompromising men — both Case protégés — squared off in a similar game, in the semifinals of the 1968 ACC Tournament in Charlotte, N.C.

Norm Sloan, an original Case recruit from Indianapolis, was in his third year of coaching the Wolfpack. Vic Bubas, who came to Raleigh from Gary, Ind., in Case's second year, was the head coach at Duke. The Blue Devils were a much better team, ranked No. 6 in the nation. The Wolfpack finished tied for third in the regular-season standings, but were hardly the same caliber as either Bubas's Blue Devils or second-ranked North Carolina, which had already advanced to the tournament championship game.

There was a history between Sloan and Bubas, as well. The two vied for the same position, and Bubas eventually won out. Midway through his junior year, Sloan quit basketball to go out for the NC State football team.

Sloan was still trying to make a name for himself as a head coach, while Bubas, who had spent some 10 seasons as Case's top assistant, had taken the Blue Devils to three Final Fours during the 1960s and was anxious to get to another.

But what happened next was more slowdown than showdown. NC State got the opening tip, and Sloan told forwards Vann Williford and Bill Kretzer to hold the ball near Case's midcourt line, hoping to draw Duke forward Bill Lewis from under the basket. The 6-8 Lewis had four inches on both Kretzer and Williford, and had pummeled the Wolfpack earlier in the season.

So, after winning the opening tap, the Wolfpack held the ball. Initially, NC State fans cheered while the rest of the Coliseum booed. Eventually, however, as Kretzer stood near midcourt dribbling the ball, passing it to a teammate only when his arm got tired, the whole place fell into a confused, and rather bored, silence. One of the officials sat on the scorer's table. Several players stood in the lane talking to each other about anything but the game. Biedenbach and Williford walked over to the NC State bench to discuss strategy with Sloan.

Sloan was trying to outwait Bubas, and Bubas refused to press. At halftime, the Blue Devils led 4-2. At one point, Kretzer dribbled the ball continuously for 14 minutes as time slowly clicked off the clock. Both radio and television broadcasts went to commercial breaks while the clock was running, and neither missed any action. UNC announcer Bill Currie, calling the game for the Tar Heel Network, told his listeners: "This game is about as exciting as watching artificial insemination."

Early in the second half, the Blue Devils pulled ahead 8-6. When the Wolfpack regained possession, Sloan ordered his troops to wait again, from the 16:15 mark to just under three minutes. For exactly 13:45 minutes, Kretzer dribbled the game away.

"I think I dribbled more that night than the entire time I played college basketball," Kretzer said in a 1973 interview. "I went back and forth across the court. I had to do something. I was afraid if I just stood there dribbling the ball I would lapse into a coma or something and bounce the ball off my foot."

With 2:29 remaining on the clock, NC State's Eddie Biedenbach hit an 18-foot jumper to tie the game at 8. Duke took a brief lead with a single free throw, but NC State junior Dick Braucher grabbed an offensive rebound and scored on a put-back basket with about 40 seconds to play to give his team a 10-9 advantage.

With 16 seconds remaining, Williford gave the Pack a two-point advantage. Duke had the chance to tie the game at the free-throw line, but missed the second of two shots. With three seconds left on the clock, Braucher hit the final free throw to seal the upset victory, with the now-infamous final score: 12-10.

Sloan, like Case four decades before, was roundly criticized for his strategy. But he was unapologetic for giving his team the chance to make the ACC finals.

For the next 15 years, coaches continued to use the stall offense, most famously in the 1982 ACC championship game between North Carolina and Virginia. The next season, the ACC adopted experimental rules, including the 3-point basket and a shot clock. By 1986, college basketball adopted uniform rules that helped eliminate the stall offense, once and for all.

LUCKY BREAK

Few players can thank a conference rule — and someone else's bad test scores — for their all-star collegiate career. But forward Vann Williford can.

NC State fans in the mid-1960s were certain that the Wolfpack would win the services of Pete Maravich, the much talked about All-America prep player at Raleigh's Broughton High School. He happened to be the son of Press Maravich, the man who succeeded Everett Case as the Wolfpack's head coach.

From the day he was born, the younger Maravich had a basketball in his hands, a chip on his shoulders and a slight sag to his gym socks. But what he didn't have when he graduated from Broughton were the test scores he needed to attend an Atlantic Coast Conference school.

"If the ACC's rule that required you to have 800 on the SAT hadn't been in effect, then Coach Maravich would have still been the coach when I graduated, Pete would have been at NC State and I would have gone to Pfeiffer," Williford said.

Instead, the matched set of Maraviches headed to Louisiana State and Norman Sloan took over the program and signed the lanky 6-6 Williford from Fayetteville, N.C.

While it might be enticing for some to think what would have happened if Pistol Pete had played for the Wolfpack and his dad had stayed in Raleigh, Sloan and Williford were outstanding substitutes.

As a player, Williford helped usher in the program's best decade, the 1970s, by leading the Wolfpack to two ACC Tournament finals and one championship. The two-time All-ACC selection capped off his brilliant college career by winning the Everett Case Award as the MVP of the 1970 ACC Tournament, as the Wolfpack upset heavily favored South Carolina in the title game.

For Williford, winning championships was nothing new. He was on a Fayetteville High School team that won back-to-back state titles in 1965–66, the first with future North Carolina All-America Rusty Clark, and the second when he was the senior captain of the team.

But the undersized forward did not draw the attention of many NCAA Division I college recruiters. By the time he graduated, he had signed a nonbinding letter of intent to play for Pfeiffer College coach Felix Essix. But the young player, a State fan since the Everett Case days, flat-out told Essix: "If I get a better offer, I am going elsewhere."

That happened when Sloan, an NC State graduate and former Case player, took over for the elder Maravich in the spring of 1966, just weeks after Case died of cancer. Sloan was looking to fill out a roster that included Eddie Biedenbach and a few other quality ACC players, and he thought Williford might be able to help.

Williford remembers how he drove straight to Pinehurst, where Sloan was attending a golf outing at Firefox Golf Club, to sign an ACC letter of intent before Sloan had a chance to change his mind.

That wouldn't have been good for the Wolfpack, who benefited from Williford's development into one of the league's toughest competitors.

Williford picked that up honestly. He grew up following his older brother Richard to industrial league games all over Fayetteville and playing pickup game on the courts around Fort Bragg.

While the Wolfpack's varsity took its lumps in 1966–67, Williford struggled on the freshman team. He was determined to improve his play and his team when he advanced to the varsity as a sophomore, and six games into the season, Williford was in the starting lineup, joining Biedenbach, Bill Kretzer and Dick Braucher on a team that finished tied for third in the ACC standings and advanced into the ACC Tournament championship game — thanks to the most famous slowdown game in league history.

The Wolfpack beat Duke 12-10 in the Char-

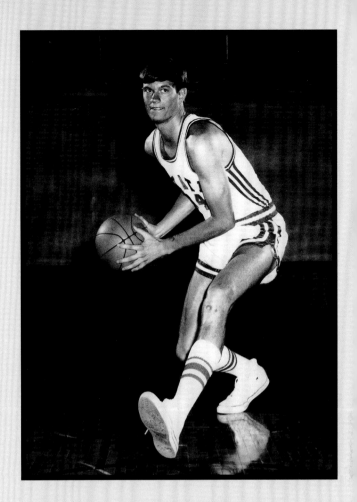

lotte Coliseum, ending the Blue Devils' hopes of another chance at the NCAA title that had long eluded their Case-tutored coach, Vic Bubas.

The next season, Williford flourished with the arrival of Rick Anheuser, a transfer from Bradley University. Williford earned first-team All-ACC honors and the Wolfpack finished third in the ACC standings.

In Williford's senior year, the Wolfpack won 16 of its first 17 games and was ranked as high as fifth in the nation. In his swan song at the ACC Tournament, the virtually unwanted player from Fayetteville led the Wolfpack past regular-season champion South Carolina, in another one of the league's great postseason upsets.

Williford, whose childhood memories were filled with watching Case lead the Wolfpack to championships, became the second NC State player to win the Everett Case Award as the tournament's most valuable player.

After a brief professional career and a stint in the U.S. Army reserves, Williford settled in High Point, N.C., using his NC State industrial engineering degree to operate a successful industrial equipment sales company.

WHAT A BARGAIN

South Carolina arrived in Charlotte for the 1970 ACC Tournament knowing, for the first time in school history, it had an open shot to win an NCAA championship.

It was the culmination of Frank McGuire's second opportunity to take a team named "Carolina" to a national title. The longtime Everett Case foe, who led North Carolina to a perfect season in 1957, had returned to the ACC in 1965 after a short stint in the NBA. He was sure five years later that he had built a team that was good enough to win it all again.

The Gamecocks, the consensus preseason choice for No. 1, were clearly the best team in the ACC. They had returning ACC Player of the Year John Roche, still just a junior. They had heady point guard Bobby Cremins. And they had a towering front line of 6-10 sophomore forward Tom Riker, 6-8 forward John Ribock and 6-10 center Tom Owens. The Gamecocks raced through the ACC regular season, becoming just the third team in league history — after McGuire's '57 Tar Heels and Vic Bubas's 1963 Duke team — to finish league play without a loss.

Few of the contests were close, as USC won its 14 ACC contests by an average of 16.2 points.

And knowing the NCAA East Regional was going to be played in front of an adoring audience in Columbia, S.C., made McGuire and his charges confident about making a trip to the national semifinals in College Park, Md.

First, however, the Gamecocks had to survive the ACC Tournament. That wasn't expected to be too difficult, though NC State and North Carolina had spent some time in the top 10 that season. The Wolfpack, led by senior forward Vann Williford, won 16 of its first 17 games to start the season but faded in February, finishing tied for second in the ACC race with a 9-5 record. Few observers expected there to be much of a challenge to McGuire's team.

Unfortunately for the Gamecocks, no one told the Wolfpack.

Sloan called this Wolfpack team his "bargain basement" squad. Williford was a lightly recruited player from Fayetteville, N.C., who signed with the Wolfpack after Pete Maravich failed to make the necessary test scores to get into school. Senior Rick Anheuser transferred to State from Bradley. Junior guard Al Heartley, the first African American player in Wolfpack history, walked on to the freshman squad three years earlier and eventually earned a scholarship. The only highly recruited player on the team was Ed Leftwich, a New Jersey native who was the first African American scholarship player in school history.

After taking its lumps late in the season, the Wolfpack had regained some confidence by the ACC Tournament. Sloan's squad breezed past Maryland in the first round, and survived a scare in the second round against Virginia, when Anheuser tipped in a missed shot with 39 seconds to play.

The Gamecocks also had a close game in the first round, as archrival Clemson played a slowdown game. But South Carolina prevailed when Roche hit a pair of free throws with eight seconds remaining. Wake Forest didn't present much of a challenge in the semifinals, but something significant did happen: with 11 minutes remaining in the game, Roche suffered a severely sprained ankle in a collision with Deacon guard John Lewkowski.

With Roche injured, the Gamecocks were hardly the same team that had dominated the league in the regular season. Sloan had his team slow the tempo of the game, further leveling the playing field. The Gamecocks jumped out to an early 11-point lead in the first half, despite Roche's ineffective play. For the game, the two-time ACC Player of the Year made just four of 17 shots and scored only nine points.

Despite trailing 24-17 at intermission, Sloan had his team hold the ball for nearly six minutes to open the second half. McGuire eventually pulled his team

out of its 2-1-2 zone, a fatal move that allowed the Wolfpack to tie the game by the end of regulation.

"Norm absolutely out-coached McGuire," Williford said. "They came into the game with the attitude that they could play with anybody on their terms. It was pure coaching genius."

More important, after State tied the score 35-35 at the end of regulation, the hobbled Roche missed a shot that would have tied the game. He missed a similar opportunity at the end of the first overtime.

"I blew it," he said after the game.

Late in the second overtime, South Carolina guard Bobby Cremins, who would later win three ACC titles as the head coach of Georgia Tech, dribbled the ball past halfcourt and was looking for an open teammate. As he took his eye off his defender, Leftwich slapped the ball out of Cremins's hands and drove down the court for the game-winning layup.

With McGuire screaming that Cremins had been fouled, the Wolfpack finished off the stunning upset when Anheuser made a pair of free throws to seal the 42-39 victory. McGuire and his team refused to accept the second-place trophy, while the Wolfpack celebrated with the traditional cutting of the nets.

Cremins went into hiding in the North Carolina mountains for weeks after the game. McGuire continued to stew. The Gamecocks weren't even allowed to participate in the National Invitation Tournament since they were also hosting an NCAA regional, which was the rule at the time. The disappointment from that season was one of many factors that pushed South Carolina to leave the ACC in 1971.

For the Wolfpack, life couldn't have been better. Just about everyone in the 11,666-seat Charlotte Coliseum had been united in pulling for the Wolfpack to beat the McGuire-coached Gamecocks. Sloan, an original Case recruit who loved the traditions established by his former coach, glowed in the spotlight that day, as he became the third Wolfpack coach to lead his team to an ACC championship.

And Williford, Sloan's first recruit, was named the tournament's MVP, becoming the second Wolfpack player to win the award after it was renamed in 1965 to honor Case.

The next week, the Wolfpack lost to Bob Lanier led St. Bonaventure in the first round of the NCAA East Regional in Columbia, which was a highly hostile place for Sloan's team to play the week after its upset of the Gamecocks.

Williford tried valiantly to lead his team to victory, with a 35-point, 12-rebound effort in his final college game.

Despite the short stay in the NCAA Tournament, the "Bargain Basement Pack" was still ACC champions.

THE GREA

Long before Star Wars, another Skywalker lifted off towards the heavens.

He flew like no one had before him, and few have since.

David Thompson's leaping ability was the stuff of legends. Lore says he could take a quarter off the top of the backboard and in the same motion leave two dimes and a nickel in its place.

He made change all right — in the fundamental way college basketball was played. Thompson was the game's first above-the-rim player, a 6-4 forward who could jump 44 inches off the ground, a fact that was verified one day in Reynolds Coliseum by *The Guinness Book of World Records*."

Deprived of the ability to dunk because of an NCAA rule, Thompson found masterful ways of laying the ball in the basket without putting his hand in the cylinder or on the rim. One day at practice, he went high in the air to retrieve an

errant pass from teammate Monte Towe and gently laid the ball in the basket.

"You know," said coach Norm Sloan. "That's a pretty good play. Let's put it in the offense."

With that, the "alley-oop" was born.

"It was an accident, really," Thompson said. "But it worked pretty well. In a lot of ways an alley-oop without a dunk was a little more artistic play. You have to have body control and be able to hang in the air a little bit and make sure you didn't get it in the cylinder.

"It was a good play, but I would have much rather been able to throw a couple of them down and shatter a few backboards."

But that would have been too flashy for Thompson's off-court persona. He was shy and quiet around everyone but his closest friends, who included Towe

and 7-2 center Tommy Burleson. Only on the court did he turn into a showman. Even there, his high-lofting jump shots and his easy lay-ins from impossibly high passes were graceful and artistic.

"David Thompson was the greatest player I ever coached, no question," said the late Norm Sloan. "But he is also the finest person."

Thompson did dunk once during his college career. Late in the final home game of his senior year, after his No. 44 jersey had been retired in pregame ceremonies, Thompson stole a pass, raced down the court and jammed the ball through the goal to the delight of the packed house. He was called for a technical foul and the basket was wiped away. Had it not been, Thompson would have become the first ACC player since Wake Forest's Len Chappell in 1962 to average 30 points a game in a season. No one has approached that average since.

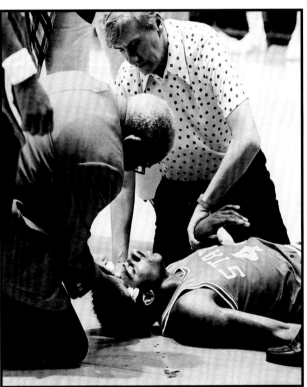

Along with Julius Erving in the NBA, Thompson showed everyone how to play the game from above the rim.

Like Icarus, Thompson almost flew too high. One afternoon during the 1974 NCAA Tournament, he tripped over teammate Phil Spence's shoulder and crashed to the floor of Reynolds Coliseum. No one considered that the horrific play might cost NC State a chance at winning the national championship. They were worried that Thompson might be dead.

But he didn't stay grounded for long. Less than a week later, he soared again, helping the Wolfpack knock seven-time champion UCLA off of college basketball's highest perch in the NCAA semifinals, scoring 28 points and grabbing 10 rebounds in the double-overtime victory. Two days later, he and his teammates beat Marquette to win the school's first NCAA championship.

Since his college career ended, no one has ever seriously challenged his place as the Atlantic Coast Conference's greatest player. Others, including NC State's own Rodney Monroe, may have eclipsed his three-year total of 2,309 points, but they all did it in four years. No one in the ACC has approached his 26.8 career scoring average since he played his last game in 1975.

"I still think David Thompson is the greatest player ever in college basketball," said former Maryland All-America Len Elmore. "David was the queen on the chessboard. He could go everywhere, inside, outside, rebounding. His impact was felt all over the floor. He changed the game.

"Everyone from then on wanted to be a Skywalker."

His high-flying act affected millions, including a young boy in Wilmington, N.C., who hoped one day he could be nearly as good as Thompson. Michael Jordan eventually eclipsed Thompson in NBA fame, but he never approached Thompson's legacy in college, even after he won his own NCAA championship in 1982 at North Carolina.

Thompson was the most highly anticipated professional player in history. He was the first player taken in the 1975 NBA draft, though he opted to play for the Denver Nuggets of the American Basketball Association. For eight years, he flew with the best basketball players in the world, until knee injuries and personal demons grounded him.

He returned to North Carolina in 1987, where he has lived as a hero to many. He lives in Charlotte, where he is the vice president of a sports ministry program that operates basketball leagues for area youth. He still receives reverential treatment from college basketball fans who remember how magical it was to see David Thompson fly so high, so gracefully.

In 2003, Thompson returned to summer school to take the two electives he needed to complete his degree in sociology, receiving his degree within days of his daughters, Brooke and Erika.

"This completes me," Thompson said.

Everett Case changed the way basketball was played in the South. He brought in great players like Dick Dickey, Sammy Ranzino and Ronnie Shavlik and played the game a different way, fast-paced and frenetic. When Thompson came to NC State, five years after Case's death, he changed the entire angle from which the game was viewed.

He played it from above.

"He changed the game"

Maryland All-America Len Elmore

GIANT,

KILLER D

The man, myth and legend, Tommy Burleson takes down Bill Walton and the mighty Bruins

There are several myths about Tommy Burleson that have persisted over the years that need to be cleared up.

First, he isn't now, nor was he ever, 7-4, his listed height during his basketball career at NC State. In his sock feet, Burleson has been measured at 7-2¼, the additional two inches added during his freshman year by folks in the athletics department to make him college basketball's tallest player.

He really isn't from Newland, N.C. He grew up in the even smaller community of Squirrel Creek, five miles to the west and just on the edge of the Pisgah National Forest. Newland is simply the home of Avery County High School, where Burleson played his prep basketball, and someone thought the "Newland Needle" would be a great nickname.

And, most important of all, he was never really gawky or uncoordinated, despite his knobby-kneed appearance when he arrived at NC State. From the first time he showed interest in sports, Burleson worked hard to make sure he could run fast and stay upright, despite the challenges of his rapid growth. He hit better than .500 as a center-fielder on the Avery County High School baseball team. He could score in the 80s on the golf course, until he outgrew his clubs. He regularly bowled over 200. Had his father allowed it, he would have played football. (Years later, Burleson's son, David, was a walk-on for the NC State football team.)

He learned to juggle to improve his hand-eye coordination.

"There are still people who don't think Tommy was a great athlete," Norm Sloan said in a 1999 interview. "But they are wrong. Opponents just liked to belittle him. We never once had to wait on him."

Burleson simply outgrew all of the other sports, sprouting four inches per year between the ages of 13 and 17. But his growth did nothing to squelch his competitive fire, as opponents learned soon after he joined the NC State varsity squad in 1971. His sophomore year, he lost the ACC scoring title to Virginia's Barry Parkhill by three-tenths of a point. He also won the first of his back-to-back rebounding titles.

After his sophomore season, in the summer of 1972, Burleson became the youngest player to ever make the United

States Olympic team, beating out Ohio State's Luke Witte for the final roster spot. He was on the bench, however, for the controversial gold-medal game against the Soviet Union, America's first loss in Olympic competition. The next summer, he and Thompson, coached by Sloan, were on the World University Games team that traveled to Moscow.

"Tommy doesn't even realize how much of a transformation that he went through, beginning with those Olympic Games," Sloan said. "He gained the confidence that he often lacked."

There was never really any doubt that Burleson would play for the Wolfpack. As a teenager, Burleson made frequent trips to Raleigh to visit his uncles, Ben and June Ware, when they were students at NC State. When Carter Stadium opened in 1966, Burleson was in the stands for the first game.

On one summer visit to campus, for the annual Agriculture and Life Science open house, Burleson stopped by Sloan's office in Reynolds Coliseum, hoping to meet the Wolfpack's new coaching staff. Sloan and his assistants, who had just been hired to replace Press Maravich, were a little busy and not eager to meet with a 6-8 center making an unannounced visit to the office. Until they found out that Burleson was just an eighth-grader.

"We almost had a heart attack," said

Sam Esposito, one of Sloan's assistant coaches.

Over the next several years, Sloan and his staff stayed in touch with their new friend from the mountains and in 1970, just after the Wolfpack surprised South Carolina for Sloan's first ACC title, Burleson officially made the announcement that he would attend NC State, and not one of the 367 other schools that had contacted him about playing.

He turned out to be the most important piece in building a program that would win the 1974 NCAA championship. He had befriended David Thompson when the two played against each other in the Western North Carolina High School Association state playoffs during Thompson's junior year. They made a pact to attend the same school, and Thompson followed Burleson to Raleigh a year later.

Burleson's only drawback was his tendency to play down to his competition. He could play like an All-America against an All-America, as he did in the 1974 ACC Tournament game against Len Elmore and in the NCAA semifinals against Bill Walton.

"He sometimes was a little slow to get going," Sloan remembered. "But once he did, he was a son of a gun."

Sloan inspired Burleson against Maryland by clipping out a newspaper article in which Elmore claimed to be the ACC's best center. In the greatest game in league history, a motivated Burleson scored 38 points and grabbed 13 rebounds against Elmore, as the Wolfpack claimed the conference's only berth into the NCAA Tournament.

Two weeks later, Burleson practically matched Walton's 29 points and 19 rebounds with 20 points and 14 rebounds of his own, as the Wolfpack ended UCLA's seven-year reign as national champions by beating the Bruins 80-77 in double-overtime in the NCAA semifinals in Greensboro, N.C.

"Burleson is one of the greatest competitors that I ever coached," Sloan said.

Burleson retired from professional basketball in 1981 and returned to the North Carolina mountains, where he owns a Christmas tree farm and is the director for the Avery County Department of Inspections and Planning.

Many times a year, Burleson comes down the mountain for NC State basketball games. And, closing in on four decades after his career ended, he still stands out among the crowd, as he cheers on the school he has loved since he was a teenager.

Floor show

Monte Towe finds his own spotlight while

Monte Towe is a living legacy for NC State's history of basketball success.

Never mind that he was the feisty floor leader of the 1974 NCAA championship team. Or that he is serving his second stint as a Wolfpack assistant, coaching young players to do the amazing things he did on the court.

What makes Towe special is that he is a living link to the earliest days of Everett Case's program. Despite what his knees tell him, Towe didn't play for Case when he took over NC State's program in the summer of 1946. But Dick Dickey, the first true superstar of NC State basketball, did.

And if it weren't for Dickey, the only NC State player to ever earn four first-team All-Conference honors, Towe would have never come from Converse,

Ind., to play for Norm Sloan, Dickey's one-time roommate.

After his playing days were done, Dickey returned home to his hometown of Marion, Ind. When Sloan became head coach of the Wolfpack in 1966, he often asked Dickey to scout players for him in the Hoosier state. It's exactly the kind of information Case got from his birddogs back in the day.

Once, Dickey told Sloan to recruit a 6-3 center named John Mengelt. Sloan flat-out refused to sign such an undersized big man. Four years later, Mengelt was an All-Southeastern Conference forward at Auburn, who poured in 40 points against the Wolfpack in a 98-51 whipping. Sloan promised he would take the next player

directing the Pack to its first NCAA title

Dickey recommended, sight unseen.

In 1971, Sloan sent Dickey to scout Indiana-born point guard Steve Ahlfeld. Dickey wasn't impressed, but he did take notice of Towe, who was playing on the other team. Dickey was impressed with the spunk of the 5-7 Towe. He also learned that the undersized player was an excellent shortstop and a quarterback who led his team to back-to-back 9-0 records.

Dickey was sold, but Sloan needed convincing.

"He'll get killed on defense," Sloan said. Dickey invoked Sloan's Mengelt promise, and insisted that his old roommate give Towe a scholarship.

Sloan appreciated Dickey's stubborn-ness many times over the years. Though he was the eighth man in a seven-player recruiting class, the Wolfpack coaches noticed that no matter who he was playing with, Towe's teams always won in scrimmages. Before anyone realized what was happening, Towe became the Wolfpack's point guard of the future, not to mention a campus heartthrob with a Davey Jones haircut.

He may not have been the most important piece on a chessboard that included David Thompson and Tommy Burleson, but the Wolfpack would not have won its first NCAA Championship without the player *Sports Illustrated* described as a "lovable lightning bug."

Burleson's 7-2 presence inside and

Thompson's shot-blocking abilities negated Towe's size disadvantage. So did Towe's own toughness. He played most of his sophomore season with a broken nose and a bandaged wrist. Towe was a master at running "The Tease," Sloan's version of the Four Corners slowdown game, and he had the fastest trigger in the history of college basketball at the free-throw line.

In the 1974 NCAA Championship game against Marquette, Towe made sure that the Wolfpack didn't suffer a letdown after ending UCLA's string of seven consecutive national championships. He scored 16 points and pushed his teammates to a 76-64 victory.

"Don't talk to me about Thompson and Burleson," Marquette coach Al McGuire said after the title game. "The key to their team is the little white kid in the backcourt. We like to think our guards are quick on defense, but he kept buzzing past them like they were standing still."

After a brief professional career, Towe returned to NC State to join Sloan's coaching staff. He eventually became the head coach at New Orleans, but returned to the Wolfpack as an assistant coach for Sidney Lowe in 2006.

Towe's goal during his career was simple.

"All I ever wanted was a chance to show I could play," Towe said.

He could, and did.

The Hawkeye

HAWKEYE WHITNEY

Of all the great things Charles "Hawkeye" Whitney did as a player at NC State, nothing compared to what he did in his Senior Day performance on Feb. 20, 1980.

The burly forward capped off his brilliant career by making 11 of his 12 shots and scoring 26 points against archrival North Carolina. In the final moments of the game, he closed out the 63-50 victory with a thunderous dunk, thanks to a through-the-legs pass from fellow senior Clyde Austin —a play Sidney Lowe and Thurl Bailey replicated three years later against the Tar Heels.

Whitney came to NC State after a standout career at Washington's DeMatha Catholic High School, where he played for Naismith Memorial Hall of Fame coach Morgan

The Pioneer

Legendary basketball coach Everett Case had considered recruiting African American basketball players as early as the 1950s to help sustain his highly successful program. He even sent representatives from NC State to New Bern, N.C., to talk to future Naismith Memorial Basketball Hall of Famer Walt Bellamy about joining the Wolfpack. But that did not work out, and Bellamy eventually became a two-time All-America selection at Indiana.

NC State was the first ACC school to integrate athletics, welcoming Walter Holmes Jr. and Manuel Crockett to the varsity track team and Irwin Holmes to the tennis team in 1956. Irwin Holmes was not only the first African American to earn a degree from NC State, he was also the first black athlete in the ACC to be named the captain of a varsity team. ACC basketball teams didn't integrate until a full decade later, though, starting with Maryland's Billy Jones during the 1965–66 season.

In the fall of 1967, a shy applied mathematics student named Al Heartley walked into the office of Wolfpack basketball coach Norm Sloan and asked to try out for the freshman team. He had been a star player at segregated Johnston Central High School in Clayton, N.C., and came from an accomplished basketball family. His brother, Harvey, was an All-America player at North Carolina Central in the mid-1950s and had won N.C. state high school championships at all-black Cooper High School in Clayton and Ligon High School in Raleigh. He later became the head coach and athletics director at St. Augustine's, the historically black college less than five miles from NC State's campus.

Heartley never mentioned his pedigree to Sloan, however, hoping to earn his way onto the freshman squad on his own ability. Sloan recognized the importance of Heartley's request, knowing the time had come to integrate his program, just as Maryland, Duke and North Carolina had done. He told Heartley to keep an eye out for tryout announcements in the student newspaper.

When those tryouts began, assistant coach Sam Esposito called Sloan over to watch the young guard play. He was not only the best of the walk-on players, he was also running circles around the seven recruited freshmen. Heartley made the fresh-

Wootten. He was part of a pipeline from the school to Norm Sloan's program in Raleigh. It began with Kenny Carr, and continued with Whitney, Lowe and Dereck Whittenburg, just to name a few.

He had a great debut for head coach Norm Sloan's program in 1977, becoming the first and so far only player in school history to win the ACC Freshman of the Year Award after averaging 14.6 points and 5.8 rebounds a game.

The next year, he helped the Wolfpack advance to the championship game of the National Invitation Tournament, where it lost to Texas at Madison Square Garden.

In four years, Whitney scored 1,954 points, grabbed 652 rebounds and set the school record with 166 steals, a record broken three years later by Lowe.

One of the first things Lowe did after becoming head coach in 2006 was reach out to all former Wolfpack players. He was especially happy to see Whitney, who went through troubled times after he left NC State, accept his offer to return to Raleigh for a reunion of former players.

"My greatest memory is being here at NC State," Whitney said. "It was the greatest time of my life. Not just being a player here, but being around the fans and the NC State family. It wasn't a fake thing. They loved us because we were here representing the school.

"Being a part of the NC State family is a great thing."

man team and averaged eight points a game, even though he played out of position at forward.

The next year, Heartley was elevated to the varsity team, becoming NC State's first African American basketball player. At the same time, Sloan recruited Ed Leftwich to become the school's first black basketball player to be offered an athletics scholarship.

In 1970, Heartley helped the team win the ACC Tournament championship and in 1971 he was named the winner of the Alumni Athletics Trophy as the school's top athlete, as voted by the students.

"He is one of the best experiences I had in coaching," Sloan said in his 1991 book *Confessions of a Coach*.

Shortly after Heartley's career ended, Sloan recruited David Thompson of Shelby, N.C., without question the ACC's greatest player. In the eyes of many, including Heartley, the exceedingly shy Thompson did not have the demeanor to break the racial barrier for the program. Heartley had already cleared the path, and Thompson's arrival caused ripples only because of his incredible talent and basketball skills, not because of the color of his skin.

The
Gold Standard

Growing up in Washington, D.C., Kenny Carr was a football player, and his burly 6-8 frame might have been the perfect prototype for the modern-day NFL tight end. But at the age of 14, Carr could no longer find football cleats in his size, so he tried a different sport.

"It was kind of by accident, to be honest, but I just fell in love with basketball," he said.

He was the first of Morgan Wootten's talented players to come to NC State from DeMatha Catholic High School in Hyattsville, Md., clearing the path for guys like Charles "Hawkeye" Whitney, Sidney Lowe and Dereck Whittenburg.

The husky forward spent three years playing for NC State coach Norm Sloan in the mid-1970s, continuing David Thompson's practice of earning scoring titles and twice earning All-America honors.

Thompson and Carr were teammates in 1974–75, when Thompson led the ACC in scoring for a third consecutive year. After the three-time All-America small forward moved on, Carr became Sloan's go-to player. He twice led the league in scoring, averaging 26.6 points as a sophomore and 21 as a junior.

So the Wolfpack duo led the ACC for five years running, a feat that has never been matched by another school.

Though he technically took over Thompson's starting position, he was a vastly different player. Thompson was all finesse, using his athletic ability to extend the height on his graceful jumper and to float above the rim. Carr was all power. He could muscle his way into the lane and clear people out of the way. He also liked to step out to the perimeter and take long jumpshots, something players of his size rarely did in those days.

Carr was a dominating player and a natural to be considered for the 1976 Olympic team, when North Carolina's Dean Smith was the head coach for Team USA. Smith held his first round of tryouts on NC State's campus and selected Carr to be one of the 12 players to represent the U.S. at the Montreal Games, where Carr became the first NC State basketball player to win a gold medal.

Carr returned from his Olympic experience knowing that he would spend only one more year in college, following in the footsteps of Maryland player Brad Davis in declaring financial hardship to enter the NBA.

"I just thought my body and my game were ready to move on," said Carr, the first Wolfpack player to leave school early for professional basketball. "I was a very physical player and I would get a lot of fouls. I was a little bigger and more aggressive than most people I played against. I got frustrated a lot."

He was the sixth overall pick in the 1977 NBA draft, going to the Los Angeles Lakers. His career got off to a rocky start, after he broke his right foot in his rookie season and his left foot in his second season. But he played for 10 years with four different franchises: Los Angeles, Cleveland, Portland and Detroit. He retired in 1987 after 674 career games, 7,713 points and 4,999 rebounds.

Carr returned to NC State during the summers of his first two years after he went to the NBA, earning a degree in education. After his playing days were over, he settled in Portland and founded a successful commercial construction company.

PERF

It was perfection, with an asterisk.

The 1972–73 NC State basketball team knew going into the season that it would not be eligible for postseason play and, no matter how dubious the players and coaches thought the charges of NCAA violations were, they were prepared to live with those restrictions.

And to be motivated by them.

The charges stemmed from the recruitment of high-flying forward David Thompson, the future three-time National Player of the Year from Shelby, N.C. Thompson, owner of a smooth, elevated jumper and a 44-inch vertical leap, had chosen NC State over North Carolina in the spring of his senior year, so he could play with close friend Tommy Burleson, the 7-2 center who was already a star for the Wolfpack.

After Thompson signed his ACC and national letters of intent in the summer of 1971, he traveled to Raleigh for freshman orientation, sleeping on the floor of two friends from Shelby, Larry and Jerry Hunt, who happened to be summer basketball camp counselors. Thompson also played a few pickup games at Carmichael Gymnasium.

However, because Thompson did not pay the

ECT*

school $8 for a week's room rental and because Wolfpack assistant and former All-ACC guard Eddie Biedenbach also participated in some of those pickup games, the NCAA found the school to be in violation of recruiting rules and handed the program a one-year probation for conducting an illegal tryout of Thompson.

"I thought the whole thing was really nitpicky and kind of harsh," Thompson said.

Burleson agreed.

"David and I felt that it was a real chintzy way of putting us on probation and keeping us out of the tournament," Burleson said. "We both had offers from other schools of cars, clothes and apartments. We came to NC State and didn't receive anything other than our scholarships."

Still, the Wolfpack players and staff went into the season knowing, no matter what, their season would end following the ACC Basketball Tournament in Greensboro, N.C., early that March.

And that was great inspiration.

"We knew going into the season that things were what they were," said Monte Towe, the fiery point guard who was a sophomore for head coach Norman Sloan. "We didn't feel like at the time that we deserved those sanctions, but we accepted them.

"We knew we could play as many as 27 games on the schedule and we made up our minds that we were going to win every one of them."

And that's what happened, as the Wolfpack joined North Carolina's 1957 NCAA championship team as only the second undefeated team in ACC history. There were a few close calls along the way, but the Wolfpack's 21.8-point average margin of victory shows just how dominant it was.

Thompson, Towe and forward Tim Stoddard were all sophomores on that team, moving up from the freshman squad to join Burleson, the team's leading scorer and rebounder in 1972. The team featured a pair of veteran leaders in senior starters Rick Holdt and Joe Cafferky.

The arrival of Thompson on the college scene was highly anticipated, after so many stories circulated about his play for the NC State freshman team in 1971–72, which earned Thompson an invitation to the 1972 U.S. Olympic Trials, along with Burleson. Thompson declined, but Burleson made the squad, to become the first NC State basketball player to make the U.S. Olympic team.

Sloan was criticized for playing a weak schedule in the early part of the season, as the Wolfpack scored more than 100 points in four early blowout wins over Appalachian State (130-53), Atlantic Christian (110-40), Georgia Southern (144-100) and South Florida (125-88). But it also proved itself by winning the Big Four championship in Greensboro with wins over Wake Forest and North Carolina.

On Jan. 14, 1973, as a lead-in to Super Bowl VII between the Miami Dolphins and the Washington Redskins, the third-ranked Wolfpack traveled to Cole Field House to face second-ranked Maryland. The Terps, featuring future NBA players Tom McMillen and Len Elmore, were the preseason favorites to win the ACC.

NC State athletics director Willis Casey worked with television syndicator Castleman D. Chesley to put together a patchwork network of 145 television stations that made that game available to more than 95 percent of the nation. It was the first national broadcast of a college basketball regular-season game in more than five years.

Thompson became a superstar that Super Bowl Sunday, scoring 37 points and laying in a missed shot by Burleson with three seconds remaining to give the Wolfpack an 87-85 victory.

"I was determined to get that one," Thompson said after the game. "If I had to jump through

the ceiling, I was going to get that one."

There were a few other close calls that season, including an 82-78 win over North Carolina in Chapel Hill after Thompson fouled out with more than five minutes on the clock. But the next real challenge came in Greensboro in the ACC title game.

State, after receiving a bye as the regular-season champion, survived a slowdown game against Virginia, while Maryland advanced with wins over Clemson and Wake Forest.

Stoddard and Thompson both hit a pair of free throws in the final minute to lead the Pack to a 76-74 win over the Terps, and Burleson won the Everett Case Award as the Tournament's Most Valuable Player.

But that's where the season ended. The Wolfpack

became just the 12th team since 1938 to finish the college basketball season undefeated. There has been only one since — Indiana in 1976. Only three teams — Kentucky in 1954, NC State in 1973 and Alcorn State in 1979 — have finished with an undefeated record and not been invited to the NCAA Tournament.

There was another undefeated team in 1973, as John Wooden's UCLA dynasty completed its second consecutive season without a loss en route to its seventh consecutive NCAA title.

College basketball fans were upset that the two teams could not meet to decide which unbeaten team was better. But they found out the next year.

GREATEST. GAME. EVER.

It was a do-or-die situation. With only one ACC team advancing to the NCAA tournament, NC State and Maryland battled for supremacy.

Basketball greatness was born with a taunt on Super Bowl Sunday.

The day was Jan. 13, 1974, and NC State had just beaten Maryland at Reynolds Coliseum, in a matchup of two top-five teams from the Atlantic Coast Conference.

Though his team lost, 6-9 Maryland center Len Elmore had a message for his 7-2 counterpart in the other lockerroom, NC State's Tommy Burleson.

Elmore had just outplayed Burleson, limiting the two-time first-team All-ACC center to just three field goals on 19 shots, despite the Wolfpack's 80-74 victory.

"You tell Burleson," Elmore said, "I am the best center in the ACC."

Not until UNLV's Sidney Green said something similar to Wolfpack forward Thurl Bailey nine years later has anyone ever put motivation quite so neatly on a platter and served it to an opponent.

In the games that followed, Elmore backed up his claim, taking the ACC rebounding title that Burleson had won the previous two years. When sportswriters were forced to choose between Elmore and Burleson for their first-team selection at that position, the cold, hard statistics pointed to Elmore, who did indeed have the better year.

But statistics don't measure heart, especially in Burleson's case.

He was the most important piece to the Wolfpack's two-year domination of the ACC. Sure, teammate David Thompson was the All-America game-changer, whose legendary leaping ability was unlike anything college basketball had ever seen. But it was the shot-blocking, rebounding and emotional leadership of Burleson that made the Wolfpack all but unstoppable.

In 1973, when the combination of Burleson, Thompson and Monte Towe first played together,

the Wolfpack was a perfect 27-0, but unable to participate in the postseason because of a one-year NCAA probation. In their second year, the Wolfpack was nearly perfect again, suffering just one loss to UCLA in a made-for-television contest between two teams that were unbeaten the year before. The seven-time national champion Bruins pulled away in the second half to claim the game, played in mid-December in St. Louis.

Since that setback, however, the Wolfpack had dominated the nationally prominent ACC, easily beating its opponents in the Big Four and continuing its dominance over Maryland, which had spent most of the season ranked in the top five.

None of that mattered, of course, when the league met in Greensboro for the ACC Tournament. Everyone was gunning to beat the Wolfpack, and both Maryland and North Carolina had teams that could do it.

And, in those days, only the tournament winner advanced to the NCAA Tournament, making the tension inside the Coliseum palpable.

Burleson didn't exactly need the extra motivation, but he got it when Wolfpack head coach Norm Sloan taped to his locker a crumpled newspaper clipping of Elmore's claim that he had saved in his wallet for nearly six weeks.

Burleson, the senior center from the North Carolina mountains, had one last chance to prove the unconvinced wrong. What happened in the 1974 ACC Championship game is still remembered as the greatest game in ACC history: NC State 103, Maryland 100, in overtime.

From the moment the teams were introduced, Burleson was on fire. He jumped off the bench with finger pistols blazing and never cooled off. For the hard-luck Terrapins, it was an unsettling sight.

Lefty Driesell might have been the most frustrated coach in ACC history. Despite a 1970 recruiting class that ranked as one of the best ever, the Terps were making their third consecutive ACC title game appearance but still had no trophy for Driesell to strap onto the hood of his car and drive around North Carolina, as he had promised to do if he ever managed to claim that piece of hardware. Elmore, Lew Alcindor's successor in high school, was joined by 6-11 fellow senior Tom McMillen and the sophomore backcourt combination of John Lucas and Mo Howard.

Two years before, the Terps lost to North Carolina in the ACC title game and had to settle for the National Invitation Tournament, a title they claimed with four straight victories. In 1973, Driesell's team lost to NC State, but represented the ACC in the NCAA Tournament because the Wolfpack was on probation. The Terps lost to Providence in the East Region finals in Charlotte.

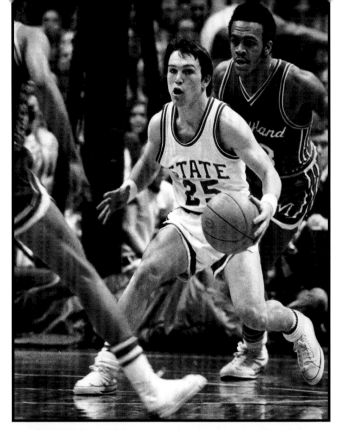

To win this time, the Terps would have to get past nemesis NC State, which had beaten Driesell's club five consecutive times going into the championship game.

The Wolfpack, still stinging from the inability to face UCLA in the tournament the previous year, wanted desperately to go back to the NCAA Tournament, especially since the Final Four would be played on the same Greensboro Coliseum floor two weeks later.

NC State wasted little energy getting into the championship game. After a first-round bye, the Wolfpack didn't need its starters the whole time in an 87-66 victory over Virginia in the semifinals. Driesell, meanwhile, played McMillen, Lucas and Elmore for a combined 104 minutes in the opening-round game against Duke (85-66) and 116 minutes in a 105-85 blowout of North Carolina.

Driesell is still criticized for playing his stars for so long in a game that was decided early.

"He thought we needed to make a statement and I think we certainly did that against North Carolina," Elmore said. "We gave them one of their biggest whippings ever in the tournament."

But at what price? State's game plan was to run the Terps ragged, which explains why Wolfpack forward Tim Stoddard took the game's first shot just four seconds after the opening tip. The pace never slowed down, as both teams shot well from the floor and made few unforced errors.

Burleson continued to keep his team in the game, while reserve Tom Roy and Elmore worked together to shut Thompson down.

"The guy we didn't want to beat us was

Thompson," said Elmore. "What we had to do in order to keep that from happening was leave something else open. I kind of had to play half and half, paying attention to Tommy and David. That left me vulnerable to some offensive rebounding by Tommy.

"And every shot he took went in. He was even taking hook shots from 15 feet that were hitting every part of the rim and falling in."

In one stretch, Burleson scored 12 of the Wolfpack's 17 points to offset the Terp guards' abuse of the undersized Towe. Burleson was practically hot-dogging it, bouncing the ball between McMillen's legs for an assist on a fast break.

The Terps could have won the game on the final play of regulation, after McMillen stole the ball away from substitute NC State point guard Mark Moeller, who was in the game because Towe was suffering from leg cramps. Rivers, NC State's defensive specialist, forced Lucas to pass the ball away to Howard, who was in the midst of the best game of his career. Howard, who had made 10 of his first 13 shots, hesitated for a moment too long and threw the ball back to Lucas, whose wild shot at the end of regulation wasn't close.

The overtime was classic slowdown basketball. Only nine points were scored in those five minutes, but there was a flurry of activity at the end that decided the game. The Terps, obviously showing their fatigue, made a pair of critical turnovers and missed the front end of a one-and-one.

Towe hit a pair of free throws just before the clock expired to secure the 103-100 victory. The Maryland players slumped to the bench, losers for the third consecutive time in the ACC finals. Oddly, it was Towe who broke down, just before his team cut down the nets on the school's eighth ACC championship, releasing all the emotions that the team had pent up inside for so long.

"He said to me, 'The hell with it, I am going to cry,'" Sloan says. "And he sat right down in a chair and cried his eyes out."

Burleson didn't shed tears then but he still gets misty-eyed talking about the performance that won him the Everett Case Trophy for the second year in a row: 38 points on 18 of 25 shooting, 13 rebounds and two assists.

"It was like a thousand pounds being lifted off my shoulders," Burleson said. "That was the only chance I had to go to the NCAA Tournament, because of the probation the year before. It was completely do-or-die and I wanted badly to win that game."

Before the Wolfpack's bus pulled out of the coliseum parking lot, Driesell flagged it down and climbed on board.

"I congratulated them," said Driesell, who never won the elusive tournament crown, "and told them I hoped they won it all."

That's exactly what happened two weeks later.

Reaching a goal never attained by legendary coach Everett Case, the Wolfpack brings the national championship trophy home

BIG
RED
ONE

No one could ever remember seeing David Thompson angry before.

For three years, Thompson flew higher than anyone else in college basketball, and no one could disturb him, not with blatant fouls, subtle digs or the lead weights of a double-team. The young man who soared on unseen wings was completely unflappable.

On the afternoon of March 16, 1974, however, Thompson was enraged in this NCAA Tournament second round game against Pittsburgh. On just about every shot, someone from the Panthers would slap Thompson on the arm, bump his legs or try to hold him. It was an unconscionable way to play the artistic game of basketball, in Thompson's opinion, if that's the way they wanted to play. . . .

While everyone else marveled at his sheer athletic ability, David's mother, Ida Thompson, was always worried that her youngest son was going to fly too high. "That boy is going to hurt himself," she frequently told head coach Norm Sloan. And, horrifically, in front of 12,400 spectators in Reynolds Coliseum and a television audience that afternoon, he did.

Thompson decided that the Panthers would not take an uncontested shot the rest of the game, if he had to block every single attempt himself. That wasn't possible, of course, but no one thought it was possible for a man to leap 44 inches off the ground, either. He had to try.

Thompson and his teammates were driven to get to the NCAA semifinals, which were being held for the only time in the history of the NCAA Tournament in Greensboro — the same place where just a week before the Wolfpack survived an overtime thriller against Maryland in the ACC Tournament championship game. All the Wolfpack needed to do was win two games on its home court and it could make the 70-mile trip down the road for a possible rematch with UCLA, the undisputed class of college basketball. The first of those two home games was easy, a 92-78 win over Providence and its All-America forward Marvin Barnes. But Pittsburgh was giving the Wolfpack some trouble.

There was no way that the team was going to let this opportunity slip through its fingers. Earlier in the season, the Wolfpack had been humiliated by UCLA, in a made-for-television showdown in St. Louis. It was the most anticipated game in the history of NC State basketball. Both teams had finished undefeated in 1973, with the Bruins going 30-0 and winning their seventh consecutive national championship. The Wolfpack was 27-0, but unable to compete in the postseason because of a one-year NCAA probation.

So over the summer, while John Wooden was in North Carolina to accept an honorary degree from Campbell University, he helped negotiate a game with NC State, to be played on a neutral court. It was the game that all college basketball fans wanted to see.

The Wolfpack rolled into town riding a 29-game winning streak. The Bruins, however, had won an NCAA-record 78 in a row. Could this be where their stranglehold on college basketball ended?

No. The game was close for the first half, but only because an overeager Bill Walton committed four fouls and was on the bench most of the game. The Wolfpack could not take advantage of his absence, however. UCLA's Keith Wilkes kept Thompson under wraps, and backup center Ralph Drollinger roughed up Wolfpack center Tommy Burleson, knocking

out two of his teeth with a forearm shiver to the face at the end of the first half.

Wooden held Walton out of the game until less than 10 minutes remained on the clock. NC State tied the game at 54 on its next possession, but in the space of just three minutes Walton led his team on back-to-back blitzes of 10 points and 9 points, with a single Wolfpack basket in between. The Bruins maintained their rule over college basketball, with an 84-66 win that embarrassed Sloan's team.

"We just weren't good enough to win that day," said point guard Monte Towe. "I think it helped us in the long run, because we knew if we played them again, we would be playing to win instead of looking at the name on the jersey."

Memories of that game were running through Thompson's mind in the East Regional final against Pittsburgh. He and his teammates had to get to Greensboro to avenge that earlier loss to the Bruins, and he was ready to take a few chances to get there.

As Pittsburgh's Keith Starr went up for a jumper, Thompson swooped in and tipped the ball. As the game official whistled him for goaltending, however, Thompson's leg caught the shoulder of 6-9 teammate Phil Spence and he flipped in midair. He came crashing to the wooden floor, landing on his neck and immediately silencing the crowd of 12,400 hometown spectators.

He lay motionless on the floor, as team trainers tried to restore consciousness. Tears streamed down the faces of teammates and fans as they wondered if anyone could possibly survive such a fall. Spence stood in the corner, thinking only one thought: "I've killed David."

The superstar forward was wheeled off the court on a stretcher and taken by ambulance to Rex Hospital, while his furious teammates slapped, mugged and powered their way to a lead against the Panthers. The game, however, became an afterthought. Everyone simply waited to hear a medical update from public address announcer C.A. Dillon.

At the hospital, while CBS News anchorman Walter Cronkite was on hold waiting to hear if college basketball's best player had died, doctors quickly determined that Thompson had miraculously suffered relatively minor injuries, other than a severe concussion. They sewed his head closed with 16 stitches, wrapped the injury in white gauze and grudgingly

allowed Thompson to return to Reynolds Coliseum.

"That just shows that you shouldn't lose control on the basketball court," Thompson said. "I had always been cool under pressure. I got a little upset, which was out of character for me, and I paid a huge price for it."

Just before halftime, Dillon made the announcement that Thompson would be okay, bringing a thunderous ovation from the crowd. A few minutes later, Thompson walked through the door and was mobbed by his teammates, who left the court mid–free throw to greet their injured friend. He was hit with a wall of noise that could not

have been good for his headache.

"Without a doubt, that is the loudest Reynolds Coliseum ever was," said Dillon, who sat behind the courtside microphone for 50 years.

No one knew if Thompson would be able to play seven days later in the national semifinals, but they did know he was alive. At the time, that's all that mattered.

Over the next week, Wolfpack player Greg Hawkins became the most popular person on campus. As Thompson's roommate, he fielded calls from all over the country, from concerned fans, media and even a few bookies who wanted to know if Thompson would be able to play in

its quick backcourt of Towe and shooting guard Morris "Mo" Rivers. He shuffled his lineup a couple of times, interchanging Spence and powerful forward Tim Stoddard. With Burleson patrolling the middle and Thompson

the rematch against UCLA. Each day, Thompson improved a little.

By the time the team went to Greensboro for the Saturday afternoon contest against the Bruins, the high-flying forward was close to 100 percent, though he did still have all those stitches in the back of his head.

UCLA, which had won seven national titles in a row and nine of the last 10, was not quite the dominant team it had been in December. Notre Dame had ended the Bruins' record winning streak at 88 games, and they had lost twice more after that. It was the most losses John Wooden's team had suffered since the 1965–66 season, which was the only time in a decade that the Bruins did not win the national title. Still, with Walton and Wilkes, it was clearly one of Wooden's best teams.

The Wolfpack had also changed, with Sloan making some adjustments that helped his team take advantage of

flying overhead, the team went to Greensboro believing it could topple Wooden's juggernaut.

UCLA, however, was not exactly convinced.

"I think their earlier win allowed them to be a little complacent in the second game," Burleson said. "They just felt they were better than us."

Early in the game, with the Wolfpack leading 14-12, Thompson proved there were

no lingering effects from his concussion. He jumped high in the air to block a shot by the 6-11 Walton, and the sellout crowd went wild. Twice in the second half, the Bruins built an 11-point lead. Twice, the Wolfpack erased it, with Burleson playing Walton on even terms and Thompson taking over the game. And twice, the Wolfpack

missed closing shots that could have won the game, one by Stoddard at the end of regulation and one by by Burleson in the first overtime.

In the second overtime, UCLA jumped out to a 74-67 lead with 3:27 remaining, and it appeared that Sloan's team had merely extended its competitiveness

from the game in December, when the Bruins blitzed the Wolfpack in the final 10 minutes.

After UCLA called timeout, however, Towe stepped in front of Wilkes for a charging call and made a pair of free throws. Thompson stole the ball and made a jumper that cut UCLA's lead to four, and Burleson, who had long played in the shadow of Walton, made a three-point play that trimmed the lead to one, all in the span of just two minutes.

When UCLA's David Meyers missed the front end of a one-and-one chance with 1:16 to play, Thompson finished off his most heroic game with a high-rising jumper and a pair of free throws that gave his team its first lead in overtime.

When the curtain fell on the game, State owned an 80-77 victory, and the Bruin dynasty was broken.

While fans celebrated around the Wolfpack at the Albert Pick Hotel, Sloan sequestered his team away from all the raucous activity. He didn't want

the Wolfpack's magnificent squad to be remembered as a footnote — the team that ended UCLA's dynasty but lost in the championship game.

Two days after the Wolfpack felled the Bruins, Marquette coach Al McGuire imploded on the sidelines, earning two technical fouls in the first half and allowing the Wolfpack to score 10 unanswered points. In the second half, under Towe's guiding hand, State built a 19-point lead that was too much to overcome. When the buzzer sounded, the Wolfpack owned a 76-64 victory and its first national championship.

Sloan, one of Everett Case's original recruits in 1946, had accomplished what his mentor never did: He cut down the nets after winning college basketball's ultimate prize.

On the ride home from Greensboro, Sloan had the bus driver pull over to the side of Highway 70 near the graveyard where Case is buried. And they all said thank you to the man who started all this madness so many years ago.

INNOVATIONS: MIRACLE

"V"

FOR VICTORY

Sir Winston Churchill first flashed the "V" for victory during WWII, but it was the Wolfpack's charismatic coach that made it stand for "victorious" during his team's magical 1983 NCAA tournament run

The dream started on Day 1: March 27, 1980.

That's when James Thomas Anthony Valvano, a brash-thinking and fast-talking New Yorker, told the players assembled in the basement locker room of Reynolds Coliseum that he was on his way to win an NCAA Championship. All he wanted to know from the questioning faces in front of him was if they wanted to come along.

He was a young guy, only 33 years old at the time. But he had always dreamed

big, and he wanted his new players to do the same.

"He came in, on that very first day, talking about championships and family," said Dereck Whittenburg, one of the players Valvano inherited the day he was hired to be NC State's basketball coach. "We all bought into that dream from the first day we met him."

It's not exactly true that this was the first time Whittenburg and teammate Sidney Lowe had met Valvano. Two years earlier, after their team won an AAU basketball tournament in Boston, Valvano nearly tackled the two guards. He wrapped his arms around their shoulders and said "I love you guys. You should come play for me. I'm Jim Valvano, Iona College."

Lowe and Whittenburg looked at each other: This guy owns a college?

That's the only thing they remembered when they heard Valvano had been hired to replace Norm Sloan, the coach who had recruited them both from DeMatha Catholic High School in Hyattsville, Md.

"Sidney, do you know who our new coach is?" Whittenburg said. "It's that crazy Italian dude who choked us up in Boston."

The crazy Italian dude always left a lasting impression.

But this was a skeptical lot of players, burned by Sloan's hasty departure to Florida. They weren't happy that the coach who recruited them had left in a dispute over salary. Lowe was ready to leave for Florida with Sloan. Whittenburg was steadfast in his desire to stay. Forward Thurl

JIM VALVANO BASKETBALL COACH
N. C. STATE UNIVERSITY

Bailey, another rising sophomore, couldn't make up his mind.

"None of us knew anything about this new guy," Bailey said. "To be honest, my mind wasn't on him. We were distraught kids who were thinking about the promise Coach Sloan made to us to be here all four years of our career.

"Then [Valvano] started talking about his dream of winning a championship and how we could come along with him. He was so passionate about it. All of a sudden, he had the attention of every single person sitting in front of him."

They all eventually decided to stay right where they were; Valvano made them a part of his dream.

"He never looked at us like we were Norm's recruits," Whittenburg said. "He just told us that we are all here at NC State, all here for the same dream and the same cause. That meant something to us."

Valvano didn't just talk to the players. He told anyone who would listen that he would win an NCAA title, often while gazing at the banner from the 1974 championship hanging in the rafters of Reynolds Coliseum. He began dreaming about it during his days as a walk-on point guard at Rutgers. The dream grew as he became a head coach at Johns Hopkins, Bucknell and Iona. And he knew at NC State, member of the powerful ACC and owner of one NCAA Tournament title already, it could be fulfilled.

In case he ever forgot, he kept a laminated 3x5 index card in his pocket that read: "Win a national championship." It was the one that remained after he fulfilled several of his other dreams, like

Jim Valvano gets his customary hug from Dereck Whittenburg after an ACC Tournament victory in Atlanta.

becoming a Division I head coach and playing the night game at Madison Square Garden during the Holiday Festival, those one-time dreams that were now no more than résumé items.

This is how confident Valvano was that it would actually happen: in his early days at NC State, he made his team practice cutting down the nets, the tradition that Everett Case brought to college basketball from the high school gyms of Indiana.

"We wanted to be prepared for winning that championship game," Whittenburg said.

That practice came in handy just three years after Valvano met with his new players in the basement of Reynolds, when the Wolfpack embarked on college basketball's ultimate joy ride. It culminated on April 4, 1983, in Albuquerque, N.M., when Lorenzo Charles dunked Whittenburg's errant jump shot to beat Houston in the NCAA Championship game.

Valvano was certainly not the first college basketball coach to dream big, but his lasting legacy to the modern era of the sport is how he inspired others to share his dream and jump on along for the ride. It is also a cautionary tale of what

happens after a dream is fulfilled. And, ultimately, it's a bittersweet reminder of how fleeting all our dreams are.

Valvano was different from most college coaches in that he was the ultimate Renaissance man, an English major who had a voracious appetite for knowledge. He tried to read 70 pages of a book every night before he went to bed. Every summer, he would pick a single topic and learn as much as he

could about it. Theories of economics. Watergate. Anything but basketball.

He often quoted poetry. T.S. Eliot's "The Love Song of J. Alfred Prufrock" was his favorite. And he didn't mind showing his emotions, whether he was laughing, crying or picking apart one of his players for making a mistake. Whenever he heard Harry Chapin's song "Cat's in the Cradle," tears streamed down his face. Every. Damned. Time.

These words, etched on his tombstone, properly reflect his life's philosophy: "Take time every day to laugh, to think, to cry."

In that regard, Valvano was one of college basketball's ultimate innovators. He ratcheted everything up a few notches, from the recruiting process to his coaching salary. But, as much as he loved basketball, he had other interests. When opportunities presented themselves for speaking engagements, product endorsements, television commercials, basketball camps and television appearances, he jumped at them, unapologetically. He liked those opportunities as much as coaching the game itself.

In the months following the '83 championship, the hyperactive Valvano, who rarely slept more than two or three hours a night, wrote a book chronicling the team's championship run and introduced his own "Jimmy V" clothing line, which included a terrycloth wrap his players could wear in the postgame locker room. He accepted more endorsements and became a celebrity in the national sports media. His personal appearance schedule jumped to 150 events per year and his

fee for corporate speeches went to $50,000 a pop. He set up his own production company, JTV Enterprises.

His weekly routine might kill a normal person. But, as former NC State football coach Dick Sheridan observed, Valvano was anything but normal. "It took tremendous energy and a lot of talent to do the things he tried, and Jim certainly had both," Sheridan said.

Here's the thing most people didn't know about the flamboyant coach: he had more than one note card in his pocket. His dreams were many, and he continued to add more until the day he died.

He signed a big shoe and apparel contract with Nike. He flew all over the country giving motivational speeches. He made weekly appearances on the "CBS Morning Show" with Phyllis George. His overscheduled calendar looked a lot like those of modern coaches, who hop from engagement to engagement, and are paid many times their actual salary from outside sources of income. They dress and act like corporate chief executive officers. In many ways, they owe Valvano and his mentor, Bill Foster of Rutgers, for their ability to be coaches who do more than just draw Xs and Os on the chalkboard.

"There are a lot of purists in the game, but I am not one of them," Valvano said. "Purists don't drink with me at four o'clock in the morning. There are a lot of guys who are coaching their brains out when the score is 16-14 with four minutes left [in the game]. Those are the guys who are always winning coach-of-the-year awards. I do other things."

Valvano drank deeply from the cup of life, and the bottle of wine that was usually next to him.

When *USA Today* reported in 1985 that Valvano was the nation's highest paid coach, making more than a half-million dollars per year, there were some people — especially academic administrators and professors on his own campus — who were shocked at just how much he was cashing in on what started as such a sweet little dream.

And that's what created so many problems for him in his final five years at NC State, when he was named athletics director and his JTV Enterprises continued to swell. The coach was certainly well-versed enough in popular literature to know what American satirist Ambrose Bierce once said: "Success is the one unpardonable sin against one's fellows."

Those fellows believed the coach took his eyes off his primary responsibility — his basketball program — while juggling so many other opportunities.

Following the remarkable run to the NCAA Championship, Valvano recruited a slew of players who rewarded him with great success: Spud Webb, Nate McMillan, Vinny Del Negro, Chucky Brown, Chris Corchiani, Rodney Monroe, Brian Howard and Tom Gugliotta, to name a few. The team shared the 1985 regular-season championship, went to the NCAA Tournament's Elite Eight in back-to-back seasons and won another ACC title in 1987. His teams were talented, and the NBA frequently plucked players from his program to become standout pros.

But Valvano, in his quest to win a second championship, also brought in other players who were gifted on the basketball court but too ill-prepared or too immature to be successful college students. They created problems internally, and the spread-thin Valvano wasn't around enough to manage the difficulties.

"Jimmy's problem at the end, and I discussed it with him many times, is that he started taking chances with too many kids," said longtime friend and television commentator Dick

Vitale. "He always felt that if you gave a kid an opportunity, gave him a lot of love and attention, things would turn out great. Bottom line, that backfired on him."

Regardless, the coach was revered by the fans who cackled at his stand-up comedian post-dinner speeches and appreciated his on-court success. They were still invested in his initial dream. But there were others who chafed that many of Valvano's recruits had weak academic records and poor graduation rates.

When Casey retired in 1986, Valvano was named to replace him. But unlike Sloan, who briefly toyed with being athletics director in 1969, Valvano was allowed to keep his job as men's basketball coach. Now, in addition to his numerous outside activities, he was in charge of the entire department.

Valvano was one of the nation's hottest commodities, constantly being wooed for other jobs. In 1986, ABC wanted him to become a full-time broadcaster. In 1987, the New York Knicks wanted him to advance to the NBA. In 1988, UCLA offered him the job every coach dreamed of, the chance to be mentioned in the same breath as John Wooden. Plus, according to Vitale, the school was offering to help the coach get his own sitcom.

He had Wooden's personal stamp of approval. The legendary coach had befriended Valvano many years earlier at a New York summer basketball camp when he was just an eager young assistant. But Valvano's family wanted to stay in Raleigh, so he continually turned down lucrative job offers.

On Jan. 7, 1989, the same day Valvano proudly unveiled Nike's uniform of the future, the unitard, *The News & Observer* of Raleigh published a front-page story of outlandish allegations about Valvano's program made in a book called "Personal Fouls," the work of New York writer Peter Golenbock and former NC State team manager John Simonds.

Two days later, Valvano and Chancellor Bruce Poulton requested that the NCAA investigate the charges, which included point-shaving, grade-fixing and drug use. UNC System president C.D.

Spangler ordered an internal inquiry. The NC State Faculty Senate ordered a third probe. After nearly a year of investigation, almost daily newspaper reports and full cooperation by Valvano and his team, the NCAA found two major violations and three minor ones.

The major violations had nothing to do with the wild allegations made by Golenbock's book, which was largely discredited because of its multiple errors and broad inaccuracies. Its original publisher, in fact, refused to release the book because it did not live up to the company's standards.

Throughout the remainder of the 1988–89 season, the Wolfpack closed ranks — and finished in sole possession of first place in the ACC standings, the only time that happened during Valvano's decade-long tenure at the school.

"That year was a blur, because there was so much going on," said Corchiani. "It was my most enjoyable year because of all the distractions and adversity. Coach V was always rallying the troops, trying to get us to keep our heads up. The life lessons from that year are something I will never forget. Our team had a special chemistry. We rallied behind Coach V. All the negativity, we put it in a bottle and when we got on the court, we let it go."

In the first round of the ACC Tournament in Atlanta, the Wolfpack became the first No. 1 seed to ever lose in the ACC quarterfinals, falling to last-place Maryland.

Valvano and his team went on the road for the NCAA Tournament, beating South Carolina and Iowa in Providence, R.I. In one of the coach's most controversial losses, the Wolfpack lost to Georgetown

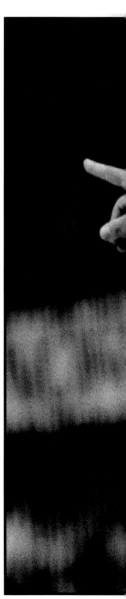

in the East Regional semifinals in East Ruther-
ford, N.J., when official Rick Hartzell called
Corchiani for traveling on a play that could have
been Hoya star Alonzo Mourning's fifth foul.
Veteran television announcer Billy Packer called
it "the worst call in the history of the NCAA
Tournament," a comment he still stands by long
after his retirement from the broadcast booth.

That was the last game Valvano ever coached
in the NCAA Tournament.

In December 1989, the NCAA announced
a one-year probation for Valvano's program,
primarily because it found that players frequently
sold complimentary tickets and shoes provided
to them by the university. Initially, Valvano felt
vindicated that although the NCAA came look-

ing for large ethical problems throughout the program, it found only relatively minor compliance issues.

But there was still the ongoing cloud of the Poole Commission, the special committee appointed by UNC System President C.D. Spangler to conduct an internal investigation into the NC State basketball program. When its findings were released, there were no substantial transgressions. Reports of grade-fixing and outright cheating were dismissed. But, just like the 1960s point-shaving scandal that killed the Dixie Classic, the system administrators were taken aback at the lack of control within the program, especially when it came to maintaining academic eligibility. "The system has been misused," Spangler said. "The spirit, not the letter of the law, has been broken."

Under intense scrutiny from media and university system administrators, Poulton resigned in the fall of 1989, primarily because he agreed with Valvano's lawyers not to cooperate with the Poole Commission. Valvano returned for the 1989–90 season, but he and his team were dogged throughout about his future with the program. Valvano offered to coach the 1990–91 season for $1, but the school's board of trustees turned him down.

On April 7, 1990, Valvano stepped down, after 10 years, one national championship, seven NCAA Tournament appearances, two ACC Tournament titles and a pair of first-place finishes in the ACC regular-season standings. His dream of winning the national title was accomplished, but his spirit was broken and his image tarnished.

He finally took a job as a color commentator for ESPN and ABC, working with Vitale and John Saunders. Not surprisingly, over the next two years, he became one of television's most popular analysts.

While on vacation in Spain in the spring of 1992, Valvano lacked energy and felt poorly, much the same way Everett Case felt throughout

1964. He returned home for a checkup and had an MRI at Duke University. The results were devastating: doctors diagnosed metastatic adenocarcinoma, an aggressive form of cancer that is almost always fatal when detected in its latter stages.

Valvano was bitterly disappointed that he was not able to chase more of his dreams, though not long before he died, his wife found a new note card in a jacket pocket: "Find a cure for cancer." Soon thereafter, his friends at ESPN founded the V Foundation for Cancer Research.

On Feb. 21, 1993, prior to a nationally televised game between NC State and Duke, Valvano returned to Reynolds Coliseum for a 10-year celebration of the 1983 Cardiac Pack. Everyone knew it was a final goodbye.

As he sat in the basement of the coliseum, not far from where he had that initial meeting with his first team, Valvano was a sick man, and nothing was going to make him better. He was unable to climb the 23 steps to the coliseum floor. Between the vomiting and the fatigue, there was no way he could possibly address the sell-out crowd that ached to see him on the court one last time.

"I can't make it," he told veteran NC State golf coach Richard Sykes. "I can't do it."

Somehow, leaning on the shoulders of several friends from the athletics department, he made it up the stairs, gaining strength as he heard the buzzing crowd, as

With the news media and Chris Corchiani in tow, Jim Valvano leaves the Reynolds Coliseum floor after his last home game coaching for the Wolfpack.

so many of his players did during the glory days of his coaching career.

On the court, most of the members of the 1983 team were waiting to shake his hand. One by one, he hugged them. When he arrived at the end of the line, he saw Bailey. The man who was ready to give up just a few minutes before found the strength to step onto a folding chair and whisper in Bailey's ear, "I love you."

For the next 20 minutes, Valvano stood in front of 12,400 sets of weeping eyes and spoke about his most famous team.

"The '83 team taught me about dreaming and the importance of dreams, because nothing can happen if not first a dream," he said. "If you have someone who never gives up, who has great hope. . . . Don't ever give up, don't ever stop fighting! The '83 team gave you hope, gave you pride, told you what hard work was about. It gave you

the meaning of believing in a cause, and lastly what they taught me is to love each other. They taught me what love means. When you have a goal, when you have a dream, and when you have belief, and you throw in that concept of never stop believing in and loving each other, you can accomplish miracles."

At 10:30 a.m. on April 28, 1993, barely 10 years after he helped cut down the nets in Albuquerque, Valvano died quietly in his room at Duke University Hospital. He was just 47 years old.

Some say the coach lost his battle against cancer that day. Today, however, the V Foundation is one of the most successful charities in the nation. In less than 20 years, it has raised more than $100 million to fund research grants to up-and-coming doctors.

Valvano didn't lose his fight against cancer when he died. He started it.

LOWE

From Valvano's floor coach to the Wolfpack's head coach, Sidney Lowe knows how to hold court

Sidney Lowe coached his first basketball game before his college playing career was even over.

Truth be told, he was so adept at running NC State's team as a point guard, he could have gotten an assistant's salary from the day he stepped on campus, had it not been against NCAA rules.

One game in particular, however, stands out as the foreshadowing of his chosen profession. It was the opening round game of the 1983 NCAA Tournament, when Lowe fouled out against Pepperdine in the first of two overtimes. With his team down by as many as six points and freshman George McClain in charge of the team, Lowe joined head coach Jim Valvano on the sidelines, giving directions for the team to make

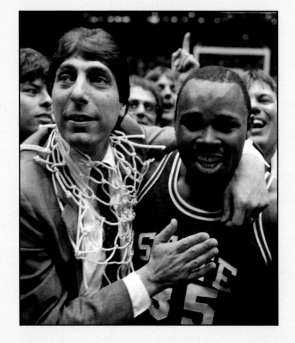

a comeback. McClain made two critical plays down the stretch, and the Wolfpack advanced to the next round.

The team didn't stop winning until it beat Houston in the national title game, thanks in large part to Lowe's guidance on the court.

Lowe, a native of Washington, D.C., was born to be a point guard, and by extension, a coach.

"He understood the game so thoroughly," said his high school coach, Naismith Memorial Hall of Fame inductee Morgan Wootten. "He made everybody else better. He made everybody else believe in themselves. He wanted to be part of something greater than himself. He left his ego at the door.

"When Sidney had

BEHOLD

the ball in his hands, you knew everything was going to be all right."

Both Norm Sloan and Valvano discovered that same comfort when they coached the stocky young guard. He entered the starting lineup as a freshman and never relinquished the job. By the time he was a senior, Lowe was prohibited from coming out of the game at all.

"You can come out when your eligibility is up," Valvano told him every time he held up the tired signal.

He split the leadership duties on the national championship team with fellow seniors Dereck Whittenburg and Thurl Bailey, but his role was to be the brains of the outfit. He had permission from Valvano to call any play at any time and was frequently

more in tune with what would and would not work against any given opponent than either Valvano or his paid assistants.

Becoming a coach was a no-brainer for Lowe, even though he took an irregular route on his way to becoming the head coach at NC State. He spent 23 years playing and coaching in the professional ranks. He won three championships in the Continental Basketball Association as a player and was twice the head coach of National Basketball Association franchises.

He eagerly accepted the opportunity to return to NC State on May 6, 2006, when he was named the 16th coach in school history.

"I know I am the right person for this job," Lowe said. "Basketball-wise, I have

had the experience of being in the game for a long time. I have played this game on [the college level] and on the highest level and in the biggest national championship game ever. That is something I can pass on to our players."

In Lowe's first season, he beat North Carolina on the Wolfpack's home court, debuting a bright red blazer that has become his trademark. It's not quite as flashy as the plaid jackets Sloan used to wear or the handmade Italian suits Valvano was known to sport on the sidelines, but it helped him establish his identity as the Wolfpack's leader. At the end of his inaugural year, the Wolfpack played in the ACC Tournament finals, falling just short of accomplishing the difficult task of winning four games in four days.

He joined Everett Case (1954), Press Maravich (1965) and Herb Sendek (1997) as coaches who played for the championship in their first ACC Tournament, something that has happened only six times in the history of the league.

Lowe has proven to be an excellent recruiter who has expanded his knowledge of the nuances of the college game. He is prepared to lead the Wolfpack into its next century, following in the successful footsteps of those who came before him.

UP PLAYER

What if Lorenzo Charles had never come to NC State? Would there have been a Cardiac Pack? Could Destiny's Darlings have pulled off one of the biggest upsets in college basketball history without him?

Fortunately for NC State fans, they will never have to find out, because then–Wolfpack head coach Jim Valvano made Charles a late addition to his first real recruiting class. The group included a pair of prep All-Americas in Mike Warren of Raleigh's Broughton High School and Walter "Dinky" Proctor from Rutgers Prep in New Jersey; highly regarded but raw center Cozell McQueen and Terry Gannon, an undersized throw-in from the baseball program.

They all made their mark on the program, but Charles will be remembered forever for his split-second decision at the end of the 1983 NCAA Championship game. Standing under the basket — badly out of position against Houston's Akeem Olajuwon — he saw that Dereck Whittenburg's 28-foot jumper was going to be way too short.

The sophomore forward leapt up and stuffed the ball through the basket to win the school's second national title. Some three decades later, that dunk is still the most famous play in NCAA Championship game history and an iconic symbol for the underdog.

Charles is a little surprised that people remember a simple reactionary play.

"I had no idea that people would still be talking about that shot for this long," Charles said.

Charles almost didn't make it to NC State. Valvano and his staff showed some initial interest in the forward from Brooklyn Tech High School, but Charles had a subpar performance in the Newsday Classic and the Wolfpack backed off, despite the claims of local reporters who called Charles "the sleeper of the East." Valvano

came back into the picture just before Charles signed with the University of Massachusetts.

Charles was badly out of shape when he arrived in Raleigh for his freshman year and rarely left the bench. He improved enough as a sophomore — thanks to McQueen's insistence that Charles join him in the weight room — to earn a starting position. But he didn't really begin to contribute until senior Dereck Whittenburg suffered a broken foot in mid-January. That forced Charles to step up his productivity in scoring and rebounding.

"After two years, I woke up," Charles said.

By the time the Wolfpack played in the postseason, Charles was a more mature, refined player, capable of doing the remarkable. In the Wolfpack's nine-game postseason run to the national championship, Charles made three game-winning plays, scoring late free throws against Wake Forest in the ACC Tournament and Virginia in the NCAA West Region Finals and the famous play against Houston.

As a junior and senior, Charles matured into one of the ACC's most feared performers, twice earning first-team all-conference honors. He was twice voted runner-up in the race for ACC Player of the Year honors, coming in second to North Carolina's Michael Jordan and Maryland's Len Bias. Charles, a second-round draft pick by the Atlanta Hawks, played professional basketball for more than a dozen years, mostly overseas.

He returned to the Raleigh area after his playing career ended, and there hasn't been a day since when someone fails to ask him about his game-winning dunk.

And he continues to be surprised when people remember.

OF MIGHT AND MAN

Head and shoulders above the rest, Thurl Bailey proves good guys finish first

Thurl Bailey was the ultimate late bloomer, a basketball player who came to NC State with high aspirations in life but never seriously considering a career in professional basketball.

"When I came to NC State, I wasn't really thinking about the NBA," said Bailey, who was twice cut from his junior high school basketball team. "I was a late starter. I didn't really start playing until I was in high school. Of course, every kid who plays sports wants to be the best. I was no different, but I didn't spend a lot of time thinking about it.

"I was more thinking that I could be governor or senator one day."

He had other options as well, including his deep baritone singing voice, his abilities to play the trombone and the trumpet or the acting abilities that once put his name in lights—when he had a lead role in the campus production of *Of Mice And Men*, which was produced at Thompson Theater, the former home of Wolfpack basketball.

Instead, the 6-11 forward blossomed so much on the basketball court that the Utah Jazz made him the No. 7 pick of the 1983 NBA draft. Wolfpack coach Jim Valvano made a personal recommendation to Jazz president Frank Layden. "Don't think of him as just a player," Valvano said. "As a person, he will be good for your team and community."

Bailey played professionally in three different countries for a total of 16 years, the longest pro career of any former Wolfpack player. Afterward, he returned

to Salt Lake City, converted to Mormonism and became one of the most high-profile speakers in the state.

Bailey credits his long career to the Wolfpack's remarkable run to the 1983 NCAA championship. During nine postseason games, the native of Seat Pleasant, Md.,

showed the world his sweet outside jumper, his remarkable ability to run the floor and his nose for making big plays. He and fellow seniors Sidney Lowe and Dereck Whittenburg were the perfect leadership triumvirate, with Bailey serving as the team's heart, freely letting tears stream down his face after emotional victories.

His efforts were particularly important in the wins over Nevada–Las Vegas and in the first half of the championship game against Houston, when he scored 15 points and helped the Wolfpack build an eight-point lead against the top-ranked and heavily favored Cougars. "It really wasn't until after we won the championship that I thought I might have a shot of being drafted," he said.

The fact is, Bailey might have profited from the Wolfpack's title more than anyone other than Valvano. His fame helped him record several inspirational albums and develop his own clothing line.

As a player for the Jazz for more than 10 seasons, Bailey is a well-known figure. He even does commentary on the franchise's postgame television show. But more often than not, when he is stopped on the streets in Salt Lake City, people ask him about his senior year at NC State, when he and his teammates surprised Houston in the championship game.

"I just always believed in a higher power, especially during the year of the championship," Bailey said. "There is no way that anybody could ever tell me that there wasn't divine intervention involved. We had to do our parts and use our God-given talents, but it wasn't just luck. I think we were instruments. I think we transcended normal basketball."

HURT SO GOOD

*An unfortunate injury
for Dereck Whittenburg turns out
to be a blessing for
the Wolfpack*

Dereck Whittenburg was the heart of NC State's 1983 NCAA championship team, a player so important that head coach Jim Valvano thought his team's season was over when Whittenburg suffered what was thought to be a career-ending broken foot against Virginia on Jan. 19, 1983.

Whittenburg never believed that. He had suffered a similar injury as a senior at DeMatha Catholic High School in Hyattsville, Md., and returned quickly enough to rejoin teammate Sidney Lowe and lead the team to the Washington, D.C., city championship.

Around the same time, Whittenburg met his famous distant cousin, former Wolfpack All-America David Thompson, when the latter came to town with the Denver Nuggets to play the Washington Bullets.

"I heard you are going to State," Thompson told the young relative he had never met before. "It's a great place. I think you will do well there. You are going, right?"

"I am now," Whittenburg said.

Like Thompson, Whittenburg was known for his hops. He didn't have the former three-time college player of the year's 44-inch vertical leap, but the 6-1 Whittenburg did get high off the ground on his jump shots. He also moved farther and farther away from the basket, taking shots from so far out because no one guarded him there.

He thrived with the ACC's experimental three-point shot during his senior year, right up until he broke his foot. In the end, it might have been the team's biggest blessing, since it allowed Whittenburg the opportunity to sit back and watch as his teammates improved and gained confidence during his absence.

"Me getting hurt really helped the development of the team," Whittenburg said.

Especially when he saw someone goofing off or loafing.

That's when he would get in their face, slap them on the butt or inspire them to work harder. He didn't want anyone loitering when he finally returned to the lineup.

By the time the postseason arrived, Whittenburg was ready to roll. Though he was relatively quiet in the ACC Tournament, his overtime performance against North Carolina helped the Wolfpack advance to the championship game. In the NCAA Tournament, his performance in the two games against Utah and Virginia in the West Regional in Ogden, Utah, earned him the regional's most valuable player award.

While Bailey and Lowe had lengthy professional careers, Whittenburg chose to return to NC State after a brief time in the pros and pursue his dreams of being a coach. He was an assistant under Valvano until 1990, then moved to Georgia Tech to work for Bobby Cremins. He has been head coach at both Wagner and Fordham.

Whittenburg doesn't mind at all that he will forever be remembered for making the most famous air ball in NCAA Tournament history.

"If you listen to the broadcasts of that play, whether it is radio or television, all you hear them say is 'Whittenburg takes the shot . . .'" he said, laughing. "They don't even have time to mention Lorenzo Charles. So I don't mind. My name is the one they mention on the most famous play in college basketball history."

In all seriousness, though, the run to the 1983 championship means everything to him.

"There hasn't been a day in my life in the 27 years since that game that someone hasn't brought that play up to me," Whittenburg said. "It grows more and more special every day. It humbles you, makes you appreciate that people can remember where they were and what they were doing when we won that game and how it has affected so many people in such a positive way."

The Road to Destiny Runs

Fittingly, the greatest three-day run, which was followed by the greatest three-week run, in the history of NC State basketball began with the Wolfpack's oldest rival, Wake Forest.

The two teams had traded blowouts in the regular-season, with the Demon Deacons winning 91-73 in Greensboro, and the Wolfpack, just six days earlier, humiliating Carl Tacy's team 130-89. It was unlikely that it would happen again.

After 35 ½ minutes of play in the first round of the 1983 ACC Tournament in Atlanta, during which both teams squandered double-digit leads, the Wolfpack and Demon Deacons were tied at 70. That's when Tacy decided to hold the ball for the last shot, the exact thing the ACC had tried to stop before the season started. The year before, North Carolina had beaten Virginia 47-45, in a slowdown championship game that forced the college basketball world to finally address stall-ball. So the ACC adopted an experimental 30-second shot clock and a 17-foot, 9-inch three-point line.

But the clock was turned off at the four-minute mark, and the Deacons could hold as long as they wanted. With 31 seconds remaining, Tacy called time out to set up his final play. Before they ever took a shot, Wake Forest forward Alvis Rogers tried a cross-court pass that was deflected by Wolfpack point guard Sidney Lowe and intercepted by Thurl Bailey.

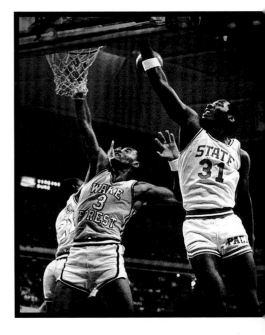

Through Atlanta

Lowe slowed down the 2-on-1 break, called a time-out and went to Valvano for advice. The coach called the same play he always used in these situations: he put the ball in the hands of his senior point guard, sent two shooters to the wings and positioned his two big men inside for a potential rebound. Then he told Lowe to make something happen.

Lowe drove into the lane, drew a double-team and bounced the ball to sophomore teammate Lorenzo Charles, who was wide open on the baseline. Charles, who had blossomed into a confident player in the absence of injured senior Dereck Whittenburg, took two steps on the baseline and drew a foul from Rogers.

A nervous Charles stepped to the line and missed the first of the two free throws. Earlier in the year, that might have ruined any chance he had of making the second, but by now the 67-percent free-throw shooter was mature enough to make a slight adjustment to his stance and calmly make the game-winning free throw.

That single point gets lost because of the two game-winning shots he made in the NCAA Tournament, but without it, the history of the 1983 postseason would have been much different.

Realistically, Valvano's team needed one more win to secure a spot in the NCAA Tournament, and that win would have to come against defending national champion North Carolina. For three years, Dean Smith's team had been Valvano's Achilles Heels. He lost his first nine games to UNC. But that changed earlier in the season when the Wolfpack celebrated a raucous win in Reynolds Coliseum, taking a 70-63 decision after Smith was hit with two first-half technical fouls and Michael Jordan fouled out of the game.

That win came without Whittenburg in the lineup — he was still on the sidelines recovering from his broken foot, but well enough to help his teammates cut down the nets following the victory.

UNC had won its first-round game against Clemson without injured All-America Sam Perkins, but he returned to the lineup against the Wolfpack. Perkins played better in regulation than Whitten-

burg did. State's senior captain had missed seven of his nine field goal attempts, whiffed on all five of his three-point attempts and scored just four points.

But a couple of things were on the Wolfpack's side when the first 40 minutes ended tied at 70. Seniors Lowe and Bailey were carrying their teammates, and Jordan, for the second consecutive game against the Wolfpack, had fouled out.

The Wolfpack's chances of going to the NCAA Tournament seemed to end in the first three minutes of overtime, as North Carolina built a six-point lead. It was the kind of run Tar Heel opponents rarely recover from, especially since Smith began cherry-picking the Wolfpack's worst free-throw shooters and sending them to the line.

Even Valvano, Mr. Never Give Up, was not sure his team could come back. "There was a time on the bench when we thought we had lost," the coach admitted to the me-

dia afterwards. "We let down a little bit, and I felt like we were going to lose."

What Valvano's team needed was a miracle. What they got was several of them. First, tiny Terry Gannon, the smallest player on the court, boxed out Sam Perkins for an offensive rebound. Perkins was called for over-the-back, Gannon made a pair of free throws and the lead wasn't quite so intimidating. North Carolina's Curtis Hunter, a 94-percent free-throw shooter, missed the front end of a one-and-one. Freshman George McClain, in for his only possession of the game because Lowe had the breath knocked out of him, found the exceedingly quiet Whittenburg on the wing for an open three-pointer that cut the lead to just one point with 1:36 to play. And UNC's Jimmy Braddock missed his team's third consecutive front end of a one-and-one.

By now, Whittenburg was fully awake. He dribbled past three Tar Heel defenders for the go-ahead layup. He scored two points on free throws when Perkins fouled out. He and Bailey added six more free throws at the end of the game.

Whittenburg single-handedly wiped out the Tar Heels' six-point lead by scoring nine consecutive points. The Wolfpack outscored its biggest rival 15-2 in the overtime, a stunning turnabout that led to Valvano's second career victory over Smith. Whittenburg scored 11 of his 15 points in the extra period and the team made 12 consecutive free throws.

Remarkably, the Tar Heels all but gave up with two minutes to play, and Valvano thought he knew why: "We had more to gain from this than they did," the coach said.

With four seconds still on the clock, Whittenburg ran to the sidelines for an extended embrace with Valvano, celebrating another comeback win. NCAA selection committee members Dave Gavitt and Vic Bubas confirmed many years later that the

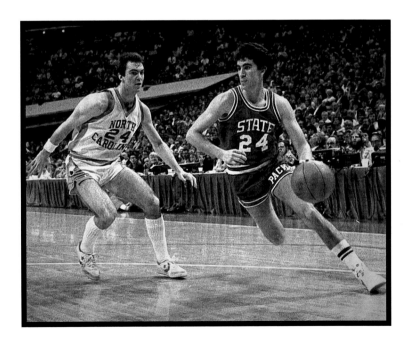

NC State win over the Tar Heels assured the Wolfpack a bid into the tournament. But Valvano wanted to make sure. "Guys, I'll tell you what — if we win this game, we are definitely in."

But, at the time, Virginia had the biggest obstacle in the nation, 7-4 senior center Ralph Sampson, who was desperate to win his first ACC Championship. And for all that had been made of Valvano's lack of success against North Carolina, the coach was also winless in his NC State career against the Cavaliers.

The Cavaliers limped into the final game, with Tim Mullen out of the lineup with a knee injury and Sampson recovering from a bruised jaw he suffered the day before. So the Wolfpack raced out to a 12-1 lead, led by point guard Lowe, who was still hot after posting a career-high 26 points against the Tar Heels.

Valvano packed a zone defense on Sampson and had Whittenburg chase Virginia point guard Othell Wilson all over the court. Sampson, despite the Wolfpack's best efforts, was all but unstoppable and he quickly erased State's early lead. He scored 18 points and had nine rebounds before the first half ended. The only way the Wolfpack stayed in the game was the outside shooting of Gannon, the sophomore guard, whose three-pointer just before the buzzer cut Virginia's lead to 40-37.

With 11:51 remaining in the game, Virginia stretched its lead to 59-51, Whittenburg picked up his fourth foul and the crowd at the Omni began to believe Sampson finally was going to win the championship that had long eluded him. But the big man needed his usual second-half sabbatical, so Terry Holland replaced him in the lineup with Kenton Edelin and told him to guard Bailey.

That proved to be an impossible task

for the 6-9 walk-on forward. Sampson was out of the game for only three minutes, but Bailey scored three quick jumpers, including his only three-pointer of the game, to give NC State the lead.

What happened next will long be remembered in ACC Tournament lore: with a little over five minutes to play, Virginia assistant coach Jim Larranaga was whistled for a technical foul for arguing about a loose ball. The free throws that Whittenburg hit were part of a 13-1 scoring run that allowed the Wolfpack to build a 75-66 lead with four minutes to play.

A tired Wolfpack offense played sloppily at the end of the game, allowing Virginia to draw within three points with less than a minute to play. So Valvano's team needed a big defensive play to secure the win, and it came from the unlikeliest source on the court. Gannon, all of 6-1,

caught Sampson unaware, and stripped the ball out of his hands.

"I had no business stealing the ball from Ralph Sampson, and V let me know it," Gannon said. "Afterwards he told me, 'That was a really stupid play. What the hell did you think you were going to do, block his shot? It was a stupid, stupid thing to do. Great job though.'"

In the end, Sampson's 24 points and 12 rebounds were not a factor in the game. Bailey matched Sampson's scoring total and Charles, for the third consecutive game, had double-digit rebounds. Over the final 7:48 — when his team needed him the most — Sampson did not score, a disappearing act that would haunt the center for years.

The Wolfpack finished off the Cavaliers at the free-throw line to secure the school's ninth ACC championship.

The NCAA Tournament was next.

Call it Fate. Call it Luck.
Call it Destiny. Call it Divine Intervention.
Does not matter what it's called, they're...

Predictions are a lot like playing the lottery: everyone forgets the outcome until you hit a big jackpot.

And that's what happened to Jim Valvano and NC State in the 1983 NCAA Tournament, a six-game miracle run that has been boiled down over the years to a single play: Lorenzo Charles's dunk of a missed Dereck Whittenburg jumpshot against Houston in the final seconds of the title game.

But college basketball's called-shot was so much more than that. It was the wildest roadshow ever created, with a cast of characters that included the loquacious Valvano, his motley group of players and a one-legged mascot named Cap'n Jim they found along the way.

Valvano picked the numbers on his personal lottery ticket late one evening in nearly empty Gill Coliseum in Corvallis, Ore., and showed them to a couple of newspaper reporters from North Carolina who happened to straggle in after the team finished its practice the day before the opening-round game against Pepperdine.

Valvano and his team were still rid-ing an emotional high from winning the ACC Tournament in Atlanta. But traveling across country to play the Waves, an excellent team from the Western Athletic Conference, was probably a bigger task than any of the Wolfpack players imagined.

"They are a scary team," Valvano told the reporters. "But I'll tell you what, if we win this game, we're going to go all the way."

There is still some dispute among the reporters about whether Valvano meant "all the way" to the Final Four in Albuquerque, N.M., or "all the way" to the national championship. Whatever the case, Valvano kind of wished he hadn't said it. He swore the reporters to secrecy.

For the next three weeks, every time Valvano led his team to another unlikely win, the reporters would nudge each other and say, "Remember what V said in Corvallis."

The start of the journey was crazy. The Pack was housed in the dumpy Riverfront Motel, with a shady proprietor on a barstool in the restaurant and a double-decker tour bus in the parking

NATIONAL CHAMPS!

Sidney Lowe and Thurl Bailey celebrate winning the West Region
championship over Virginia and their impending trip to the Final Four.

lot. It was about as far from the Marriott Marquis, where the team stayed for the ACC Tournament, as the players thought possible.

Pepperdine was indeed a difficult first-round opponent, with a trio of tall, athletic players who created mismatches for the Wolfpack. And Valvano's team was hardly into the game, after a draining transcontinental trip and the overall lack of enthusiasm in an arena that was only three-quarters of the way full.

The Pack missed its first 12 shots and played lethargically throughout the game.

Whittenburg popped off at an official late in regulation and was hit with a technical foul. Fortunately for the Wolfpack, Pepperdine played no better and with 12 seconds remaining in regulation, the game was tied. Valvano went to his standard play, the same one he used against Wake Forest to win the first round of the ACC Tournament and the same one he would use on final possessions in two more games in coming weeks: point guard Sidney Lowe with the ball, guards Whittenburg and Terry Gannon on the wings and Lorenzo Charles and Thurl Bailey under the basket.

But Lowe, the Pack's quarterback for four consecutive seasons and the ACC's newly crowned career assist leader, was trapped on the sidelines and his team never even managed to take a shot.

In overtime, Pepperdine jumped out to a quick, seemingly insurmountable six-point lead, mainly because the Wolfpack fell apart. On the sidelines, the Waves' bench broke into an early celebration. When Lowe tried to make a backcourt steal with 48 seconds left on the clock, he was called for his fifth foul and the Wolfpack's fate was all but sealed, as the Waves had a four-point lead.

Valvano was forced to insert rusty freshman George McClain, who had barely played 20 minutes in the team's last eight games, into the lineup to replace Lowe. On his first offensive possession, the nervous youngster threw the ball right into the hands of a Pepperdine player, who was so surprised at what happened, he stumbled and turned the ball right back over to McClain. The Wolfpack scored on Gannon's long jumper, but, really, all Pepperdine had to do was make a few free throws and the game was over.

As several Wolfpack opponents discovered in the 1983 postseason, that was easier said than done. On back-to-back possessions, Pepperdine's Dane Suttle, an 84.6-percent free-throw shooter, missed the front end of one-and-one opportunities. On the first, McClain zipped the ball downcourt to Thurl Bailey for a dunk. On the second, McClain found a wide-open Whittenburg near the baseline, where he was fouled by Suttle before he could take a shot with nine seconds to play. Whittenburg missed his first free throw, but sophomore center Cozell McQueen reached above all the other players on the court for the rebound and hit a soft fadeaway jumper to tie the game. It was his only basket of the game.

In the second overtime, Pepperdine stopped celebrating. Whittenburg made eight free throws and the Wolfpack sneaked away with a 69-67 win.

"Of all the games we played that year, Pepperdine was the most important," Bailey said. "I still don't know how we won that game."

Two days later, an inspired Bailey helped the Wolfpack beat an even more formidable opponent, No. 3 seed Nevada–

Las Vegas. Bailey had been taunted by UNLV forward Sidney Green, who brashly said Bailey didn't much impress him.

Bailey was certainly impressed as Green helped his team build a 12-point second-half lead. Lowe was in foul trouble again and Whittenburg was struggling from the field, so Bailey took over the game, hitting three quick jumpers. The Runnin' Rebels, leading by one, could have put the game out of reach with 32 seconds to play, but Valvano had his team foul UNLV freshman Eldridge Hudson for a one-and-one opportunity.

Hudson, just like Suttle, missed and the Wolfpack had a chance to win the game. Whittenburg raced down the court and took a 16-foot jumper that missed its mark. But Bailey, even though he was blocked out by Green, was there to tip the ball up towards the basket twice, with the second one falling in to give his team a 71-70 win.

Even Green was impressed.

Valvano decided to keep his team out West instead of traveling back to Raleigh, so he sent them on to Ogden, Utah, site of the West Region finals, while he and his wife went to Las Vegas for a few days. History doesn't record if Valvano won any money while he was there, but if there was ever a time in his life to roll the dice, this was it, since he was in the middle of a three-week turn at the table in which he never crapped out.

Though they trailed by double digits in the second half of both games, the Wolfpack rolled over Utah and squeaked by Virginia in the regional championship game. In the latter, the Wolfpack again took advantage of poor free-throw shooting by an opponent in the final stages of the game to eliminate their familiar foe and end the career of All-America center Ralph Sampson.

Valvano brought his team back to Raleigh briefly, basically so everyone could get a new set of clean clothes. They received a huge send-off from students and fans around Raleigh, just before they headed to Albuquerque for the Final Four.

With Whittenburg suffering from a bout with the flu, the Wolfpack qualified for the national championship game by beating Georgia with relative ease in the Saturday semifinals. But it also caught a glimpse of the day's marquee game, Houston vs. Louisville. Rarely has there ever been such a display of athleticism as Houston's "Phi Slama Jama" faced off against Louisville's "Doctors of Dunk." Houston, the nation's top-ranked team, eventually pulled away in the dunk fest for its 26th consecutive victory, behind the play of center Akeem Olajuwon and forward Clyde Drexler.

Everyone who watched the game was convinced that the winner could be easily penciled in as the national champion. NC State had no chance. The only real competition remaining was among the sportswriters, who struggled to find new ways to preview the Wolfpack's doomed fate.

Dave Kindred of *The Washington Post* wrote: "Trees will tap dance, elephants will ride in the Indianapolis 500, and Orson Welles will skip breakfast, lunch and dinner before State finds a way to beat Houston."

Joe Henderson of *The Tampa Tribune* wrote: "Rain would make it perfect. It always rains at an execution."

David Casstevens of *The Dallas Morning News* said, with authority: "Anyone who watched Houston dunk over Louisville either is blindly partisan or kidding himself to think the Cougars can be beaten. Once upon a time they could. But not now. No way."

Ah, just what college basketball needed: a fairy tale that started with "once upon a time."

Houston coach Guy Lewis made a snarky prediction, saying the team with the most dunks would win the championship. Valvano told everyone who listened that if the Wolfpack won the tap in the national title game, it would hold the ball until sometime early Tuesday morning. But he had a completely different game plan for his team.

"If you think we have come all this way, won all these close games, and made it to the national championship just to hold the ball in front of 50 million people," Valvano said, "you are out of your [expletive] minds."

The team bolted out of the locker room and charged right at the most fearsome opponent they faced all season, the top-ranked Cougars.

Valvano's strategy did not work. His team missed 15 shots in the first six min-utes of the game. The only reasons the Wolfpack stayed in the game were Bailey's 15 points, which began with a dunk on the game's opening play, and the fact that Lewis left a future Hall of Fame player, Drexler, on the court after he picked up his third foul. Drexler grabbed a rebound and went one-on-one with tiny Terry Gannon, who stood his ground on the fast break, wrapped his arms around the high-flying Drexler and waited to see what kind of foul would be called.

The officials said charging, waving off the basket and sending Drexler to the bench with his fourth foul well before halftime. Despite Valvano's pre-game pep talk, the game was indeed played at a slow pace and the Wolfpack owned a 33-25 lead at the half.

Houston raced out of the gates in the second half, scoring at will during a 17-2 run that included a dunk by Olajuwon that tied the game's total of dunks at one apiece. More important, midway through the second half, the Cougars led by as many as seven points.

Lewis, a hard-luck coach who was making his fourth appearance in the Final Four with the Cougars, made the decision to slow the game down, because his players were winded in Albuquerque's mile-high altitude. Olajuwon and several teammates were on the bench during a time-out sucking on an oxygen tank, something the Wolfpack players were forbidden to do by trainer Jim Rehbock.

The slowdown allowed Valvano to reset his strategy. He stopped trying to go inside and put the ball in the hands of his three guards, Lowe, Whittenburg and Gannon. Houston covered the latter two, but the scouting report said to leave Lowe open. He burned the Cougars with three straight jumpshots at one point, and Whittenburg added another two to tie the game at 52-52 with two minutes to play.

Houston hoped to hold the ball for a final shot, but Valvano, the master of the fouling strategy, wasn't about to let that

happen. With 1:05 left on the clock, Whittenburg fouled Houston freshman guard Alvin Franklin, a 60-percent free throw shooter. Franklin nervously stepped to the line and badly missed the front end of a one-and-one. McQueen snagged the rebound while falling out of bounds, getting the ball to Lowe.

With 44 seconds showing on the clock, the Wolfpack called a time-out. Valvano set his usual strategy, putting the ball in Lowe's hands, putting Whittenburg and Gannon on the wings and Bailey and Charles under the basket.

What followed was the worst possession of the season for Valvano's team, which was not prepared when Houston came out in a 1-3-1 half-court trap. As the clock slowly ticked down, the frustrated Wolfpack made 19 passes, four of which were nearly intercepted.

The players not only passed — they passed up opportunities to take shots.

Bailey, caught in the corner with seven seconds to play, hurled the ball outside to Whittenburg, who made a two-handed catch to prevent Houston's Benny Anders from stealing the ball and making an uncontested layup.

Most college basketball fans know what happened next — Whittenburg put up a desperation jump shot from 28 feet away that came up two feet short. He likes to say it was the 20th pass in the possession, but deep inside, everyone knows the truth.

Lorenzo Charles, who had made just one basket all night long, grabbed the airball and in one quick motion dunked it into the basket.

The Wolfpack not only won the game, 54-52, it also won the dunk contest, 2-1, making the predictions of both coaches come true.

Valvano went on a looping trot around the court looking for someone to hug. And the city of Raleigh began a celebration that has never been matched.

Nearly three decades later, that title is still

remembered as a turning point in the history of March Madness. It made the underdog fashionable, just like three years before, when the United States hockey team upset the Soviet Union in the Olympics.

No team in college basketball history has ever had a run through its conference tournament and the six games of the NCAA Tournament that could match what the Wolfpack did, from the one-point win over Wake Forest in the opening round of the ACC Tournament to the last shot of the final game. In eight of the nine games, the Wolfpack trailed at some point in the second half. Seven of the games either went into overtime or were decided in the final minute.

What Valvano and his team — nicknamed the "Cardiac Pack" and "Destiny's Darlings" — did was give hope to every underdog that followed. Now, every David who hears his name called on Selection Sunday knows there is chance to knock out Goliath.

Because NC State did it in 1983.

The Dunker

He was the high-flying satellite that nearly cost NC State assistant coach Tom Abatemarco his job.

Anthony Jerome "Spud" Webb arrived on a plane from Dallas, Texas, just weeks after the Wolfpack won the 1983 NCAA Championship, a highly touted point guard who head coach Jim Valvano hoped would be a capable replacement for the linebacker-like Sidney Lowe.

Valvano was anxious to meet the 1983 JUCO All-America who had led Midland (Texas) Junior College to the 1982 NJCAA championship, mainly because Abatemarco insisted he would be a worthy successor to the most prolific point guard in ACC history. Webb was a driving madman, who had nearly 100 dunks and several goal-tending calls from the point guard position during his junior college career.

Valvano had big — and tall — expectations.

But when a 5-6 kid who looked like he was from a junior high, not a junior college, walked off the airplane at Raleigh-Durham International Airport, Valvano turned to Abatemarco and said: "If that's Spud Webb, you're fired."

What Valvano didn't see in that first glance at Webb — whose family called him "Spud" in honor of the tiny Russian satellite "Sputnik" — was just how high he could jump and just how motivated he was, after being told countless times that he was too small to succeed.

Both in college and in a dozen NBA seasons, Webb always elevated himself above the competition.

In his first game with the Wolfpack, a rematch of the 1983 title game against Houston in the Tip-Off Classic, Webb showed that there will always be a place for small players with big hearts. The Wolfpack repeated its upset of the Cougars and All-America center Akeem Olajuwon, 76-64, thanks to the speedy Webb's hustle.

For two mercurial years, Webb guided the Wolfpack offense, using a different approach than what Valvano was used to. He could hit an outside shot, but he preferred to penetrate, thrusting his frail-looking body against the redwoods.

Why? "Because that's where the basket is," Webb explained.

His pickup game antics became campus legend — he and massive NCAA heavyweight champion Tab Thacker once had their own private dunk contest, a 5-6 guard going head-to-head with a 460-pound behemoth.

But his contributions on the court were even more impressive. In a February 1985 thrashing of Duke at Cameron Indoor Stadium, Webb stole the ball and stunned the abusive crowd with an uncontested, 360-degree slam at the end of the first half.

Along with seniors Lorenzo Charles, Cozell McQueen and Terry Gannon, Webb helped the Wolfpack earn a share of the 1985 ACC regular-season title with North Carolina and Georgia Tech and advance to the NCAA Tournament Elite Eight, where it lost a narrow decision to Lou Carnesecca's St. John's team for a chance to go to the Final Four.

Like college recruiters, NBA scouts weren't convinced that Webb could continue to play against the big guys. The Detroit Pistons drafted him in the fourth round of the 1985 NBA Draft, making him the shortest player ever taken. He was cut by the Pistons and picked up by the Atlanta Hawks.

When the 1986 NBA All-Star Game was played in Webb's hometown of Dallas, he was a surprise entry into the dunk contest, an event made famous by former NC State All-America David Thompson. Among his opponents was Hawks teammate and defending champion Dominique Wilkins, who had never seen Webb dunk before. That night, however, those paying attention saw just how high Webb could fly. He received perfect scores on two of his five dunks. He outperformed the stunned Wilkins to become the shortest player to ever win the dunk contest, sending the crowd at Reunion Arena into orbit.

Hey, that's what satellites do.

Over the next 12 years, Webb played for four different NBA franchises before retiring to his hometown of Dallas in 1998.

The Reach

Few players in basketball history have made as many stops as former NC State standout Chucky Brown. In 13 years as a professional player, Brown played for a dozen NBA teams, tied with two others as the most in league history.

At NC State, Brown helped the Wolfpack win the 1987 ACC Tournament championship during his sophomore season and the 1989 ACC regular-season title as a senior. As a professional, Brown is one of a few former Wolfpack players who have won a NBA Championship, joining John Richter, Chuck Nevitt and Josh Powell on the short list.

After his career ended, Brown returned to NC State, earned his bachelor's degree in sociology and embarked on a professional coaching career in the National Basketball Association Development League. In 2010, he was the head coach of the Los Angeles D-Fenders.

Brown, from tiny Navassa, N.C., was a rare home-state recruit for head coach Jim Valvano. Though he was a raw young talent with little basketball experience, Brown impressed Valvano during his senior year at New Brunswick High School. The coach watched proudly as Brown developed into a player who led the ACC in rebounding and earned first-team all-conference honors.

He was a second-round pick of the Cleveland Cavaliers in 1989. Over the next dozen years, he played all over the NBA, from Charlotte to Los Angeles. In fact, he shares the NBA record for most teams played for in a career with former Maryland player Tony Massenburg and

Jim Jackson. In 1994–95, he spent time with the NBA's Houston Rockets and the Yakima (Wash.) Sun Kings, both of which won championships.

For a player who was a professional vagabond, Brown has always made his off-season home in Raleigh.

"Out of all the players I ever played with, on all

the different levels, I can tell you this about Chucky: he was the greatest teammate I ever had," said Chris Corchiani, who played two years with Brown at NC State. "He would do anything for you, on or off the court. It's one thing to be a great scorer, or a great shooter, or a great passer, but to be someone who is always there for you is a great, great talent."

The Player/Coaches

In the fall of 1984, two relatively unknown basketball players arrived at NC State without much fanfare. Sure, they were part of what was being called the Five Fabulous Freshmen, a class that was recruited immediately after the Wolfpack's remarkable run to the 1983 NCAA Championship.

But these two guys were overshadowed greatly by Parade high school All-America center Chris Washburn, point guard Quentin Jackson and forward John Thompson.

One was a local kid, a graduate of Raleigh's Enloe High School, who had some success in junior college and was ready to join backcourt veteran Spud Webb in what Valvano hoped was a rebound year after missing the 1984 NCAA Tournament.

The other was a skinny guard from Springfield, Mass., birthplace of basketball, who was seemingly recruited by the Italian coach because the kid's name ended in a vowel.

Who knew back then that Nate McMillan and Vinny Del Negro would become two of the school's most successful basketball alumni? After long, productive professional playing careers, both became coaches in the National Basketball Association, McMillan with both the Seattle Super-Sonics and the Portland Trailblazers and Del Negro with the Chicago Bulls.

They are among the four former NC State basketball players who have been head coaches in the NBA. Horace "Bones" McKinney was the player/coach of the Washington Capitols in 1951 and current Wolfpack coach Sidney Lowe was the head coach of both the Minnesota Timberwolves and the Vancouver/Memphis Grizzlies.

McMillan spent a dozen years playing for the SuperSonics, the team that selected him as the 30th overall pick of the 1986 NBA draft. He began his coaching career shortly after his playing days were over. After two years as an assistant, he was elevated to head coach of the team for which he was a beloved player for a dozen years.

Valvano had long predicted that McMillan would be a successful NBA player.

He moved to the Trailblazers in 2005, leading the team to back-to-back postseason NBA appearances in 2009 and 2010. He also became active with USA Basketball, serving as the assistant coach for defense for head coach Mike Krzyzewski at the 2008 Olympic Games in Beijing.

214

McMillan played two years for the Wolfpack, after transferring in from Louisburg Junior College. He was a do-everything swing guard who could play four different positions for head coach Jim Valvano. In both of his seasons, the Wolfpack advanced to the Elite Eight of the NCAA Tournament, losing to St. John's in 1985 and Kansas in 1986.

Del Negro, after more than two years of patiently waiting for his opportunity to play, was one of Valvano's best success stories, sitting on the bench as a freshman and sophomore and seeing precious little time as a junior until midway

through the season, when Valvano needed to shake up his lineup. Del Negro went on to become the hero of the Wolfpack's 1987 ACC Championship in Landover, Md., earning the Everett Case Award as the Most Valuable Player following NC State's win over top-ranked North Carolina in the championship game.

After earning first-team All-ACC honors as a senior, Del Negro embarked on a 14-year professional career as a player, spending two years in Sacramento and two years playing for Benetton Treviso of the Italian A League. He came back in the early 1990s and found his greatest success with the San Antonio Spurs. In all, he played for five different NBA franchises over 14 years before retiring in Phoenix in 2001 to begin broadcasting games on the Suns' radio and television networks.

He quickly moved into the front office, becoming the team's assistant general manager in 2007. Less than a year later, Del Negro became the fourth former Wolfpack player to become an NBA coach. He led the Chicago Bulls to the NBA playoffs in both his seasons as coach, before taking over the Los Angeles Clippers in July 2010.

Del Negro was always a popular player and in 1994 was named by USA Weekend as one of the country's "Five Most Caring Athletes."

Both McMillan and Del Negro credit their time under Valvano as the foundation of their personal coaching careers.

"When I think about Coach Valvano, I just wish he was still here with us to bounce things off of and to be a confidante," Del Negro said. "He had so much experience and knowledge about the game.

"We all learned a lot from him."

Surprise (victory) PARTY

Jim Valvano said his 1986–87 team just wasn't good enough to win games in the Atlantic Coast Conference.

During the regular season, that statement was true enough. But in the postseason, where Valvano's teams often excelled, the Wolfpack made the coach look a little ridiculous.

The Wolfpack, coming off back-to-back appearances in the Elite Eight, had high hopes that season, even though the coach knew it would be a rebuilding year. The team had lost one of its top players, center Chris Washburn, to the first round of the NBA draft. Do-everything guard Nate McMillan was also gone after two years as the team's floor leader.

Couple those losses with preseason injuries to Charles Shackleford, Walker Lambiotte and Vinny Del Negro, and Valvano was facing as big a challenge as he had in 1984, when his defending national champion team failed to make the NCAA Tournament field. Nevertheless, the season started on a promising note, as the Wolfpack won eight of its first nine games.

Del Negro, a little-used junior guard from Springfield, Mass., came off the bench in his hometown in the season-opening Hall of Fame Tip-Off Classic to lead the Wolfpack to a remarkable 84-80 win over Navy and its All-America center David Robinson. The Wolfpack played well at the Great Alaska Shootout, losing to Iowa, but beating Texas and Utah State.

By then, the Wolfpack had risen to No. 11 in the nation. Then came an ill-fated trip to Florida, in which the Wolfpack lost to Division II Tampa, in a game that Valvano missed because of a viral infection. Not long after, Valvano's team lost to Clemson and at North Carolina. Then, in a brutal string of league and non-league games, the Pack lost consecutive games to Kansas, Virginia, Oklahoma, DePaul, North Carolina again and Louisville.

To make matters worse, the Wolfpack embarrassed itself on national television. In a game at Virginia's University Hall, State led by a single point with Del Negro on the free-throw line. Cavalier coach Terry Holland called a time-out, and the teams went to their respective benches.

After a single warning horn, Virginia returned to the court, but the Wolfpack did not. The game officials put the ball in play, and when Del Negro rushed into the circle to shoot his first free throw, he was whistled for a violation. Virginia's John Johnson scored a layup at the buzzer, giving the Cavs a controversial 61-60 victory.

Not long afterwards starting point guard Kenny Drummond, in his first year with the Pack after transferring from a California junior college, abruptly left the program, leaving Valvano without an experienced floor leader.

Even Valvano was challenged to think that this team could do something special.

"Our kids are trying very hard, but we're not

216

winning because, to be honest, we're just not good enough," the coach said of his team at one point late in the season. "It's just a down year. A bad year."

During one stretch, the Wolfpack lost seven consecutive games to ACC opponents, a record during the coach's tenure.

But Valvano began adjusting his lineup. He put Del Negro and Quentin Jackson together in the backcourt, with speedy Kelsey Weems coming off the bench. Lambiotte, Shackleford and Ben-

nie Bolton handled the frontcourt. Mike Giomi, in his only season at State after transferring from Indiana, and freshman Chucky Brown, came off the bench.

The Wolfpack managed to end its ACC losing streak and win its final three regular-season games. Del Negro, who had spent a frustrating two-and-a-half years on the bench awaiting his opportunity to play, excelled in his new role.

Valvano's team was seeded sixth when it arrived in Landover, Md., for the 1987 ACC

inspired play, scoring 15 points and grabbing a career-high 12 rebounds.

The Wolfpack's reward for surviving three overtimes in two days was a championship game meeting with North Carolina, which had won 16 straight games against ACC opponents, sweeping 14 in the regular season and beating Maryland and Virginia in the first two rounds of the tournament. Like the Wolfpack, however, the Tar Heels were pushed to double-overtime in the semifinals, before finally vanquishing the Cavaliers, 84-82.

Both teams were a little winded for the Sunday afternoon championship game. Valvano had his team control the tempo on a high-scoring Tar Heel squad that had averaged 91.3 points per game that year. With a minute left to play, the Heels were holding on to a slim 67-66 advantage. The Wolfpack had made all of its free throws in the game and shot better than 56 percent from the field in order to stay with the heavily favored Heels.

With 14 seconds to play, Del Negro was fouled and sent to the free-throw line. The 89 percent free-throw shooter calmly hit both shots, giving the Pack a 68-67 lead. But the Tar Heels had one final chance to win the game.

Valvano replaced Jackson with Weems and told the speedy guard to make sure that UNC All-America guard Kenny Smith didn't touch the ball. Weems did his duty, and a pair of UNC jumpshots by Joe Wolf and Ranzino Smith both fell short, giving the Wolfpack its 10th ACC title and 17th overall conference championship.

Del Negro, an unlikely winner of the Everett Case Award as the tournament's most valuable player, gave Valvano all the credit for keeping the team calm in the final minute against an opponent that was loaded with talent.

"In the time-out before the free throws, his mentality wasn't 'Let's see if Vinny makes these

Tournament with a 17-14 overall and 6-8 ACC mark. It didn't really matter, though: top-ranked North Carolina was the prohibitive favorite to roll through the weekend.

But, as happened in 1983 under Valvano, there was a little tournament magic going on. The Wolfpack upset No. 17 Duke in overtime in the first postseason meeting between Valvano and Duke's Mike Krzyzewski, thanks primarily to the eight points Del Negro scored in overtime.

Then it survived a double-overtime thriller against Wake Forest and diminutive guard Muggsy Bogues, in part because Valvano made a late change in his starting lineup, replacing Lambiotte with Brown, who scored 13 points and grabbed nine rebounds. Del Negro continued his

free throws,'" said Del Negro, who later had a long professional career. "It wasn't 'If he makes them' or 'What are we going to do when he misses.' It was always 'After Vinny makes these free throws, Kelsey, I want you to deny the ball, keep your man in front of you.'

"He was just so good at instilling confidence in a young player in a tense situation. It was a huge moment because we needed to win the tournament just to get into the NCAA Tournament. And beating North Carolina is always a huge thing, especially in a game of that magnitude.

"For me, it was the great culmination of a frustrating first couple of years at NC State. It was a great feeling."

Brown was also a hero of the championship game, scoring a career-high 18 points and grabbing 11 rebounds against the Tar Heels.

"That was one of the most gratifying things in my career," he said more than two decades later.

Valvano's team, despite all of its troubles earlier in the season, played a near perfect game, hitting all 14 of its free-throw attempts and shooting 56.6 percent from the field.

As a reward, the Wolfpack received the ACC's automatic bid into the NCAA Tournament, but didn't last long, losing in the first round to Florida in Syracuse, N.Y. It was a game that paired the Pack against former Wolfpack coach Norm Sloan and his top assistant Monte Towe, who both helped NC State win the 1973 and '74 ACC titles and the 1974 NCAA Championship.

Nothing, however, detracted from winning the unlikely ACC title, and beating the heavily favored Tar Heels.

The Fire

Of the many quality point guards churned out by head coach Jim Valvano, none played with more passion than Chris Corchiani.

Forever known to NC State fans as the emotional half of the famed "Fire & Ice" backcourt combination, Corchiani was a four-year starter who became the first guard in NCAA history to amass more than 1,000 assists in a career. He may never have won first-team All-ACC honors, but Corchiani remains one of the most popular players in the history of Wolfpack basketball.

Like all of Valvano's point guards, he held a special place in the heart of the coach, who himself had been an all-star point guard at Rutgers University. It didn't hurt that Corchiani shared Valvano's ethnic background.

"He doesn't play because *he's* Italian," Valvano used to say. "He plays because *I'm* Italian."

The stocky 6-1 guard with a plucky demeanor arrived in Raleigh in the fall of 1987, earning a starting job early in his initial season. Over the next four years, he made 112 career starts and was one of college basketball's best playmakers.

"The great thing about Coach V was that he gave me full control of the team during the game," Corchiani said. "I was able to call all the plays I wanted to run and do the things I wanted to do. Sometimes, he would rip into me for making the wrong call, but generally he let me do what I wanted to do."

He handed out more than 230 assists each season, usually getting the ball to Monroe, his prolific teammate who broke David Thompson's career scoring record at the school.

"It was a fun ride being able to play with someone like him," Corchiani said.

But it was also fun following the coach's instructions. During a famous game during the 1988–89 season, Valvano told Corchiani to guard 6-9 Georgia Tech center Tom Hammonds. Corchiani was an excellent defender and he denied Hammonds the ball throughout the game

The Ice

Not long after Rodney Monroe moved into his dormitory on his first day on campus at NC State, he, his parents and a family friend walked into Reynolds Coliseum, where they saw David Thompson's No. 44 jersey hanging in the rafters. Then they walked over to Case Athletics Center, where they saw a display highlighting Thompson's remarkable career, in which he scored a school record 2,309 points.

"You see that record?" said the friend, Billy Sellers. "Rodney's going to break it."

It was never Monroe's goal, but the former high school All-America from Hagerstown, Md., made it a reality on Feb. 15, 1991, when he scored 26 points in a 60-51 win at Connecticut and finished his career with 2,551 points, which still ranks as the fourth-most in ACC history in 2010.

Monroe knows that the two records are completely different: Thompson scored his points in just three years, while Monroe needed four. And Monroe, a 6-3 shooter, had the advantage of the three-point line, which was not around during Thompson's career. But those things don't matter to him.

"I knew all about David Thompson before I came to NC State," Monroe said. "You couldn't follow college basketball in the 1970s and '80s and not know about him. I eventually became good friends with him.

"But I didn't set out to break his record. I just wanted to be the best player I could be. David Thompson is still the greatest player to ever play

in the ACC. To have any part of the record, to share in his name in any way, was a great honor for me."

Monroe averaged more than 20 points a game his final three years, including a 27 points per game average as a senior, when he was named All-America by several organizations and was the 1991 ACC Player of the Year.

As a sophomore, he had two remarkable games—playing 59 minutes of the Wolfpack's four-overtime victory over Wake Forest and a in Reynolds Coliseum, and the Wolfpack shocked the Bobby Cremins–coached Jackets, 82-68.

While the program went through a difficult transition during Corchiani's career — the team was on probation in 1989–90 and Valvano stepped down after Corchiani's junior season — he still remembers his role as "Fire" as the best time of his life.

"I get goose bumps thinking about some of the times we had," Corchiani said. "Whether it was a bus ride from Reynolds to the airport or just time together in the locker room, V was always holding court. He was always animated, always upbeat. Never saw him down, even the worst times of my junior year."

Corchiani had a long professional career, mainly overseas, but he settled down with his family in Raleigh, where he owns a mortgage finance company and is a regular spectator at all Wolfpack home games.

40-point performance in a double-overtime win over Iowa.

Some of his games during his senior year were amazing. He scored 48 points against Georgia Tech, with Thompson sitting in the stands showing his approval. With the Wolfpack trailing by 12 at intermission, Monroe scored 31 points after halftime to lead the Pack to a 90-83 upset. A few days later, Monroe outscored Virginia 30-28 in the second half for another conference win.

By the end of his career, he had 21 games of 30 points or more.

Monroe, of course, is inextricably linked to point guard Chris Corchiani, his backcourt teammate who dished out an NCAA-record 1,038 assists during his own record-breaking career. The two were known as "Fire & Ice" because of their opposite personalities.

The two were recruited by NC State coach Jim Valvano, arriving in the fall of 1987 at the height of Valvano's popularity. They spent three years playing for the coach, winning the ACC regular-season title as sophomores in 1989, the year NCAA investigators began looking into Valvano's program for possible violations.

Monroe was a second-round pick of the Atlanta Hawks in the 1991 NBA draft, but he played only 38 games before beginning an overseas professional career that took him to Greece, Israel, Australia, Spain, the Philippines and Italy before he retired in 2007.

Monroe settled in the Charlotte area after his playing days were over, and began a coaching career at Lake Norman Christian School.

UNIFORM DISSENT

Not every idea Jim Valvano came up with was a good one. Take the unitard, for example. It was a one-piece body suit made out of extra-clingy spandex. Like a wrestling singlet, it left nothing to the imagination.

Valvano thought it was great. He made arrangements to have his team debut the "uniform of the future" on Jan. 7, 1989, when the Wolfpack hosted Temple at Reynolds Coliseum. Nike took measurements and sent a batch of the stretchy togs to the team a few days before the game.

When they arrived, there was a near revolt among the players.

"The unitards were absolutely horrendous," said Rodney Monroe. "I think the only two teams in America that were wearing them were NC State and UNLV. They wanted us to wear those things without shorts over the top.

"No way was that going to happen."

Monroe, like most players today, liked wearing loose-fitting clothes. The unitard was the total antithesis of basketball's future fashions.

"For me, it was very uncomfortable," Monroe said. "I didn't even think they looked that great."

He's not the only one who felt that way.

"The players just really didn't like it," Chris Corchiani said. "We didn't mind being a little tight up top, but down below, we wanted to wear something a little looser."

Still, more than two decades after the Wolfpack tried and abandoned basketball's newest fashion after only two games, both Corchiani and Monroe still have their original NC State unitards tucked away in storage.

Sometimes, their kids use them to play dress-up.

INNOVATIONS:
THE MODERN ERA

One of the saddest days in the history of NC State's basketball program was one of the happiest of Les Robinson's life.

Robinson, a Wolfpack player in the early 1960s, was a graduate assistant for NC State's basketball team when legendary head coach Everett Case announced on Dec. 7, 1964, that he was stepping down after 18 years and 10 conference championships. It was the program's very own Day of Infamy.

Robinson had played one year on the freshman team and two years of varsity basketball under Case, and was just getting started in his coaching career when the ailing coach stepped down because of the effects of multiple myeloma, a bone cancer that would eventually take his life. When assistant head coach Press Maravich was elevated to replace Case, he gave Robinson his first full-time job, as coach of the Wolfpack's freshman team.

Robinson lost that job when Maravich

bolted after just two seasons for Louisiana State. He moved to Florida, where he became a high school basketball coach and volunteer fire chief in the small town of Cedar Key. Learning to put out fires was a skill he needed, a quarter-century later, when he returned to NC State.

By the spring of 1990, Robinson had cobbled together an impressive résumé as a college coach, beginning as an assistant at Western Carolina in 1974 and at The Citadel in 1975. He was eventually elevated to head coach of the Bulldogs, a job that was once held by Norm Sloan. In 11 years, he became the school's career leader in coaching victories. From there, he moved on to East Tennessee State in 1985, taking a program just coming off probation to back-to-back NCAA Tournament appearances and winning two more Southern Conference Coach of the Year awards.

One of the wins in his final year with the Buccaneers was a pre-Christmas upset of his alma mater at Reynolds Coliseum. The NCAA had just levied a one-year probation on the Wolfpack, and there was already speculation that Robinson might be a good successor for embattled NC State coach Jim Valvano.

"[Valvano] said precisely, and I will swear this on the Bible: 'This might be a good place for you to coach, because my ass is out of here at the end of the season,'" Robinson said.

Indeed, Robinson was the school's first choice to take Valvano's place. But he knew that it would be an almost impossible job, replacing a coach whom fans loved and had won a na-

tional championship and two ACC titles. Not only that, because of the ugly break with Valvano, there was open distrust and outright hostility at the time between the NC State faculty and the athletics department. He knew he would face some unprecedented academic restrictions that would likely make it impossible to succeed in the rugged ACC.

"At the time, the faculty absolutely hated men's basketball," Robinson said. "That's not overstating it one bit."

Besides self-imposed scholarship reductions and off-campus recruiting limitations that were part of the NCAA sanctions, the school required all freshmen basketball players to have at least a 1.8 grade point average after their first year, a restriction above NCAA limits that no other school had to follow. Before he ever coached a game, he lost one of his earliest recruits over a clerical error regarding that rule.

Most coaches facing similar situations might have run. But Robinson jumped at the opportunity to take over the program once led by Case and to return to the school he loved, even if it ultimately meant sacrificing his coaching career.

Robinson built good relations with a skeptical fan base. He dug out the old wooden floor from the basement of Reynolds Coliseum and replaced the rubberized Tartan surface that had been inflicted on the arena more than two decades before. He brought back the spotlighted introductions that Case used during the Dixie Classic and early ACC Tournaments.

But Robinson never managed to cut

down the nets.

He actually inherited a good first team from Valvano, including seniors Rodney Monroe and Chris Corchiani and future NBA first-round draft pick junior Tom Gugliotta. Monroe averaged 27 points a game and broke David Thompson's career scoring record, while Corchiani became the first player in NCAA history to reach 1,000 career assists. The Wolfpack won 18 games in the regular season and advanced to the second round of both the ACC and NCAA Tournament, eventually losing to Oklahoma State.

But it would be a full decade before the Wolfpack returned to postseason, as the program struggled to compete with the restrictive rules imposed by the university administration.

"We just got killed in recruiting," Robinson said. "Players didn't want to come here and other coaches were using our rules against us. It made it difficult to play against ACC competition."

It didn't help that next door neighbors Duke and North Carolina combined to win three NCAA titles from 1991–93.

The Wolfpack had losing seasons for five consecutive years under Robinson, though he did record five wins during that span over archrival North Carolina. In the end, however, Robinson's career at NC State should not be judged by his 78-98 record in six years, but by the healing that occurred during that time.

"I always hoped that I would be someone who helped bring people back together," he said.

The academic standards were eventually relaxed, though Robinson did not benefit from it.

After his sixth season, the Wolfpack finished with a 15-16 record. He had returned the program to academic integrity, personified in two-time All-Academic ACC center Todd Fuller, who graduated with honors in applied mathematics and led the league in scoring and was second in rebounding his senior season.

But supporters were eager for more success on the court, and the school needed a little momentum to help fund construction of a new basketball home. Ground had been broken in November 1993, in a parking lot adjacent to Carter-Finley Stadium, but construction did not move forward for nearly four years as the school, the North Carolina legislature and Wake County discussed how to proceed with the joint venture.

nobody else had and most people don't know about. Les never for a minute would say it was not a level playing field.

"I think he did an admirable job with it. We couldn't recruit the way everybody else did, but he would never sit up and say: 'This is why.'"

In March 1996, following a quarterfinal loss in the ACC Tournament, Robinson relinquished his dream job. Though he had been offered a two-year extension, he chose not to accept it. Instead, he accepted an associate athletics director position within the department.

"A lot of people don't appreciate the job that Les did," said former Wolfpack star Vann Williford. "He had restrictions that

Athletics director Todd Turner immediately began a national search for Robinson's replacement, a 25-day adventure that led him to Miami of Ohio head coach Herb Sendek. Fans knew little about the school's new coach, other than he was a Rick Pitino protégé who was known for his recruiting skills. At the time he was hired, Sendek was 33 years old, the same age as Valvano when he took over the Wolfpack program more than 15 years earlier.

Ironically enough, less than six months after Robinson stepped down as men's basketball coach, Turner left to become the athletics director at Vanderbilt and Robinson was elevated to his position. Robinson had athletics director experience — he served in that role in his final four years at East Tennessee State.

As the ACC's youngest coach, Sendek took over a program that was still struggling to attract players on par with the rest of the ACC. In his first season, however, he earned the affection of the Wolfpack faithful by taking his inaugural team to the ACC Tournament championship game. Along the way, the eighth-seeded Wolfpack upended top-seeded and seventh-ranked Duke in the quarterfinal, in one of the tournament's most memorable upsets. The Wolfpack became the first team since the ACC expanded in 1992 to advance to the championship game with three wins.

The Wolfpack made its first postseason appearance since Robinson's inaugural year when it was selected for the National Invitation Tournament, which helped in Sendek's efforts to attract top-flight talent

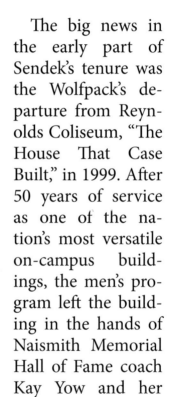

to the school, like his first McDonald's All-America, Damien Wilkins.

After his first season, Sendek was the toast of west Raleigh. Over the next three years, he made three more appearances in the NIT, advancing to the semifinals in Madison Square Garden in 2000. However, that wasn't exactly on even par with Case's appearance in the same tournament in his inaugural season of 1946–47.

The big news in the early part of Sendek's tenure was the Wolfpack's departure from Reynolds Coliseum, "The House That Case Built," in 1999. After 50 years of service as one of the nation's most versatile on-campus buildings, the men's program left the building in the hands of Naismith Memorial Hall of Fame coach Kay Yow and her Wolfpack women's team, which had also played in Reynolds since the program began in 1974.

The school's $160 million RBC Center seats 19,700 for basketball. Like Reynolds, it is a multi-purpose facility, but it is operated outside the control of the university, in a partnership with the NHL hockey franchise, the Carolina Hurricanes.

Not long after the doors opened for the 1999–2000 season, Robinson left his alma mater to become the athletics director at The Citadel. The school hired Lee Fowler from Middle Tennessee State as his replacement.

But neither the new building nor the new boss gave Sendek's program an immediate boost. The coach posted his only losing season in 2000–01, with a 13-16 overall record and a 5-11 mark in the ACC.

Late in the season, Fowler gave a strong endorsement for Sendek to continue as head coach, based on a solid recruiting class that was ranked as high as No. 5 nationally and included Mc-Donald's All-America Julius Hodge, a high school player from Harlem, N.Y.

Hodge was more than just a player during his all-star four-year career. He was a life force, injecting the program with energy and personality that Sendek did not outwardly show.

Sendek, a young father, was a thoroughly normal person, though slightly more on the academic side than most coaches. His personality hardly mirrored Case's gregarious demeanor, Sloan's fiery temperament, Valva-no's emotional glibness or even Robinson's homespun charm. So sometimes he paled in comparison.

"People always want a witty, funny, charismatic coach," Pitino once said about one of his all-time favorite assistants. "For some reason, they don't always like overly bright, intelligent people who don't make many mistakes.

"That's the thing about Herb: you aren't going to outwork him. You are not going to have more focus than he does. You are not going to be smarter than him. The man has never gotten anything other than an A in his life."

Hodge helped, with a brash attitude sharpened on the playground courts of Harlem and the Bronx. He was joined by Bulgarian-born Ilian Evtimov, future NBA champion Josh Powell, Levi Watkins and Jordan Collins to lay the foundation for the Wolfpack to make five consecutive NCAA Tournament appearances and two more runs at the ACC Tournament championship.

The Wolfpack lost to Duke in the finals of

both the 2002 and 2003 ACC Tournaments, as part of the Blue Devils' unprecedented run of six consecutive championships.

By the time Hodge was a junior, the Wolfpack moved up to second place in the ACC regular-season standings, he was named the league's player of the year and Sendek was named coach of the year. But for the second year in a row, the team had a disappointing showing in the NCAA Tournament, losing to Vanderbilt in the second round.

Hodge considered going pro, but kept a promise he made to his mother to get his college degree. Plus, he wanted a chance to finally win a championship. He did not duplicate his ACC-leading numbers as a senior, but his three-point play against defending national champion Connecticut in the second round of the 2005 NCAA Tournament sent the Wolfpack to its first Sweet Sixteen since 1989, when Valvano made his final appearance in the Big Dance.

The Wolfpack remained in the upper half of the ACC in Sendek's final year, but lost to Wake Forest in the opening round of the ACC Tournament and to Texas in the second round of the NCAA Tournament. Just before the 2006 title game, Sendek announced he was leaving for Arizona State.

Fowler, like Willis Casey and Les Robinson before him, was a former chairman of the NCAA Basketball Selection Committee whose background was in basketball. He conducted a national search to replace Sendek.

On May 6, 2005, Fowler introduced one of NC State's most popular heroes, Sidney Lowe, the point guard on Valvano's 1983 national championship team, as the latest leader of the Wolfpack. Lowe had spent much of his time since leaving school in the NBA, either as a player, an assistant coach or his two opportunities as head coach.

Lowe's ties to and knowledge of basketball were strong. He played at DeMatha High School for Naismith Memorial Hall of Fame coach Morgan Wootten. He was recruited by Everett Case protégé Sloan and played for Valvano.

While he wasn't as familiar with the college game, Lowe made an immediate impact on the program. In his first shot at playing North Carolina, he broke out a red blazer and whipped the Tar Heels at the RBC Center, improving his personal winning streak over the Wolfpack's archrivals to three games.

In the ACC's first trip to the state of Florida for the post-season tournament, Lowe's inaugural team had a magnificent performance. Redshirt freshman Brandon Costner led the 10th-seeded Wolfpack on a wild run that included back-to-back-to-back wins over Duke, Virginia and Virginia Tech, all of which were seeded higher in the tournament.

He became the fourth NC State coach to reach the title game in his first ACC Tournament, joining Case (1954), Press Maravich (1965) and Sendek (1997). The Wolfpack fell to the Tar Heels in the championship game, but were rewarded for their late-season run with a bid to the NIT.

Lowe worked hard in his early seasons with the team to build a foundation with the players he inherited. He recruited and developed a first-round NBA draft pick in J.J. Hickson, who left for professional basketball after one season.

As the school celebrated its 100th season of basketball in 2009–10, Lowe welcomed back a number of players, coaches and others who helped build the tradition of NC State basketball.

Some of the most important people could not be there, of course. Many of the men who initially built the program have long ago faded from memory. Even Case, the man most responsible for the passion of ACC basketball, is no longer the automatic answer when young fans consider the game's greatest and most influential coaches.

But the spirit of NC State basketball lives on in the championship banners that hang in the rafters of one of the nation's best basketball arenas.

And that would make Case smile.

The Favor

Tom Gugliotta was a recruiting favor by NC State coach Jim Valvano for an old friend.

The skinny forward from Huntington Station, N.Y., was barely a mid–major level recruit during his senior year of high school. But he performed well enough at a summer basketball camp that his father, Frank Gugliotta, called Valvano, his old buddy from Long Island basketball camps some two decades earlier, to see if there might be any interest in young Tom.

Valvano wasn't particularly impressed, but he offered Gugliotta a scholarship anyway.

After Gugliotta's freshman year, Valvano basically told him that he wasn't an ACC player, an assessment that both angered and inspired the young forward. He hit the weight room, added 30 pounds to his growing 6-8 frame and became one of the best all-round basketball players in Wolfpack history. He still ranks in the top 15 of every major statistical category.

"Tom worked harder than anybody I have ever seen in the weight room," said teammate Chris Corchiani. "He was a madman when he did his workouts."

Gugliotta was the No. 6 pick in the 1992 NBA draft, chosen by the Washington Bullets. However, his best seasons were with the Minnesota Timberwolves, averaging double-figure scoring in his first eight years in the league. He was a 1997 All-Star selection, when he averaged 21.4 points per game for the Timberwolves.

He was also selected to represent the U.S. on the 2000 Olympic team, but a major knee injury ended his hopes of becoming the third former NC State player — after Tommy Burleson in 1972 and Kenny Carr in 1976 — to make an Olympic roster.

He retired from the NBA in 2005, after playing for seven franchises, scoring 9,895 career points and grabbing 5,589 career rebounds.

Valvano only coached Gugliotta for two years, since the coach left in 1990. He had already begun to improve as a sophomore, but Gugliotta blossomed under new head coach Les Robinson.

"Jim Valvano was not wrong when he told Tommy that he was not an ACC player," Robinson said. "To me, it is a great story: you can get better or you can whine about it. He wanted to prove his coach wrong.

"Thirteen years in the NBA and about a $100 million later, I think he did it."

The Brain

Todd Fuller played professional basketball on every continent except Antarctica, but his home will always be NC State, where his No. 52 jersey hangs in the rafters in celebration of his standout career.

Fuller played under Wolfpack coach Les Robinson from 1992–96, leading the ACC in scoring as a senior in 1995–96 with 20.9 points and 9.9 rebounds per game. He earned first-team All-ACC honors and the endearing gratitude of a fan base who appreciated what this high school valedictorian from Charlotte meant to the program as both a student and athlete.

Even more impressive than his basketball career was that Fuller was a summa cum laude graduate of NC State with a degree in applied mathematics. He graduated with a 3.96 grade point average and was named both Academic All-America and GTE Scholar-Athlete of the Year. He turned down the possibility of a Rhodes Scholarship to play professional basketball.

He was taken as the 11th overall pick in the 1996 NBA draft by the Golden State Warriors and played five seasons for four different NBA franchises. He then embarked on a long career of playing overseas, where he represented teams around the globe, from Spain to Australia to Brazil.

Fuller has remained close to his alma mater. After he retired from basketball, he sponsored the "Todd Fuller Wake County Math Competition" through NC State's College of Physical and Applied Mathematics, and served on the PAMS Alumni and Friends Advisory Board.

He also continues to do global volunteer work. In 2008, he traveled to Tasmania for the Australian National Baptist Basketball Carnival and spent three weeks in Micronesia on a mission to train basketball players to become coaches.

The
Harlem Knight

The hallways of Reynolds Coliseum were never quiet during Julius Hodge's four-year career at NC State. Hodge actually only played a few heritage games in the old coliseum, but it was the team's primary practice facility when Hodge competed for the Wolfpack from 2002–05.

The tireless worker had his own key and knew where all the appropriate light switches were. Frequently, he would come home from a road game and head straight to Reynolds, where he would take 1,500 jump shots before he wandered off to bed.

"He is extremely driven," said NC State coach Herb Sendek. "He cares a great deal about basketball. He works very hard at it. With all his heart, he wants to do well. You can never question his intent."

Fans might remember Hodge as a gregarious swing player who came to Raleigh from Harlem, N.Y. and entertained them with his style of play, his on-court antics and his postgame comments. He led the program on a fun ride, going to the NCAA Tournament in all

The Quotable Mr. Hodge

"New York is the place to be. I could wake up there at three in the morning and decide to go to the store for some chips and Snapple and there would be cars racing down the street and people walking around everywhere. If I do that here, I'd probably get attacked by a deer."

"When you're hungry, you eat; when you're a frog, you leap; if you're scared, get a dog."

"I see us as the 'lunch-baggers' of the ACC. We just go to work every day, try to get the job done."

On having the ball stolen from him by Florida State's Tim Pickett:
"I was peeved. I had some turnovers like I was in the seventh grade. One time, Pickett took my cookies."

four of his seasons after a year team absence.

But his legacy is the work he put in to make the Wolfpack relevant in the ACC, with help from coach Herb Sendek's breakthrough recruiting class of 2001, which also included Josh Powell, Ilian Evtimov, Levi Watkins and Jordan Collins.

Hodge was the centerpiece of that highly rated class and from the day he first stepped on campus, he was a lightning-rod player who made things happen, usually by driving straight to the basket. He ached to win championships and put his team in position to do so in his freshman and sophomore years at the ACC Tournament. But the Wolfpack lost both years to Duke in the title game.

As a junior, when the Wolfpack finished second in the ACC regular-season standings, he became NC State's fifth ACC Player of the Year, joining the likes of Ronnie Shavlik, Lou Pucillo, David Thompson (three times) and Rodney Monroe. After earning All-America recognition, Hodge considered leaving for the NBA after that junior season, but his mother, Mary Hodge, insisted that he return to complete his degree in communications.

He did not have the same kind of regular-season success, but he was responsible for returning the Wolfpack to the Sweet Sixteen for the first time since 1989, thanks to the last-second drive he made against defending national champion Connecticut in the second round of the 2005 NCAA Tournament.

Hodge's dream of going to the NBA finally came true after he graduated from NC State, as he was taken as the 20th pick of the first round by the Denver Nuggets. However, his rookie season ended when he was involved in a near-fatal drive-by shooting on April 8, 2006, that ended his rookie season and, for all intents and purposes, his NBA career.

He did return to play the game he worked so hard to perfect after recovering from the shooting, but most of that time was spent playing professionally overseas.

"It really just made me appreciate everything," Hodge said. "People always thought I had a lot of fun on the court, but now I try to look at everything as fun. I could not be doing this — or anything else.

"I am just always trying to look at the bright side." Even if he has to work hard to do so.

ON THE AIR

The voices are silky, intelligent and memorable.

"Hello, Wolfpack radio is on the air. . . . "

Their familiar words often echo among the banners that are stitched with the names of players they helped make famous. The men behind the microphone on the Wolfpack Sports Network are yet another NC State innovation — the area's first collection of stations dedicated to broadcasting the games of just one school.

No real Wolfpack fan can hear Wally Ausley's call of the final moments of the 1983 NCAA title game — "Lorenzo Charles! . . . State! . . . The Cinderella team has done it. The glass slipper fits. . . . The Wolfpack has won the national championship!" — without sprouting a few cold chills.

The Wolfpack Sports Network began in 1961, not as a revenue stream, but as a way for fans across the state to hear about the Wolfpack, even if they couldn't be in Reynolds Coliseum, Riddick Stadium or traveling with the teams.

At the time, radio stations in the area broadcast games at random and were not associated with a particular school. Sometimes different stations in the area would broadcast the same game. That changed in February 1961, when a basketball game between Clemson and the Wolfpack was not aired by any station in Raleigh. As he often did, NC State sports information director Frank Weedon thought the Wolfpack was getting the short end of coverage in the local media. He and *Technician* editor Jay Brame organized NC State fraternities to flood Raleigh radio station WPTF-AM 680 with calls asking for broadcasts of basketball games.

Soon after, WPTF became NC State's flagship station and Weedon was traveling across the state lining up stations for the area's first radio network. A small network of just three stations broadcast the 1961 football season.

"We weren't in it for the money," Weedon once said. "What we wanted was exposure."

While initially a joint partnership between the athletics department and WPTF, the network was taken over by Capitol Broadcasting Company's Capitol Sports Network in 1983. Since 1996, the network has been owned by Wolfpack Sports Marketing, a division of Capitol Broadcasting and a separate entity from the athletics department.

In 2007, the network moved to a new flagship station, WRAL-FM 101.5, in order to increase its coverage area, ending one of the longest associations between any college and its flagship station. What fans remember the most, however, are the voices that described the action.

Wally Ausley (1948–90): The native of rural North Carolina's Harnett County made his first radio appearance on WPTF during the station's weekly 4-H show at the age of 12. His first job was as the public address announcer at UNC's Woollen Gym. He called his first game on the radio in 1948, just after he graduated from North Carolina. On Dec. 2, 1949, he called the first game ever played at Reynolds Coliseum for a Durham station. He continued to broadcast throughout the 1950s, when he was WPTF's farm director. His friendly, folksy style was an immediate hit with his listeners, both on Wolfpack broadcasts and his morning farm reports on WPTF. After broadcasting more than 1,100 NC State football and basketball games, Ausley retired to Holden Beach, N.C., following the 1990 ACC Tournament, after nearly 30 years as the "Voice of the Wolfpack." He died at the age of 65 on April 8, 1994.

Bill Jackson (1961–74): Another former farmer who was the leader of the morning "Gabfest," Jackson handled play-by-play duties from 1961 until his death in 1974. Though no one can say for certain, the Jackson-Ausley pairing is believed to be the first two-man broadcasting crew for basketball and football games. "Back in those days, everyone would have the play-by-play man on the air during the game, and the color man would only talk during the pre-game and halftime shows. Bill and I worked as a team, with him doing play-by-play and I did the color throughout the game. I can't say we were the first, because I wasn't listening to everyone, but I don't know anyone else who was doing it at the time," Ausley said.

Garry Dornburg (1975–97): Like many Wolfpack basketball players, Dornburg was born in Indiana, but spent most of his life in North Carolina. Dornburg began working as a part-time disc jockey in Elkin, N.C., at the age of 16. He was first hired as a part-time announcer by WPTF two years before he enrolled at NC State in 1967 and stayed at the station after he graduated three years later with a degree in English. Among his many duties at the station, Dornburg hosted a call-in sports show and a weekly opera program. Following Jackson's death, Dornburg was picked from more than 100 national candidates to be the Wolfpack's new color commentator, a position he held for nearly 25 years. A year after leaving the network, on Feb. 2, 1998, the 51-year-old Dornburg died of leukemia at Duke Medical Center in Durham, N.C.

C.A. Dillon (1950–61): Though he is better known as the public address announcer at Thompson Gym, Reynolds Coliseum and, for its opening game, the RBC Center, Dillon was a longtime radio announcer, calling various games for local stations.

Jim Reid (1950-61): A regular member of the radio crew for the Tobacco Radio Network in the 1950s, Reid worked with longtime public address announcer C.A. Dillon broadcasting Wolfpack football and basketball games. But Weedon replaced Reid and Dillon with Ausley and Jackson when he formed the school's network. Reid ended up getting a job with more responsibility, but less prestige — he was elected mayor of Raleigh, serving from 1963–65.

Reese Edwards (1973–74): The long-time Triangle radio broadcaster only did one season of play-by-play announcing for the Wolfpack, but he picked a pretty good year. He was behind the microphone during the 1973–74 season, calling every game of the Wolfpack's ACC championship football season and its run to the ACC and NCAA Championship.

Gary Hahn (1991–present): Hahn is the only regular broadcaster on the Wolfpack Sports Network who  doesn't have ties to the state of North Carolina. The Pennsylvania native graduated from Butler University in 1974 and had a variety of sports broadcasting jobs, from Ohio State football and basketball play-by-play to color on the Louisville and Alabama networks to NBC Radio in New York. Selected from more than 120 applicants in a nationwide search, Hahn took over as the Wolfpack's play-by-play announcer when Ausley retired in 1990.

Tony Haynes (1998–present): Like Dornburg, Haynes is an NC State graduate who began his broadcasting career during his days as a student, calling baseball play-by-play for campus radio station WKNC. The graduate of Raleigh's Millbrook High earned his degree in speech communications in 1984. His work after he  left NC State helped land him a job as a sideline reporter for Duke football, a position he had for 12 years. He also worked as a member of the Duke basketball broadcast team from 1993–98. In 1998, a year after Dornburg passed away, Haynes was offered the opportunity to return to his alma mater.

Howard Baum (1968–present): Few people have ever heard Baum's raspy voice on the radio. That's because, as the network's long-time statistician, his job is to crunch numbers, not wax poetic over the airwaves. The Fayetteville, N.C., bowling center owner began as a spotter and stat-keeper during football games in 1968. He added basketball to his repertoire in the late 1970s.

LOUD & PROUD

Long before coliseums had piped-in anthems blaring over loudspeakers, Everett Case wanted something that would help create an unparalleled home-court atmosphere in Reynolds Coliseum. So, thanks to a couple of students at NC State's acclaimed engineering department, Case created a technological marvel, a gleaming red-and-white meter that measured just how loud the crowd was during crucial points of a home basketball game.

The 10-foot long meter, which hung in the rafters of Reynolds Coliseum for at least 50 years, had 14 rows of lights on four sides. As the noise level increased, the 13 white lights would come on from the bottom up, inching slowly toward the top. When the noise reached its crescendo, the red light on top would flicker, spurring the crowd to yell even louder.

"No question about it, you could hear when the game was revving up because the crowd saw the lights go higher and higher and they would get louder and louder and louder to get it up to the top," Sidney Lowe said. "It was one of the great traditions of Reynolds Coliseum and NC State basketball."

Opponents may not have known what it was, but Wolfpack players could tell when the light turned red, without even looking.

"You couldn't really see when the top light came on," said Rodney Monroe, the Wolfpack's all-time leading scorer. "But you sure could feel it."

And here's the brilliance of this Case innovation: it was completely fake. In reality, the state-of-the-art device was just four pieces of quarter-inch plywood nailed over a 10-foot frame. A standard light socket was installed for each bulb, with the wiring hidden inside the meter.

There was a 100-foot electrical cord attached to the top that snaked from the rafters to one of the eight barges in the upper regions of Reynolds, where a crude control panel of 14 light switches manipulated the lights. It was the job of the Reynolds Coliseum maintenance and facilities staff to manually operate the meter during every home basketball game. They ran a specially made wooden block over the switches to turn each row off and on during the course of the game.

Three of the people who used to manually operate the old meter in their younger days — Ray Brincefield, Richard Sykes and Shannon Yates — eventually became associate or assistant athletics directors at NC State. Brad Bowles, whose family has long taken care of NC State's athletics facilities, often sat in one of the upper level barges in Reynolds operating the old meter, even when he was too young to drive. Imagine, he says, what it was like to be a 10-year-old kid, drunk with power, whipping the crowd into a 135-decibel frenzy.

BIG, BAD WUFS

*"For the strength of the Pack is the Wolf,
and the strength of the Wolf is the Pack"*
Rudyard Kipling

There have been many
incarnations of the NC State
mascot through the years, but in
every case the unknown cheerleader
donning the giant head has brought life to
every athletic event they get up and howl for.
From the single Mr. Wuf to the present day married
Mr. & Ms. Wuf, fans love their big, bad mascots.

The Wolfpack shoots and scores with a new home

BANK SHOT

Each time NC State has needed a new basketball home, there have been some long delays. But on every occasion, the wait has been worth it.

For the first 15 years, the school didn't have its own place to play the new sport of "basket-ball." Home games were held in downtown Raleigh's 2,000-seat Municipal Auditorium, which was plenty large enough during the early days.

After World War I, the school received funding to build its first on-campus facility, the multipurpose Frank Thompson Gymnasium, one of the campus's first buildings south of the railroad tracks.

Even before Everett Case arrived and fans started sitting two-to-a-seat, the school knew it needed to replace the aging Thompson, if only to host its annual Farm Week for farmers across the state. Construction on a new armory/coliseum began before World War II, but was halted for more seven years. William Neal Reynolds Coliseum finally opened in 1949 as the South's biggest home for college basketball.

In the mid-1980s, the school started looking into the possibility of revamping or replacing "The House That Case Built," which had hosted more basketball games and spectators than any on-campus building in the country.

In 1984, Raleigh mayor Avery Upchurch commissioned a study to explore the possibility of building a multipurpose facility in downtown Raleigh, an idea that was eventually decided to be unfeasible. When Jim Valvano became athletics director in 1986, he decided the cost of renovating and upgrading Reynolds to modern codes was too prohibitive.

In 1988, the NC General Assembly and the university contributed $1.5 million each to plan for a new arena adjacent to Carter-Finley Stadium; the next year, the NC State Board of Trustees approved plans for a 23,000-seat arena that would cost $58.5 million. The project was delayed due to Valvano's messy departure from the school in 1990, but restarted two years later, with a strong push from

Raleigh real estate developer Steve Stroud.

Ground was broken in November 1993, and was graded into a large bowl by the next spring, but the site sat idle for nearly four years as the city, state and school worked out the details for the new arena. In 1997, the NHL's Hartford (Conn.) Whalers began looking for a new home. They agreed to help finance major changes to the already-designed coliseum, committing some $40 million for facility upgrades and offices.

By the time the facility — then called the Entertainment and Sports Arena — opened on Oct. 29, 1999, with a game between the newly-named Carolina Hurricanes and the New Jersey Devils, the cost had risen to nearly $160 million, some 780 times the cost of Thompson Gymnasium and 64 times more than Reynolds Coliseum.

NC State — after 589 victories in Reynolds — made its debut in its new home on Nov. 19, 1999, in front of a sold-out crowd of 19,722 spectators with a 67-63 season-opening victory over Georgia. The state-of-the-art facility, featuring 19,700 red seats and 61 luxury suites, maintains its home-court advantage with 3,000 courtside seats for students.

For three years, the building was simply known as the ESA, but in 2002 the Royal Bank of Canada agreed to a 20-year naming rights deal for a reported $80 million to rename the arena the RBC Center.

Again, the building is more than just a basketball arena, with a collection of concerts and other events like the circus, monster truck shows and community events. The Hurricanes have twice hosted the Stanley Cup finals, claiming the franchise's first championship on June 19, 2006, with a 3-1 victory over the Edmonton Oilers, and the 2011 NHL All-Star game.

NC State has hosted both NCAA men's and women's basketball regionals at the RBC Center.

As with all of its permanent homes over the years, the Wolfpack may share the stage but is always the featured attraction when it's time for basketball.

EPILOGUE

Somewhere, Everett Case is smiling and Adolph Rupp is burning with envy.

The two Hall of Fame coaches faced each other only once on the basketball court, more than six decades ago, but they went head-to-head often on the recruiting trails they forged in the early days of big-time basketball. Their battles over the best players of that time were the stuff of legend.

So they would have appreciated the national interest in C.J. Leslie, a high school basketball player from Raleigh, whom recruiting experts considered to be one of the best players in the class of 2010.

The fact that there are "recruiting experts" would tickle the two old goats, who knew how to mine basketball talent without slick highlight DVDs, internet scouting services or any of the other tools at the disposal of modern college basketball coaches. They did it old school, with great success.

They surely would have known about Leslie, a 6-8 forward with advanced skills. And they would have taken keen interest in his final decision of whether to play for NC State or Kentucky.

On May 4, 2010, Leslie called a press conference at a restaurant less than a mile away from Reynolds Coliseum, known locally as "The House That Case Built." With future teammate Ryan Harrow at his side, Leslie signed his national letter of intent to play for the Wolfpack, completing a recruiting class that analysts believe will be one of the nation's best.

The next 100 years of NC State basketball had begun.